21 YEARS OF WORLD CUP

# SKI RACING

BY SERGE LANG

mazda

**GRAFTON BOOKS**
A Division of the Collins Publishing Group

LONDON GLASGOW
TORONTO SYDNEY AUCKLAND

Grafton Books
A division of the Collins Publishing Group
8 Grafton Street, London W1X 3LA

Published by Grafton Books 1986



*British Library Cataloguing in Publication Data*

Lang, Serge
Twenty-one years of world cup ski racing.
1. World Cup (*Ski racing championship*)
—History
I. Title
796.93 GV854.1

ISBN 0-246-13116-0

*21 Years of World Cup Ski Racing* was conceived, edited and designed by James Wotton Limited, 7 Stafford Mansions, Albert Bridge Road, London SW11 and Graham Davis Associates, 10 Amwell Street, London EC1.



Printed and bound in the Netherlands by Royal Smeets Offset, BV Weert.

# CONTENTS

# FOREWORD

This book is about the contribution the World Cup has made to the history of ski racing. It tells the story of its inception in Portillo in 1966 and its growth into one of the major institutions of the sport. It also dispels many of the misconceptions there are about the competition.

For example, the Alpine World Cup has led to a reduction in the number of races, not an increase. When it received the official sanction of the International Ski Federation (FIS) in 1967, it took over all the existing agreements between the leading skiing nations for their teams to visit each other every winter. And although the World Cup has extended the calendar to include events in Japan and South America, it has cut back the Alpine season to four months – December to March. The great spring races at Gross Glockner, the Stelvio Pass, Zugspitzblatt, the Grimsel Pass, the Jungfrau Pass and other venues have been dropped. This has allowed the year to be divided into roughly three equal periods for competition, rest and preparation.

The World Cup is not without its problems though. Snow conditions, the demands of winter tourism, the start of the school term and other outside factors mean that the ideal World Cup calendar is still a dream. But the beneficial influence of the World Cup on skiing, its popularity and its growth, both as a mass pastime and a competitive sport, has never been questioned in the 21 years of its existence. The fact that the father of the World Cup is now presenting his successful progeny – with all its growth problems – to a wider public is of benefit to all of us. For that reason, thanks and congratulations are due to Serge Lang, his son Patrick and the others involved in bringing out this book.

MARC HODLER
*President, International Ski Federation*

# INTRODUCTION

This is the story of World Cup ski racing and of those who created it, first in their heads and later on the slopes.

It is a saga of long nights spent in Portillo, Chile; of superb feats of skiing – like the fantastic gambles of Jean-Claude Killy who, in 1967, wrought havoc in the ranks of his rivals at every race.

It is also a homage to "Tigress" Nancy Greene, who confronted Marielle Goitschel, the era's most brilliant champion, and went on to crown her career by winning the last slalom of the season, in the final event of the 1967 World Cup at Jackson Hole, Wyoming.

With its inception, the Cup impetuously turned all established order upside down, before settling on it a new order: that of the World Cup itself. It showed no respect for historically entrenched great events, insolently upstaging the Winter Olympic Games and the World Championships.

We could barely believe our ears when, in February 1968 at the Grenoble Olympics, Jean-Claude Killy told the press: "Of course, I'm thrilled to have won a gold medal . . . I dreamed of it for years. My hopes for the future? To win the World Cup. It's even more important."

His sentiments were echoed by most of the winners including Marielle Goitschel and Nancy Greene, who still had Olympic events left to race in.

Skiing history was already long and rich before year one of the World Cup. This allowed the Cup to quickly reach its exceptional form, taking root in a soil already made fertile by so many champions, so many great feats.

The dashing victories of Rudolf Rominger, Edi Reinhalter, Emile Allais, James Couttet, Stein Eriksen, Jean Vuarnet, Toni Sailer and many others, cleared the way for Jean-Claude Killy, Karl Schranz, Bernhard Russi, Gustavo Thoeni, Ingemar Stenmark, Pirmin Zurbriggen, Marc Girardelli, Maria Walliser, Rok Petrovic, and all their successors.

This book then is as much the story of the World Cup as that of skiing in general – the sport so many of us around the world love with such passion.

It is in that spirit that I dedicate this work to Marc Hodler, faithful and indulgent friend, a representative of skiing's big family and of its champions – companions in our fine adventure.

Riehen, May 1986.

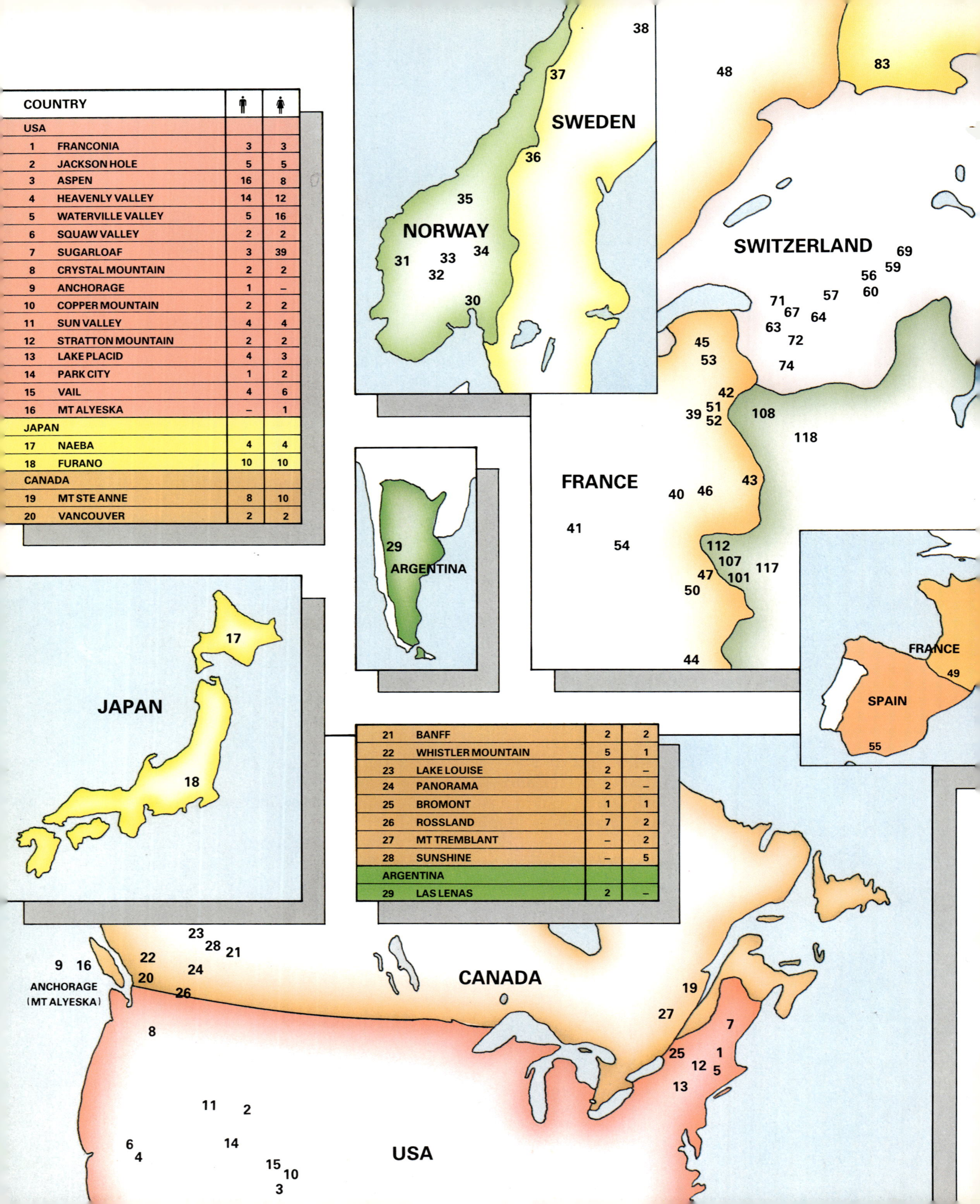


| COUNTRY | | Men | Women |
|---|---|---|---|
| USA | | | |
| 1 | FRANCONIA | 3 | 3 |
| 2 | JACKSON HOLE | 5 | 5 |
| 3 | ASPEN | 16 | 8 |
| 4 | HEAVENLY VALLEY | 14 | 12 |
| 5 | WATERVILLE VALLEY | 5 | 16 |
| 6 | SQUAW VALLEY | 2 | 2 |
| 7 | SUGARLOAF | 3 | 39 |
| 8 | CRYSTAL MOUNTAIN | 2 | 2 |
| 9 | ANCHORAGE | 1 | – |
| 10 | COPPER MOUNTAIN | 2 | 2 |
| 11 | SUN VALLEY | 4 | 4 |
| 12 | STRATTON MOUNTAIN | 2 | 2 |
| 13 | LAKE PLACID | 4 | 3 |
| 14 | PARK CITY | 1 | 2 |
| 15 | VAIL | 4 | 6 |
| 16 | MT ALYESKA | – | 1 |
| JAPAN | | | |
| 17 | NAEBA | 4 | 4 |
| 18 | FURANO | 10 | 10 |
| CANADA | | | |
| 19 | MT STE ANNE | 8 | 10 |
| 20 | VANCOUVER | 2 | 2 |
| 21 | BANFF | 2 | 2 |
| 22 | WHISTLER MOUNTAIN | 5 | 1 |
| 23 | LAKE LOUISE | 2 | – |
| 24 | PANORAMA | 2 | – |
| 25 | BROMONT | 1 | 1 |
| 26 | ROSSLAND | 7 | 2 |
| 27 | MT TREMBLANT | – | 2 |
| 28 | SUNSHINE | – | 5 |
| ARGENTINA | | | |
| 29 | LAS LENAS | 2 | – |

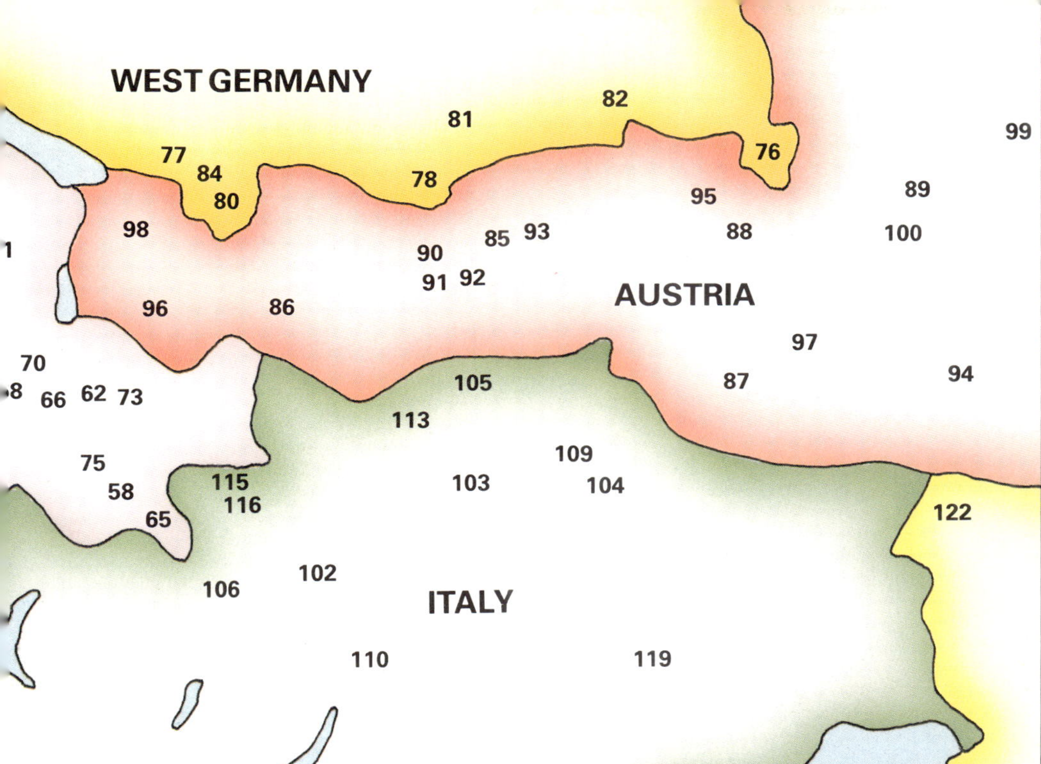


# ALPINE WORLD CUP VENUES

Since its inception in 1967 the Alpine World Cup has visited 127 locations in 16 countries. This chart shows the number of ski races that have been held at each venue for men and for women.

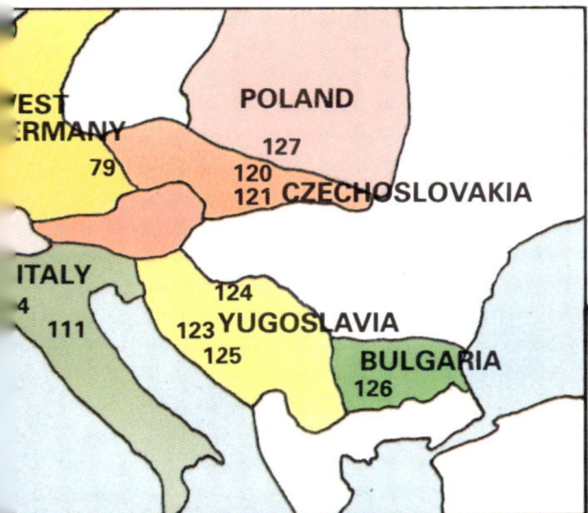


| UNTRY | Men | Women |
|---|---|---|
| RWAY | | |
| OSLO | 6 | 3 |
| VOSS | 7 | 2 |
| GEILO | 1 | – |
| HEMSEDAL | 2 | – |
| LILLEHAMMER | 1 | – |
| OPDAL | 1 | – |
| EDEN | | |
| ARE | 15 | 1 |
| TARNABY | 1 | – |
| GAELLIVARE | 2 | – |
| ANCE | | |
| MEGEVE | 13 | 10 |
| MERIBEL | 1 | – |
| GRENOBLE-JO | 3 | 3 |
| CHAMONIX | 5 | 5 |
| VAL D'ISÈRE | 29 | 31 |
| PRA-LOUP | 3 | 4 |
| MORZINE | 12 | – |
| COURCHEVEL | 1 | – |

| | | Men | Women |
|---|---|---|---|
| 47 | MONTGENEVRE | 1 | 1 |
| 48 | MARKSTEIN | 2 | – |
| 49 | LA MONGIE | 1 | – |
| 50 | PUY ST VINCENT | 2 | 5 |
| 51 | ST GERVAIS | – | 20 |
| 52 | LES CONTAMINES | – | 1 |
| 53 | LES GETS | – | 7 |
| 54 | ALPE D'HUEZ | – | 2 |
| SPAIN | | | |
| 55 | SOLYNIEVE | 1 | 1 |
| SWITZERLAND | | | |
| 56 | WENGEN | 30 | – |
| 57 | ADELBODEN | 20 | – |
| 58 | ST MORITZ | 6 | 2 |
| 59 | MURREN | 1 | 1 |
| 60 | GRINDELWALD | 1 | 21 |
| 61 | EBNAT-KAPPEL | 2 | – |
| 62 | AROSA | 1 | 5 |
| 63 | VILLARS | 1 | – |
| 64 | CRANS-MONTANA | 6 | 6 |
| 65 | LAGALB | 1 | – |
| 66 | PARPAN | 4 | – |
| 67 | LES DIABLERETS | 1 | 8 |
| 68 | LAAX | 5 | – |
| 69 | MEIRINGEN | – | 5 |
| 70 | WANGS PIZOL | – | 2 |
| 71 | LES MOSSES | – | 2 |

| | | Men | Women |
|---|---|---|---|
| 72 | NENDAZ | – | 1 |
| 73 | DAVOS | – | 3 |
| 74 | VERBIER | – | 4 |
| 75 | SAVOGNIN | – | 1 |
| WEST GERMANY | | | |
| 76 | BERCHTESGADEN | 9 | 8 |
| 77 | HINDELANG | 2 | – |
| 78 | GARMISCH-PARTENKIRCHEN | 21 | 3 |
| 79 | ZWIESEL | 3 | 4 |
| 80 | OBERSTAUFEN | 3 | 15 |
| 81 | LENGGRIES | 1 | 1 |
| 82 | BAD WIESSEE | 2 | – |
| 83 | TODTNAU | 1 | – |
| 84 | PFRONTEN | – | 11 |
| AUSTRIA | | | |
| 85 | KITZBUHEL | 45 | |
| 86 | ST ANTON | 9 | 1 |
| 87 | LIENZ | 2 | 2 |
| 88 | ZELL AM SEE | 1 | 5 |
| 89 | SCHLADMING | 9 | – |
| 90 | INNSBRUCK | 1 | 1 |
| 91 | FULMPES | 1 | – |
| 92 | STEINACH | 1 | – |
| 93 | KIRCHBERG | 1 | – |
| 94 | BAD KLEINKIRCHHEIM | 2 | 5 |
| 95 | SAALBACH | 3 | 7 |
| 96 | SCHRUNS | – | 18 |
| 97 | BADGASTEIN | – | 23 |
| 98 | MELLAU | – | 1 |
| 99 | ALTENMARKT | – | 2 |
| 100 | HAUS IM ENNSTAL | – | 3 |
| ITALY | | | |
| 101 | SESTRIERES | 7 | 6 |
| 102 | MADONNA DI CAMPIGLIO | 27 | 3 |
| 103 | VAL GARDENA | 23 | 5 |
| 104 | CORTINA D'AMPEZZO | 7 | 6 |
| 105 | VIPITENO | 2 | 2 |
| 106 | APRICA | 1 | 2 |
| 107 | SANSIOCARIO | 1 | 2 |
| 108 | COURMAYEUR | 2 | 2 |
| 109 | LA VILLA | 1 | – |
| 110 | MONTE BONDONE | – | 1 |
| 111 | ABETONE | – | 8 |
| 112 | BARDONECCHIA | – | 1 |
| 113 | CERVINIA | – | 1 |
| 114 | LIMONE PIEMONTE | – | 5 |
| 115 | BORMIO | – | 1 |
| 116 | VALFURVA | – | 2 |
| 117 | VALZODANA | – | 1 |
| 118 | PILA | – | 1 |
| 119 | PIANCAVALLO | – | 12 |
| CZECHOSLOVAKIA | | | |
| 120 | VYSOKE TATRY | 2 | 7 |
| 121 | JASNA | 4 | 2 |
| YUGOSLAVIA | | | |
| 122 | KRANJSKA GORA | 16 | 3 |
| 123 | SARAJEVO | 1 | – |
| 124 | MARIBOR | – | 19 |
| 125 | JAHORINA | – | 2 |
| BULGARIA | | | |
| 126 | BOROVETZ | 4 | – |
| POLAND | | | |
| 127 | ZAKOPANE | 1 | – |

# SKI RACING – HOW IT ALL STARTED

At the end of the nineteenth century, many sports were being rediscovered and modernized. This explosion of interest in leisure gave birth to Alpine skiing, a sport that seemed made to match the new age. It was swift and daring. And once it was established among the snowy peaks of Switzerland and Austria, the idea of slalom and downhill racing could not be far behind.

Norwegian ethnologist Fridtjof Nansen's account of his 1888 crossing of Greenland's icefields on skis-written as he chafed at his bit as curator of the Bergen Museum – was the seminal work. But while it was being read by budding skiers in the Alps, racing of a kind already existed in Scandinavia and the American West. Skiing of the cross-country Nordic kind had existed for centuries. Soldiers, trappers and merchants used coarse, home-hewn boards for exclusively utilitarian purposes, simply to get about in the snow. But they made legendary heroes out of men like Mikkyel Hemmesveit who leapt 23 meters – nearly 70 feet – off an improvised ski jump at Huseby near Oslo in 1879. Ski jumping too is Nordic in origin.

In California, Swedes and Norwegians drawn to the Sierra Nevada by the discovery of gold, organized downhill races with wild mass starts. Cash prizes were awarded from the substantial betting pools. But though a number of such races are recorded, they were not the origin of a lasting sporting trend. When the gold miners left for new strikes in other territories, ski racing vanished with them. Skiing was only to be reborn in California seventy years later with the beginning of modern-day winter tourism on the West Coast of America.

It was the inception of skiing in the Alps that led to modern ski racing. And that in turn sprang from a new interest in mountaineering. As early as the eighteenth century certain city-bred gentlemen were gripped with the craze of conquering the Alpine peaks. While the more daring were scaling Mont Blanc and the Matterhorn, other tamer nature lovers flocked to the high Alpine valleys for the bracing air, mountain walks and the breathtaking

*Above:* Skis were used in Scandinavia from the earliest times. *Opposite:* People from many countries played decisive roles in the promotion of ski racing. Austria's Hannes Schneider (*top left*), Britain's Sir Arnold Lunn (*top right*) – seen here with Austria's Rudi Matt in the ski band – and France's Emile Allais (*bottom*) were three of the most influential pioneers. Schneider was a famous ski instructor from St. Anton. Lunn created the first slalom competition and Allais was the first to use metal skis.

scenery. This led to the rapid development of boarding and lodging facilities. And soon there were not just hotels, but cable cars and cog railways which brought the towering peaks within effortless reach. Mass tourism in the Alps had begun.

It was the railway – built long before the arrival of the first skier – that helped popularize the sport. The most active pockets of winter tourism often developed along the routes of the European expresses which crossed the Alps from West to East. St. Anton and Kitzbühel are two examples. But local railways to smaller health resorts with sanatoriums – like Chamonix, Davos and St. Moritz - also played a decisive role. Almost all the facilities were already in place when the ski craze began to grow to such dimensions that Alpine hotelkeepers opened their establishments in winter.

This process, which took place over a period of forty years, did not happen evenly across the countries that border the Alps, or within the countries themselves. The presence of a large number of British tourists in the Bernese Oberland after the First World War helped a handful of villages – among them Wengen and Mürren – to become bastions of skiing. In Graubunden, Arosa quickly made a name for itself. But while in 1928, when the winter Olympics were held there, St. Moritz advertised a dozen winter sports – among them tobogganing, bob-sledding and skating – there was was no mention of skiing.

The advent of Alpine ski racing took place thanks to a young Englishman whose father owned the Lunn Travel agency in London. For years, Lunn senior had shepherded thousands of tourists around some of the Alps' most spectacular scenery. The English, who by this time had discovered Interlaken, had a romantic attachment to picking edelweiss and were irresistibly drawn to the Mer de Glace in Chamonix.

Born in 1888, it was as a young boy that Arnold Lunn first visited the Alps. By the time he was an adolescent, he was spending most of his time between Chamonix, Crans and Montana in Valais, Adelboden and Mürren in the Bernese Oberland. In love with the Alps and the snow, Arnold Lunn somehow managed to convey his passion to thousands of his countrymen. And it is thanks to him that Alpine ski racing as we know it today finally took root.

In 1905, Kitzbühel had already organized its first downhill ski race. The event was so successful that the following year special trains had to be laid on to bring spectators from Innsbruck and Bavaria. In 1922 Lunn invented the slalom – skiing's first properly codified event. It derived from the gymkhanas he organized for

tourists in need of exercise and amusement. In 1924 he organized the first combined event, a downhill and a slalom. Then he fought hard within the International Ski Federation (FIS) – founded that same year in Oslo – to endorse Alpine ski races, a battle he did not win until 1930.

But it was the meeting of – by then – Sir Arnold Lunn and another giant of skiing lore, Hannes Schneider of St. Anton, which gave birth to the first of the great classics – the Arlberg-Kandahar. This event was to become the real starting point of international Alpine ski racing.

The name of the race itself reflects the collaboration between the two men. Schneider contributed the Arlberg after the mountain range he turned into the Mecca of skiing. It was there, from his ski school in St. Anton, that the mysteries and techniques of skiing were first taught to graded classes, each grade addressing a different stage of the skier's development.

Lunn added the Kandahar in honour of Lord Roberts of Kandahar, the hero of the British raj who distinguished himself in battle during the relief of Kandahar in southern Afghanistan in 1879. In 1911, Roberts donated a magnificent trophy for the race organized by Lunn, on 19 January that year, from the Glacier de la Plaine Morte to the hotels and chalets of Crans-Montana. It was a downhill with the then traditional mass start. And it was called the Roberts of Kandahar Challenge.

Thus was born, in the Arlberg, one of the most majestic skiing terrains, the Arlberg-Kandahar race.

Inaugurated in St. Anton, the Arlberg-Kandahar was to be alternately run there and in Mürren, where Lunn had made one of his homes. In 1938 it was once again St. Anton's turn to host the race. But, a few days before the event, Nazi Germany annexed Austria and the Gestapo arrested Hannes Schneider who they considered

Jumping and cross country were the first competitive ski events. Jumping competitions date from the middle of the nineteenth century. It took all Arnold Lunn's persuasive ability to get the International Ski Federation to recognize Alpine events.

François Bonlieu was one of the best technical skiers from 1954 to 1965. Silver medal winner in 1954, he became Olympic champion ten years later at Innsbruck.

to be hostile to Hitler's regime. In retaliation, Lunn cancelled the race. But he kept up negotiations with the Germans over the next year's event long enough for Schneider to flee with his family to the United States. There Schneider created a new ski school modelled on the Arlberg school he'd been forced to abandon in Austria.

Once Schneider was safe, Lunn refused to let the race return to German-occupied St. Anton. Instead he offered friends from Chamonix, in France–including the young world downhill champion James Couttet – the chance to include their town on the Arlberg-Kandahar circuit. After the Second World War, Sestrière and Garmisch were also included on the circuit, but the original Lunn-Schneider formula was to remain as that era's ski racing model.

Rankings in the Arlberg-Kandahar – and the other events conceived along the same lines: the Lauberhorn, the Grand Prix of the Paris Ski Club in Megêve and Alpine skiing's debut at the Garmisch Winter Olympics – were exclusively based on combined downhill-slalom performance. So when Birger Rudd the multi-talented Norwegian (he won an Olympic ski jump gold medal in addition to the Alpine World Championships) won the 1936 Olympic downhill on the Krezeck course, he did not win a medal. Individual downhill awards were first presented in the 1948 St. Moritz Winter Olympics – where France's Henri Oreiller capped his career with a gold medal – irrespective of the slalom results the next day.

The apparent even-handedness between downhill and slalom in those days was misleading. Downhill still held the whip hand. Ranking in the downhill event determined which competitors would go on to the slalom event on the second day of these two-day competitions. To qualify for the slalom – and thus have a chance to win any prize at all – a competitor had to finish among the top forty in the downhill. Further, the slalom's starting order – which is often crucial – was determined by the downhill rankings. The first five in the downhill tackled the slalom in reverse order, the second five, and so on, in eight seeds of five.

The abandonment of this original Lunn-Schneider formulation, where competitors had to qualify for the slalom with a respectable downhill performance, has led to the modern-day sport's emphasis on specialists. Under the old rules every competitor had to perform well in both downhill and slalom.

Just before the Second World War, at a time when sports in general seemed to be in their Golden Age and Alpine skiing was burgeoning, ski racing reached its first historic summit with the 1938 World Championships in Engelberg, Switzerland. The event was a rite of passage for a sport only codified a decade before.

Until then, the annual duels of the era's best skiers – including professional ski teachers who were thus barred from the Olympics – were demurely called the FIS races, though there had been a World Ski Games in the Mont Blanc valley in 1924. But by 1937 when the races were held in Chamonix, the full passion of international competition was to enter the games.

It was the first time the championships had been organized by France. And the French coach, Paul Gignoux, entrusted the preparation of his team to the most prestigious champions of the time, Toni Seelos of Austria and Rudi Rominger of Switzerland. Both were true professional world champions several times over.

Seelos from Seefeld, whose artistry in the slalom produced the

In the early years of ski racing, the Arlberg-Kandahar was Alpine skiing's greatest event. Until 1970, the starting order of the slalom was determined by the results of the downhill, in order to encourage the all-round skier.

The American Andrea Mead Lawrence was one of the greatest skiers of the early 1950s. She won two gold medals in the 1952 Oslo Olympics. This achievement was matched by another North American at Cortina d'Ampezzo in 1956, Canada's Lucie Wheeler.

parallel turn, drilled his secrets into the French squad while Rominger from Graubunden – the most elegant stylist of his generation – had them glued to his wake as he plunged down progressively steeper and more daring slopes. With such fine coaching, the French, led by Emile Allais who won three gold medals in the slalom, the downhill and the combined, dominated the "mundial" of Chamonix,leaving only crumbs for the foreign skiers including Rudi Rominger himself!

Switzerland – sometimes in concert with Austria, Germany and Italy – had dominated the FIS meets since they were first held in Mürren in 1931. But now France had taken its place as a real contender in Alpine skiing, a fact which the French were to trumpet far and wide, much to the annoyance of their German-speaking neighbours who regarded the French as nothing more than poachers on their private reserve.

Insult was added to injury with the publication of the book, "The French Method" by Emile Allais, Paul Gignoux and G. Blanchon, secretary general of the French Ski Federation. The *mèthode française* was based on the style of their world champion.

At the same time the French were developing their own tourist infrastructure, ski schools and techniques – and announcing to the world that if people wanted to learn to ski they had better come to France to do it.

For months the bitter and argumentative Swiss contested the validity of the French method in the press. The timing was perfect. With the Engelberg World Championships coming up, acrimonious debate in the Swiss papers was a promoter's dream. The slalom race – where the French technique was to be particularly evident – was to be run on the final Sunday of the meet. It attracted more than 20,000 spectators.

In the end, the sport itself was the best judge. James Couttet of Chamonix was crowned downhill champion at the age of seventeen, Rudi Rominger took the slalom title and Emile Allais took the combined crown home to Megêve.

The outbreak of war in the summer of 1939 cut skiing in half and brutally ended the brilliant careers of the current champions. The Lauberhorn races were run uninterrupted each winter in Wengen, Switzerland, but their international character was sometimes only guaranteed by a handful of Frenchmen from Chamonix or Megêve. Shortly before the end of the war some of Italy's best skiers – including Zeno Colo – also raced. Many had crossed the border into Switzerland in 1943 and had been interned. But their political status did not technically allow them to participate in civilian events, so they raced under pseudonyms like Donner (Thunder) and Blitz (Lightning).

The Germans twice organized an International Week in Garmisch. Skiers from the neutral countries and the Axis Powers, including Japan, took part in races there in 1940 and 1941. And after occupying Norway, the home of the International Ski Federation in Oslo, Nazi Germany and Fascist Italy even organized World Championships in Cortina d'Ampezzo in the Italian Alps.

This was to be a last moment of triumph for the German champion Christl Cranz and a last taste of the exhilaration of skiing for her brother Caro, a champion of great charm and brio. He was to die a few months later on the Russian front.

Though the medals were awarded amid great pomp and ceremony by the son of the Italian king, they are no longer listed in any official records. Freed at the end of the war, the International Ski Federation simply erased those World Championships from their books.

Once the war was over ski racing took off again with zest. In Wengen, Ernst Gertsch – who'd won the slalom segment of the first Lauberhorn Cup he'd helped create in 1930 – worked tirelessly to make the event the most important of that era. And in France and Switzerland, International Weeks galvanized skiers long starved of big-time competition.

In 1948, the Winter Olympics were hosted by St. Moritz for the second time – the first had been in 1928. Henri Oreiller became the first hero of the post-war games by taking both the downhill and the combined titles. For a good number of the pre-war champions, the long lay off during the war had hastened their retirement, as was the case with Rudi Rominger and Emile Allais. Some had paid for the war with their lives. The Austrian and German teams, especially, boasted many new faces. But many of the pre-war champions – such as James Couttet, Zeno Colo, Karl Molitor, Ralph Olinger and Edi Reinalter who won the gold medal in the slalom – were still on form. Indeed, Colo – who had already had a glorious past – went on to win the 1950 World Championship downhill at Aspen, Colorado, and the 1952 Olso Olympic downhill.

But new blood was pumping into the sport. Switzerland's Georges Schneider, loose-limbed and easy-going in life, superbly stylish on skis, became the world slalom champion at Aspen. Blond Norwegian Stein Eriksen won the giant slalom – an event initiated in 1946 at the suggestion of Paul Gignoux – at the Oslo Olympics.

Italy's Zeno Colo was one of the all-time great all-round skiers. In 1950 he won the downhill and the first giant slalom of the World Championships at Aspen and finished second in the slalom. He also won the Olympic downhill in 1952, but was disqualified by the FIS the following winter for being a professional.

The champions of the 1950s were all great characters and their achievements helped promote Alpine ski racing all over the world. Skiers like triple Olympic champion Toni Sailer (*left*), Canada's Lucie Wheeler (*centre*), Christian Pravda (in ski bib) with the hero of the 1952 Oslo Olympics Norway's Stein Eriksen were famous even in countries where it never snows.

The charismatic Eriksen soon became the post-war ski king. François Bonlieu, who came from the north of France, and learned to ski by aping others, came second to Eriksen in the giant slalom at Åre's 1954 World Championships. Ten years later, at Innsbruck, Bonlieu became Olympic gold medalist in the same event.

This was a period of great progress, with Christian Pravda at the core of an Austrian team built along simple and modern lines by Fred Roessner, a geography and physical education teacher. Under his tutelage, the Austrians dominated international skiing for six winters. So powerful was the "Wunderteam" that even after Roessner abandoned it to its own destiny after the 1956 Winter Olympics at Cortina d'Ampezzo, it kept on winning. One of the greatest ski epochs had begun, with Austrians Christian Pravda, Anderl Molterer, Fritz Huber, Ernst Hinterseer, Toni Sailer and Karl Schranz on one side. On the other were the American Buddy Werner, the Swiss Willy Forrer and Roger Staub, the Japanese Chibaru Igaya, the French Charles Bozon, Adrien Duvillard, François Bonlieu, Jean Vuarnet and James Couttet who had been in competition since 1937.

It is thanks to this extraordinarily high level of competition that Toni Sailer's three gold medals in the Cortina Winter Olympics had such an unprecedented reception – at a time when television was still playing only a marginal role in image making. Even in countries where snow only existed in picture books, skiing – and Sailer – gripped the public imagination.

Germany's Ludwig Leitner, Austria's Karl Schranz and France's Guy Périllat then began to take their place among the ranks of the champions. Like their predecessors, these heroes still raced, more often than not, simply for glory. Some enterprising athletes sometimes managed to cadge a few thousand Swiss francs from the ski manufacturers whose equipment they used. But most were happy enough to keep a few pairs of skis at the end of the season which they resold at half-price to tourists in their home town resort.

For some, financial security only came later, once their career was already over. A handful of champions learned to market their names and their technical know-how. Stein Eriksen, Jean Vuarnet, Anderl Molterer, Pepi Steigler, Willy Forrer, Ernst Hinterseer, Toni Sailer, Karl Schranz and Jean-Claude Killy were among them – with Killy and Schranz being lucky enough to cash in on the beginning of the World Cup circuit.

It was to be the advent of television coverage that made the Lauberhorn in Wengen, the Grand Prix of Megêve, Kitzbühel's Hahnenkamm, the Arlberg-Kandahar, the women's races in Grindelwald and, of course, Innsbruck's first Winter Olympics in 1964 powerful media events – first on a national scale, then internationally thanks to the Eurovision network. Soon the broadcasts spread to Eastern European countries, then to such unlikely places as Algeria and Morocco. By 1966 television had turned skiing into an international spectator sport – and everything was set to usher in the World Cup.

In the 1950s Alpine skiing crossed new frontiers. Japan's "Chick" Igaya (*left*) was one of the best international slalom specialists. He won medals at the 1956 Olympics and the 1958 World Championships. Even Louis Armstrong (*centre*) learnt to ski. The legendary Karl Schranz won his first classic, the Kandahar at Chamonix, in 1957.

# We're working for you full time.

**Introducing the new Mazda 323 with full-time 4-wheel drive.**

When the Front-Wheel-Drive Mazda 323 was first introduced, it was an instant hit with drivers, journalists and engineers the world over. Its balance of sporty handling, comfortable ride in a roomy, yet compact and stylish car set the trend that others are still trying to follow.

Meanwhile, Mazda engineers weren't just resting on their laurels. Their advances in engine technology have increased power. And their advances in suspension technology, like the award-winning Twin-Trapezoidal Link system, have helped to handle this power. But Mazda engineers felt that the best way to really take full advantage of an engine's zip was to build a car with real grip; so they set out to develop a Mazda 323 with full-time 4-wheel drive.

**A traction-packed story**

Mazda engineers have been exploring 4-wheel technology for many years; going beyond 4-wheel drive to include 4-wheel steering as well on the MX-03 prototype. Th idea behind this breakthrough technology i simple; the more control you have over all four wheels the better the car's agility, stabi braking and acceleration.

Short of 4-wheel steering, the best wa to enjoy these advantages is to have full-tin 4-wheel drive. The problem, however, was that the system's centre differential was too heavy and bulky, lowering efficiency and stealing cabin space. That's one reason wh many car makers have abandoned full-tim

impractical. Mazda, however, decided to ve full-time the time it deserved. It took four ars of testing and research, but the results ve you the driving pleasure you deserve.

**e difference is the differential**

By developing a centre differential that volved around planetary gears, Mazda gineers not only saved space and weight, ey were able to adjust the system for a rfectly even distribution of torque. And to easure up to the system's capabilities, the azda 323 4WD gives you plenty of torque to play with in its new 1600cc 16-valve DOHC intercooled turbo engine. But, of course, that's just what the 323 4WD was designed for; to play with.

**Full-time fun**

Tear down the highway in confidence. Take the tight turns with a smile. Stop sure. Surely this is the sporty performance you've been looking for; zip and grip.

The Mazda 323 4WD is the result of Mazda's full-time commitment to drivers. And we think it's time well spent, because the result for you is full-time driving fun.

*The Mazda 323 4WD*

*Models and features shown may not be available in your area. Please consult your local Mazda dealer.*

10

# THE APPROACH OF THE WORLD CUP

The World Cup was to be brought into being by a near-perfect conjunction of events and the support of a handful of important people. The very name chosen to designate it was of the utmost importance. World Cup, *Coupe du Monde, Weltcup, Coppa del Mondo* echoed like a fanfare in all the languages of the world.

Even before the first race, the World Cup was to assume significance thanks to its name.

At that time, other than in soccer, there were no other World Cups. And soccer's international trophy had only been dubbed the World Cup by the British that same year. Today, of course, there are a hundred-odd world cups, in everything from sailing to cycling, fencing to volleyball, rugby to bob-sledding. In skiing alone – including jumping and cross-country – there are half a dozen, all inspired by the name and, sometimes, by the spirit and the formula of the Alpine skiing World Cup which I and my colleagues created.

The World Cup was not a journalistic creation. I can confirm that having been a journalist since 1940. But it was an event devised with the media in mind – not just the mass circulation newspapers and the sporting press – but radio and especially television.

Audiences, readers and sponsors have shown this to be right. The World Cup has become a massive worldwide attraction. But in the early days there were only three journalists who were prepared to put their professional weight behind the project. Those three were: Michel Clare of *L'Equipe,* the famous French sports paper; John Fry, then managing editor of *Ski Magazine* in New York; and Austria's Kurt Bernegger, a reporter for *Salzburger Nachrichten,* now with Austrian television and to my mind the most far-sighted commentator of that era. I might never have dared push our project forward had he and I not shared a similar approach to sports.

And what of all the other sportswriters and broadcasters? While they were not really against the World Cup, neither were they ready to support it. Later I was to read with great interest that a good many of them had, for a long time, imagined a similar rank-

If the World Cup (*above*) had existed in the 1965-66 season, Karl Schranz (*opposite*) would have won it. He dominated all the classics that year including the unofficial "Challenge de *L'Equipe* ", the competition sponsored by a French sportspaper and a forerunner of the World Cup.

The US coach Bob Beattie (right), pictured here in Vail with Serge Lang during the 1965 ski World Series, played a crucial role in the creation of the World Cup. His idea to organize a series of international races in the US that March, enlarged the frontiers of the sport.

ing system. Well, such a system was not unique. Other sports had adopted a point-based ranking system for some time. The Desgrange-Colombo Challenge and the Prestige Pernod in cycling, and the Golden Ski of *L'Equipe,* awarded ten years earlier, all used similar systems.

However, the World Cup borrowed its format from sailing. It followed its system of only counting a limited number of finishers from each discipline towards the overall ranking. "That way, our skiers won't feel obliged to participate in every race," said French team coach Honoré Bonnet.

He was wrong. That was, we were all to realize very soon, giving too little credit to racers' tactical sense. Even after having accumulated their maximum number of points in any given event, they still raced to deny rivals the chance. After all the first place was worth 25 points.

The story of the World Cup began late one January morning in 1966, less than a hundred metres from Hinterseer Farm, halfway down Kitzbühel's Hahnenkamm downhill course. Struck by sudden inspiration, I turned to French coach Honoré Bonnet and US coach Bob Beattie, who were also there to watch the practice runs.

"What we are going to do," I said, "is hold a World Cup."

I was speaking in English for the benefit of Bob Beattie, so "World Cup" was the actual phrase I used. In a way, of course, I can take no great credit for this. For several weeks the British had been using the term, for soccer's world championship being played in England that summer.

That year, skiing and football seemed to travel a good way down the same road. Even in Portillo, Chile, where the Alpine World Cup was effectively to be launched a few days later, I found myself on the edge of the downhill course at 10 am – listening to the soccer final between England and West Germany at Wembley.

It was thanks to Bonnet, Beattie and Dr Sepp Sulzberger, a lawyer who, since 1958, was in overall charge of the Austrian Alpine skiing teams, that the Cup was launched. However, it was Marc Hodler, president of the International Ski Federation (FIS) since 1950 who had the courage to shoulder the heavy responsibility and declare that the first World Cup would be raced under FIS patronage on the 1967 winter schedule.

I once read that history knows how to choose the men and the women it needs to carry out its destiny. Perhaps it is true. After all, I held no mandate in any ski federation. The only office I held was as newly elected president of the International Association of Ski

Journalists. But this was enough to enable me to have official – and usually friendly – relationships with the executives of the various ski federations, the FIS and, more importantly, its president.

Even though Hodler had long been enthusiastic about such a project, nothing was certain in Portillo. Even after long days and nights of negotiations with my three partners and with the project finally ready, Bob Beattie doubted that we would get FIS approval. For a week he had set out possible objections while still being one of the World Cup's greatest supporters. Then one evening he got up from the table, pointed to a piece of paper on which we had noted the various points of our agreement – the dates of the first schedule, the rules and the points system and so on – and said: "Marc Hodler will never accept this proposal."

Fortunately this was a gross misreading of Marc Hodler, of his sportsmanship, enthusiasm, goodwill and far-sightness. The next day, around noon, and in the same bar where – with the aid of much "Pisco" and coffee – we'd just spent a good part of our Chilean nights, Marc Hodler studied the proposal for a few minutes then asked simply: "What time do you want me in the Press Room to announce the creation of this World Cup?"

So everything was set. In the heart of the Andes, thousands of miles from the Alps, the old era of pre-World Cup ski racing died on 11 August 1966. And another, new era, whose outlines we could not yet make out, was about to begin.

The simultaneous naming of Bonnet, Beattie and Sulzberger as the three head coaches of their respective national teams, lent them considerable credibility. Since the retirement of Fred Roess-

The 1966 World Championships took place in the small resort of Portillo, Chile. It only had one hotel. But it is unlikely that the World Cup could have been created elsewhere. The Italian, Carlo Senoner, was the surprise winner of the slalom at Portillo.

ner in 1956, no coach had attained their stature. This could also lead one to believe that, they too, were destined to fundamentally alter the face of Alpine skiing.

At that time international ski racing was in the doldrums – except for its natural peaks, the Olympic Games and the World Championships which kept their dominating role thanks to the media and popular support. However, there was a new medium to contend with. At about this time, the growing interest of television highlighted the need for change in the ski racing format. It had already begun to make its presence felt in the skiing world, making its own stars out of what had formerly been simply ski racing champions. Racers like Jean-Claude Killy, Karl Schranz and Leo Lacroix clamoured for TV attention. International racing was desperately in need of a new showcase.

Bonnet and Beattie had come up with the idea of the Alpine Countries Cup some time before The concept had played down individual victories and elevated nation-by-nation racing. This was an excellent idea in itself, but not likely to generate mass support. Ski racing is a sport of individuals, not a team game. And TV wanted to concentrate on the stars.

However, that same year, 1964, Beattie, Bonnet and Sulzberger decided to create a tournament in Vail, Colorado, restricted to the American, French and Austrian teams. To justify this three-country "World Series", Beattie stated that the contest would exclude nations whose athletes had not won medals in the Innsbruck Winter Games the previous year. This was the case for the Swiss, who had been freewheeling since the tragic death of Georges Schneider in the summer of 1963, and for the Canadians.

While the Americans, French and Austrians battled it out in that memorable encounter in Vail, the Swiss, left to their own devices, turned the snub into a question of prestige. Many of their racers then skied on American-made Head skis. Then there was the matter of FIS points: the athletes competing at the three-nations contest at Vail were reaping points by the sackful. It was in mid-March 1965, with the Vail series still in progress in Colorado that a powerful Swiss team descended on Sun Valley, Idaho, where the North American circuit was continuing with the Harriman Cup. Despite the antagonism generated by the limiting of the Vail contest, all Alpine countries had, by coming to Sun Valley, implicitly accepted the idea that the American circuit was worthy of their best racers.

But something else was also triggered during 1965. It happened in summer, far from the slopes, in the heart of Roubaix where a

From 1964, Jean-Claude Killy (centre) was one of the best slalom skiers in the world. But he had to come to Portillo to win his first downhill. His team-mate Leo Lacroix (right) finished second and West Germany's Franz Vogler was third.

dense crowd had gathered to witness the morning start of one of the stages of the Tour de France. Through the confusion of the cycling teams' arrival, Jacques Goddet – owner of *L'Equipe* and head of the Tour de France itself – strode towards me in pressed khaki pants like central-casting's idea of a British officer.

"Hello Serge," he said. "Listen, dear friend, no-one can make head nor tail of this ski racing business any more. One day Killy is winning, the next it's Schranz, Marielle or Tom, Dick or Harry. Come on, get me something together. A challenge to decide the winner, a gimmick or something, like the Super Prestige Pernod. Fix it with Albert de Wetter and get me the outline before the end of the Tour de France."

At that time, Albert de Wetter, a noted journalist, was one of *L'Equipe's* two representives in the Publicis group, the main advertising agency of this important sports paper. De Wetter shouted over an awful cacophony of car horns: "I've found a client

Billy Kidd, second in the Olympic slalom of 1964, was one of the world's best skiers in the mid-1960s. But his many accidents prevented him from winning the World Cup. He retired in 1970 after becoming combined World Champion in Val Gardena.

who wants to spend a quarter of a million to link his logo with skiing and snow – it's Evian mineral water. You get the picture – drink Evian and feel like you're in the French Alps. Set up a challenge with a ranking over a number of races . . . See you in Bordeaux."

In Saintes, on the eve of our next meeting, I drafted my project. There was to be a points system: 25 for first place, 20 for second, 15 for third and so on. There would be a dozen races. Everything was to begin at Hindelang in West Germany and to end, at the beginning of March, in Mürren with the Arlberg-Kandahar where all the points would be added up. It was a simple idea and, including the schedule, it fitted on two double-spaced pages.

I gave my outline to de Wetter the night of the Bordeaux stage of the Tour de France. But it did not seem to interest him as much as it had a few days earlier in Roubaix. The challenge was, however, to begin – as scheduled – a few months later. It was won by Karl Schranz and Marielle Goitschel. But it was called "Challenge de *L'Equipe*" and not "Challenge Evian". Because of a banal misunderstanding, the original sponsorship agreement had never been completed.

The "Challenge de *L'Equipe*" survived one year. A wasted year? Hardly. That season was a great prelude to the World Cup. After Billy Kidd, who led the Challenge after his slalom victory at Hindelang, injured himself during the Hahnenkamm slalom in Kitzbühel, no-one talked of anything but the World Cup – the name which had struck a chord a stone's throw from Hinterseer's farm.

The first World Cup would, however, be graced by the Evian Trophy – the famous crystal globe. Once Evian learned that what was at stake was no longer a challenge but an authentic World Cup under the aegis of the FIS, the company wanted to share in it.

I have good reason to believe that had the 1966 World Championships – then held every four years – taken place anywhere but in Portillo, Chile, in the Southern hemisphere far from the Alps, the World Cup would never have seen the light of day. The Southern Cross were to be our lucky stars. If those World Championships had been awarded to a more traditional European venue – Davos, Garmisch or Kitzbühel, for instance – our proposal for a World Cup – which would run throughout the season from country to country – would not have overcome the opposition of the most conservative voices in skiing. But in Portillo, they were of no consequence. They did not come.

The move to Portillo was itself revolutionary. Think of it . . . what kind of idea was it, to go and hold World skiing championships, in mid-summer, at the far end of the world, let alone to discuss a new idea for a World Cup? Anyway, at the crucial moment, the stick-in-the-muds were not there to bray that a World Cup would serve no purpose and would only cause additional problems. Of course, they made their positions known, but much later – too late, once everything had begun.

The whole set-up in Portillo was of vital importance too. The small resort was situated a few kilometres from the Chilean-Argentine border, perched at nearly 9,000 feet. All the skiers and officials had to live together in a single hotel offering only 100-odd beds. This excluded battalions of unwelcome visitors.

Everything had to happen either in the hotel or on the slopes. While the Andes offered an admirable diversity of skiing, in the hotel everything was confined to dining room, bar and the basement night club where those who professed to find sleeping difficult because of the altitude spent their nights.

It was in that bar, which was deserted after dinner, that Bonnet,

Marc Hodler, (right) president of the International Ski Federation since 1951, was soon convinced of the potential of the World Cup. His support was vital to its creation in 1966 and its official recognition in 1967.

Beattie, Sulzberger and I sat day in, day out. Later, I was to chide myself for not having invited a fifth man to our meetings – Switzerland's Peter Baumgartner, a man whose advice would certainly have been useful.

With his experience as a coach and an organizer, Baumgartner had begun to rebuild the Swiss squad, demoralized by lack of success since Georges Schneider's untimely death in 1963. He was to make the Swiss into one of skiing's great powers. But I did not know him well enough then to confide in him the details of our ambitious project. He never held it against me and really helped when, less than a year later, our World Cup was submitted to the FIS for approval.

Would the World Cup have seen the light of day without these World Championships staged in the Andes, thousands of miles from Europe? Probably not. The same powers-that-be who opposed this Mundial in mid-summer in South America were in no mood 20 years ago to discuss a skiing World Cup. And they were certainly not interested in a Cup whose creators came from outside their own ranks.

So how did the World Championships ever turn up in Portillo?

The miraculous string of events that led to the successful delivery of the infant World Cup began with the vote designating Portillo as the site of the 1966 World Championships – and a particularly massive vote it proved to be.

In the beginning, it seemed that Portillo did not have the remotest chance. A few weeks before the FIS convention in Athens, representatives of all the Alpine countries met in Zurich and publically proclaimed that there would be no question of assigning the World Championships to a country where they would have to be held in the middle of summer and that, in any case, no Alpine country would support such an odd-ball candidate as Chile.

I must say that such an opinion was also that of the general public and that, when I learnt the result of the vote which gave Portillo the Championships while covering a bicycle race in Italy, I too asked myself what madness incited the delegates to the Athens convention. How could they have staged such a drastic about-face and opted for staging the World Championships so far out of the European season? Later, I was enthusiastically converted to the choice of Portillo, not just because I associated it with the birth of the World Cup, but because the Championships there were such a great success.



So how did Chile's candidature get such unexpected approval?

Essentially, it was due to two people – Sergio Navarete, Chile's delegate to the World Championships, and his attractive young wife who was a member of the Santiago Opera. The couple spent practically all winter in Europe, visiting resorts, going to all the races, meeting hundreds of journalists and executives from all the federations. They then visited all the Eastern European countries, staying in East Berlin, Moscow, Prague and Sofia. There Navarete, a persuasive communicator, swung the Eastern bloc's votes behind Portillo. With all these in his pocket, he had a stable base of support in the first round of balloting.

But it was in Athens itself that Navarete brought off his most brilliant coup. With his beautiful wife by his side, he met all the International Ski Federation delegates, including those who had taken the solemn oath to vote against Chile, at all costs, in Zurich.

"Gentlemen," he said. "I know it's all over. We have no chance. But at least spare me the shame of going home to Chile empty handed. Imagine what will happen if I don't get a single vote. They're capable of shooting me."

*Above:* Jean-Claude Killy, the first hero of the World Cup, jumped into the swimming pool of the hotel in Portillo after he won the downhill and the combined. In 1967, Killy won all the World Cup titles and 12 races out of 17. His fantastic achievements lent weight to the World Cup.

Ernst Gertsch, the father of the Lauberhorn races at Wengen which he created in 1930, was one of the strongest supporters of the World Cup in 1967. The fact that those races counted towards the World Cup was promoted in his programme.

At these words, Mrs Navarete batted her long eyelashes. Urbain Cazaux, President of the French Ski Federation, later told me in his gravelly Pyrenean accent: "I was looking at the girl. God, she was pretty. And he was such a nice guy. And dammit, I wasn't going to leave them in a mess. So I decided France would give them a vote. What the hell, I'd give them two – that way they wouldn't lose face. What a rascal Sergio was. He really took me for a ride."

A few days after the Athens vote, 10,000 Chileans greeted the triumphant Navaretes as they stepped off the plane in Santiago. Alas, three years later, stripped of all his responsibilities, Sergio Navarete was even declared persona non grata in Portillo.

In Portillo, the French feasted on medals – 16 out of a possible 24 and a World Championship record. Only one crown slipped from the grasp of Jean-Claude Killy, Guy Périllat, Louis Jauffret and Leo Lacroix – the Italian Carolo Senoner's slalom victory. Mindful of an assured combined victory if he simply avoided a fall, Killy had played it too safe in the slalom's second heat, leaving the way open for Senoner.

The French women did equally well, better in fact, considering that the only gold medal not won by Marielle Goitschel, Isabelle Mir or Annie Famose was the downhill, which was won by a man. But this was only discovered much later.

While the racers' attention was fixed on the events of the World Championships, most of them greeted the idea of a World Cup with enthusiasm. Jean-Claude Killy, who was to be the big winner of the Portillo World Championships, told me a few days before their start: "None too soon, this World Cup! I seethe at the idea of what could happen at these World Championships. Take Karl Schranz, for example. This winter he had a fantastic season. Here he's in a series of one-day races. And if he doesn't win a single one ... what will we look like?" And that is exactly what happened. In Portillo, the "Black Eagle" from St. Anton who, a few months earlier had eclipsed all his rivals, had to settle for a consolation medal in the giant slalom.

A few months later, as the opening date of the first World Cup approached, I had misgivings. How would it be greeted by the countries with long skiing traditions, whose races were already classic events long before the World Cup was thought of. Later the Cup not only helped all the classics but proved to be crucial in the development of many other races and many other resorts.

The first inkling of how the traditional skiing countries would react came from Ernst Gertsch, the father of Wengen's

Lauberhorn races. The name "World Cup", he announced, would be on the whole range of official programmes, posters and result sheets, as would be the Cup's rules and regulations. Adelboden – through Dr Fred Rubi, director of the tourist office and a high Swiss government official – gave proof of its co-operation a few days later. But Kitzbühel – the Mecca of Tyrolean Alpine skiing where the people are wary of anything they have not thought of and created themselves – would be the moment of truth. I discovered the answer as I arrived in the centre of town. In front of the Hotel Tenne a banner spanned the main street proclaiming the magic word: *"Weltcup."*

In Germany, where Berchtesgaden organized the first two World Cup events on the slopes of the Jenner, no notice was taken of it. But it is true that we did not take care to inform Berchtesgaden of its presence on the World Cup calendar. Kurt Bernegger of the *Salzburger Nachrichten* saw it coming though. The day before the Berchtesgaden races, he headlined his January 5 article: "Historic Day for Skiing – The World Cup is Coming." And in Madonna di Campiglio in Italy, the organizers realized too late that a slalom, run in their traditional "3-Tre" event was to count towards the Cup. In the event, the Cup would only fire the Italian imagination in December 1969, with Gustavo Thoeni's first victory in the Val d'Isère giant slalom.

The Governor of Massachussetts, Napoleon Volpi, was to make no mistake about it, however. When the Pan-Am flight landed in Boston in March 1967, he was there to greet the World Cup racers heading for Franconia, New Hampshire, where the World Cup was to make its American debut.

Jean-Claude Killy's achievements (back-to-back wins in

Guy Perillat was one of the few skiers who could beat Jean-Claude Killy in 1967. He won the slaloms at Megêve and Madonna di Campiglio and finished third in the overall World Cup standings.

*Right:* In the mid-1960s it was a great adventure to race in the US. The World Cup's last event in 1967 was at Jackson Hole, Wyoming.

*Above:* Goitschel and Killy fight it out, this time with guns and not skis.

Europe's then most prestigious downhills: Wengen, Kitzbühel, Megêve and Sestrière, plus first-ever back-to-back slalom wins at Wengen and Kitzbühel after the downhills) certainly helped his own personal prestige by winning the first overall World Cup title. But, perhaps even more, he helped the prestige of the World Cup which motivated him so strongly.

But it was with the dramatic duel in America between Marielle Goitschel and the Canadian Nancy Greene later that season that the World Cup really took off. By the time of the final slalom at Jackson Hole, Wyoming, only an outright win by Nancy Greene could deprive the French girl of her overall points lead and the Crystal trophy. To the delight of the North American audiences, Nancy Greene took the slalom by seven-hundredths of a second, and with it the overall World Cup. As a dramatic event, the World Cup had proved itself beyond all our expectations.

The endless Portillo nights, the hours and hours of discussion, the tired old arguments, the rehashing of issues we'd thought already solved had proved worthwhile. The face of Alpine skiing had been changed at a stroke. During that 1967 season, the downhills, slaloms, giant slaloms, whether great classics or races until then of modest importance, had all suddenly become star events.

The celebration of the World Cup's successful first year took over Jackson Hole, the season's last stop. And some party it proved to be. No-one had seen anything like it in Wyoming since the days when, after six months of hunting and trapping along the Snake River, the rugged mountainmen of yesteryear would come to town to let off steam.

It all happened in the Cowboy Bar. With no food served before 7 pm, the house staved off the racers' hunger with round after round of stiff shots of Scotch and Bourbon. When the prize-giving finally rolled around, a good number of the competitors were joyfully participating from the floor and under tables. The ceremony, which FIS vice-president Bud Little and Evian's Baron de Soultrait struggled to bring to order, looked like nothing so much as an out-take from Hellzapoppin. Guy Perillat appeared on stage disguised as a ghost, and Jean-Claude Killy as something utterly unrecognizable. The surrealistic staging was directed by Britain's Jeremy Palmer-Tomkinson, complete with a model airplane on his head, its propellers spinning, its engine backfiring and the whole thing surrounded by winking red lights.

Then it was time to prepare the World Cup's second season. Firstly, we realized it was crucial to place it officially under the aegis of the International Ski Federation. This was to happen in June 1967, in Beirut, only a few days before the Six Day War. Beirut was chosen – over many other sites – by the preceding FIS general assembly. As the meeting began, Beirut was still a magic city of great beauty and peace, but high in the skies, the vapour trails of the Israeli Mirages were visible above the ruins of Baalbek.

Backstage at the FIS, the in-fighting began immediately. I was shocked. The World Cup which had come so far still annoyed a lot of people. Only two months after Jackson Hole, Bob Beattie was already unsure that we had made the right move. I was too. We wondered what would happen if we simply took the World Cup back and ran it ourselves, selling the individual races to local organizers as does the Tour de France? And why not? Setting up such a structure independent of the FIS would have been possible. Legally, the World Cup still belonged to those who had invented it

Aspen hosts the greatest American World Cup race, the Roch Cup – now known as the Winternational. World Cup races have been held there every year since 1981 and the downhill is the most exciting of the tour.

Nancy Greene (*left*) and Marielle Goitschel were the great women contenders of the early World Cups. Their fight for the 1967 overall title remains one of the most dramatic contests of all time. They both retired in 1968 after winning Olympic gold medals at Grenoble.

and promoted it, not to a federation filled with voices which called for it to be banned. Bob and I became involved in seemingly endless discussions again about the World Cup, just as we had done the year before at Portillo. But we both eventually came to the same conclusion: if we wanted to take the World Cup back and run it ourselves, it could be done.

Nevertheless, we also concluded that it was unthinkable to act in a way which Honoré Bonnet, Sepp Sulzberger and, most of all, Marc Hodler, would have seen as an intolerable departure from the spirit of the initial project, and perhaps even, as a betrayal of its ideals. Bob and I abandoned our dreams and got down to the difficult task of putting the case for a World Cup circuit under the aegis of the FIS.

I had spread myself thin in the first hectic days in Beirut, reassuring those delegates who needed reassuring, enlisting those who needed enlisting. By 2 pm on the final day, everything seemed to be settled.

In a restaurant on the Beka Plain cooled by a waterfall, I walked over to Marc Hodler who was finishing his lunch.

"They're all agreed," I told him. "If you get them together over coffee, everything can be settled in a few minutes."

Hodler looked at me.

"Out of the question," he snapped. "The downhill-slalom committee wants to debate the World Cup's FIS ratification – pretending that they weren't advised – well, let them go back to Beirut and debate it then. They deserve it."

I too left that cool oasis to return to Beirut only to find a worried-looking Peter Baumgartner pacing outside the room. "Don't join it," he said, "don't go in. They're furious at having had to come back to Beirut. If they see you, they'll be even less favourable."

The discussion lasted several hours. Finally, as expected, the downhill-slalom committee members agreed. There was one additional tangible result: Bibbo Nordenskjoeld from Sweden was elected to the World Cup committee. Thankfully, he is still in it.

Next day the convention ratified the downhill-slalom committee's motion. And so, at last, the World Cup became an official FIS event. As the delegates left Lebanon, unconsciously living through its last hours of happiness, the Six Day War was beginning. But for the World Cup, the danger was over and ski racing was on its way to becoming a major international sport.

Annemarie Moser-Proell and Gustavo Thoeni won ten overall World Cup titles between them from 1971 to 1979. She was unbeaten from 1971 to 1975 and won again in 1979, clocking up a total of 62 victories. He took the Cup from 1971 to 1973 and again in 1975 after a dramatic duel with Ingemar Stenmark.

# THE FOUR ALPINE DISCIPLINES

The first Alpine skiing events, and more particularly the Arlberg-Kandahar created in 1928, consisted of only two contests – the downhill and the slalom. But these days, with increased speeds, better equipment and improved techniques, the number of competitive Alpine skiing events has been increased to four: downhill, slalom, giant slalom and the Super-G which is a longer and faster version of the giant slalom. Each demands a different approach and even different equipment.

The downhill is the freest form of Alpine competition – it is longer and has fewer gates. Initially it consisted simply of getting down from the top of a mountain into the valley or resort in the quickest possible time.

The preparation of the piste, the regulations, the training methods remained for a long time at this very uncomplicated level. It was not until the end of the 1950s that the regulations became more exacting, obliging the competitors to wear crash helmets and to complete at least one downhill non-stop, without a pause.

They were also forbidden to take shortcuts and the number of gates was increased. The FIS required, moreover, that the organizers have their speed runs approved and provide safety nets, straw bales and foam padding at the most dangerous points of the course. A technical delegation mandated by the FIS is responsible for the application of the regulations.

According to its layout, a downhill course might favour either the gliders, that is to say the very fast athletes who build up speed on the easy straight sections, or the technicians who are most at home in turns or traverses where it is essential to put balanced pressure on the edge of the skis.

The downhill has gone through a number of phases since the institution of the World Cup. There has been the constant increase in speed which has been the logical outcome of improved conditions on the course, better training for the skiers and the technical progress made in their equipment which changed considerably at the end of the 1970s. The quality of the equipment has now assumed a decisive role. Just as pneumatic tyres often made all the difference to Formula One motor racing, skiing victories depended more and more on the qualities of ski soles.

At one time members of the technical committees and the organizers became worried about the ever-increasing speed attained by skiers. So they put a stop to this development by making courses more technical, slowing the pace with more turns.

This is why the pure specialists are often challenged and even beaten by more versatile champions like Andreas Wenzel, Phil Mahre, Pirmin Zurbriggen or Marc Girardelli, who are just as much at home on twisting slaloms as they are on the straighter downhills.

The fact that Zurbriggen was able to take the World Championship title in 1985 after having won twice in succession in Kitzbühel has led trainers and skiers to question their training methods and their approach to ski racing. Nowadays, the downhill specialists spend more time working at the technical disciplines – the giant slalom and even the slalom – during their training period and even during the course of the season.

The giant slalom, designated an official event by the FIS in 1946, was originally a downhill controlled by a larger number of gates whose function was to slow down the competitors and give them a more precise route to follow. Its other function was to provide a spectacular and demanding race for those resorts whose mountain slopes were too short or too steep for a downhill.

To differentiate between the two events – the downhill and the giant slalom – precise standards were introduced by the FIS and each course has to be approved by an FIS inspector.

Since its inception the giant slalom has been considered by many experts to be the most modern form of slalom. It has, in effect, tended to become more acrobatic, yet controlled. Indeed, the giant slalom seems destined to turn into a contest appealing to racers with a highly developed technique coupled with immense physical strength.

During the 1950s, it was by no means rare for a giant slalom to last more than three minutes and for the winner to be several seconds ahead of the field. In 1956, Toni Sailer won the Olympic giant slalom at Cortina d'Ampezzo by more than six seconds.

From 1966, giant slaloms forming a part of the World Cup, were organized in two parts with reverse-order departure for the second run. At that time, each seed consisted of 15 skiers.

The philosophy underlying this contest changed rapidly during the seventies. Speeds increased and courses that used to be covered in three minutes were soon being covered in two. In 1972, the Frenchman, Roger Rossat-Mignod took just 2.07.65 minutes to cover the two parts of the giant slalom at Berchtesgaden in which Patrick Russel broke a leg after the finish line.

Insufficiently long pistes and the growing number of skiers specializing in just one event had effectively turned the giant slalom into just another slalom event. So the FIS created the Super-G – or Super Giant Slalom – which aimed to be the meeting point between the best slalom skiers and the best downhillers. It was, in fact, nothing more than a modern form of the old giant slalom in one part. Staged for the first time in December 1981 at La Villa in Italy, the Super-G has been part of the World Cup since 1983 and joined the World Championships during 1987.

The development of the slalom has also been noticeably influenced by the World Cup. The slaloms of 1986 bear little resemblance to those of the 1960s even though the number of gates and the average vertical drop remain the same.

The slalom was once a race of speed and skill which allowed the competitors to exhibit their technique. Now it is a type of boxing match fought over a steep piste which has usually been iced up with thousands of litres of water and where articulated plastic poles reel from the skiers blows – the old ash and bamboo poles which splintered under the pressure of the skiers' edges have long since been replaced.

At one time competitors completed the slalom without touching a pole. Arnold Lunn, the creator of the Arlberg-Kandahar, even recommended placing a ping-pong ball on the top of each pole and awarding penalty points to those who knocked them off. And in the past, time penalties were given to the racer who straddled or missed a gate. Now they are simply disqualified in these cases.

The slalom is currently the discipline that requires the most specific preparation. The champions frequently pass through more than 10,000 gates during training. But these days form is no longer enough. Aggressiveness, concentration and cool-headedness play as important a part as physical strength or technique.

The great slalomer Phil Mahre, who also raced in the downhill from 1978, contrasts the disciplines. The giant slalom, he reckons, is the most difficult and demanding test of technique. "It demands as much precision as perfection and great physical strength," he says.

Downhill, in his opinion, is the easiest as it is possible to achieve an excellent time while committing faults or drifting from the ideal line. And slalom is the most acrobatic – but it also demands a greater amount of courage and determination. During training the skier receives violent blows all over his body when he strikes the poles, until he learns to ward them off with his forearm or knees.

In addition to the four main disciplines, there is the parallel slalom, which is only occasionally raced. It is a slalom where two or more competitors race simultaneously side by side down two or more courses. Unlike the other disciplines it is not raced against the clock.

## SLALOM

Slalom competitions must be raced on snow that is as hard as possible to permit maximum speed with precise execution of technique. A slalom is raced against the clock. FIS rules decree that a slalom is always decided over two runs on two different courses. Both courses must be used one after the other. The vertical drop of the course should be 180 to 220 m for men; 130 to 180 m for women. The course must be at least 40m wide if two runs are set on the same slope.

**Number of Gates**
Men: Minimum 55 gates Maximum 75 gates.
Women: Minimum 45 gates Maximum 60 gates.

A gate is made from two separate, self redressing plastic poles of the same colour. Each gate is coloured either red or blue and has matching flags. Consecutive gates must have alternate colours. A gate has a minimum width of 4m and a maximum of 6m. The distance from turning pole to turning pole of successive gates may not be less than 0.75m and not more than 15m.

A slalom course must contain open and vertical gates as well as a minimum of two and, whenever possible, three vertical combinations (consisting of three to five gates) and at least four hairpin combinations.

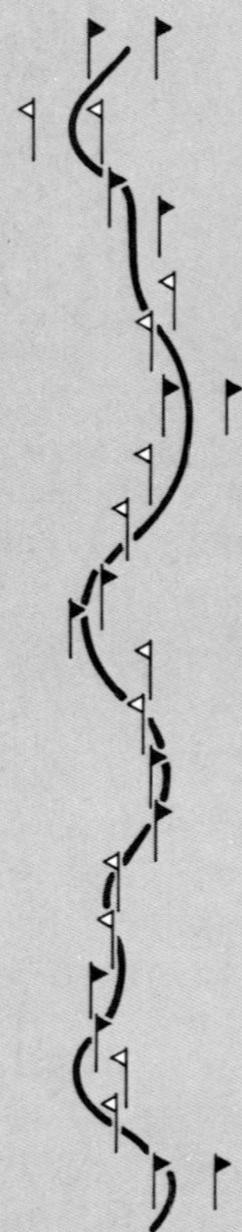

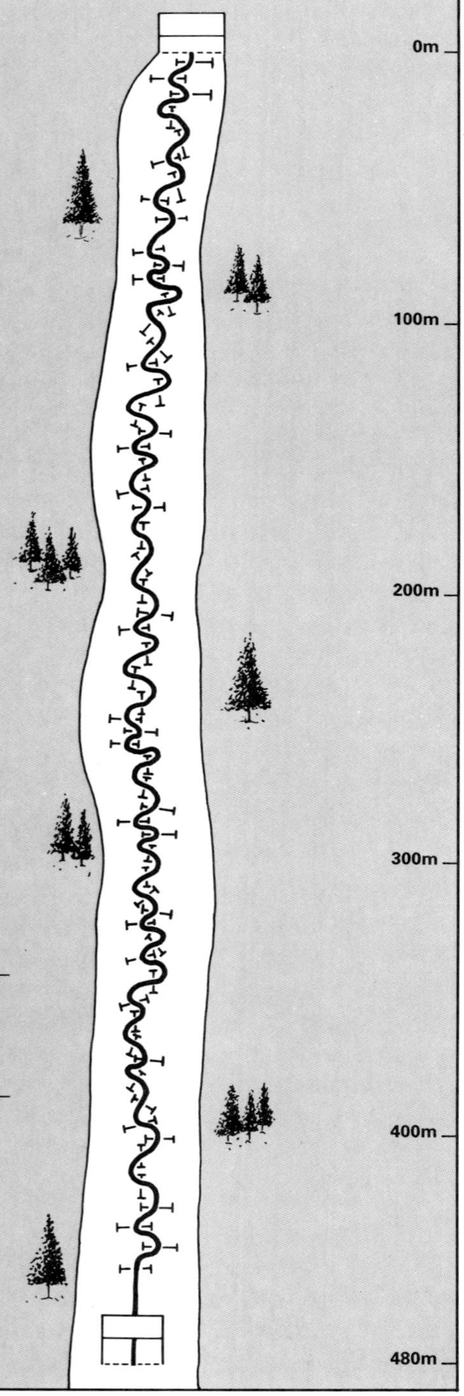


The diagram shows a typical slalom course with overall length measured in metres.

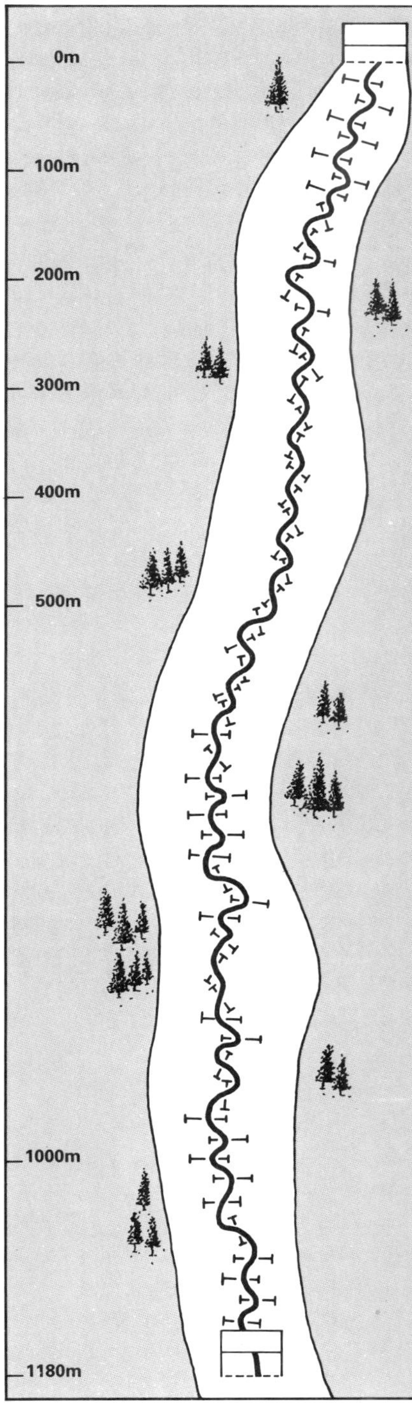


The diagram shows a typical Giant Slalom course with overall length measured in metres.

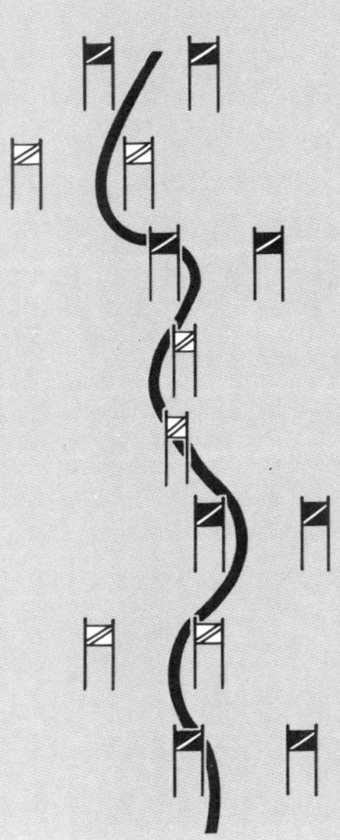

## GIANT SLALOM

In the World Cup the vertical drop for the men's and women's courses is 300m. The terrain should be undulating and hilly and the course at least 30m wide. The course must be prepared as for a downhill race. The parts of the course where gates are set and where competitors have to turn must be prepared as for a slalom.

A giant slalom should present a variety of long, medium and small turns. The competitor should be free to choose his own line between the gates, which must not be set down the vertical line of the slope. The full width of the hill should be used wherever possible. The race is decided, against the clock, over two runs set in such a way that there is as little difference as possible between the best times of each run.

Giant slalom race flags are fixed between the poles so that the lower edge of the flag is at least 1 metre above the snow. The flags are at least 75cm wide and about 50cm high. The turning pole of the gate is a self-redressing pole.

Gates must be alternately red and blue, the blue flags preferably with a distinctive mark, ideally a diagonal white stripe to aid visibility.

A course consists of single and double gates. Double gates must be at least 4m and at the most 8m wide. The distance between the nearest poles of two successive gates must not be less than 10m. The gates must be set so that the competitors can distinguish them clearly and quickly at high speed. The two flags of a gate should be at right angles to the racing line.

## SUPER GIANT SLALOM

The 'Super G' has some of the characteristics of a downhill, combined with some of the giant slalom's features. A men's giant slalom has 56 gates, a vertical drop of 300m and an overall length of approximately 1,180m. A downhill's length is around 3,300m with sufficient gates to guide the competitors safely down the course and a vertical drop of between 800 and 1,000m. A Super-G course has only 35 gates but an overall length of 2,000m and a vertical drop of around 600m.

A Super-G competitor wears the same body-hugging suit and crash helmet as a downhiller but normally uses slalom ski poles.

The diagram shows a typical 'Super G' course with overall length measured in metres.

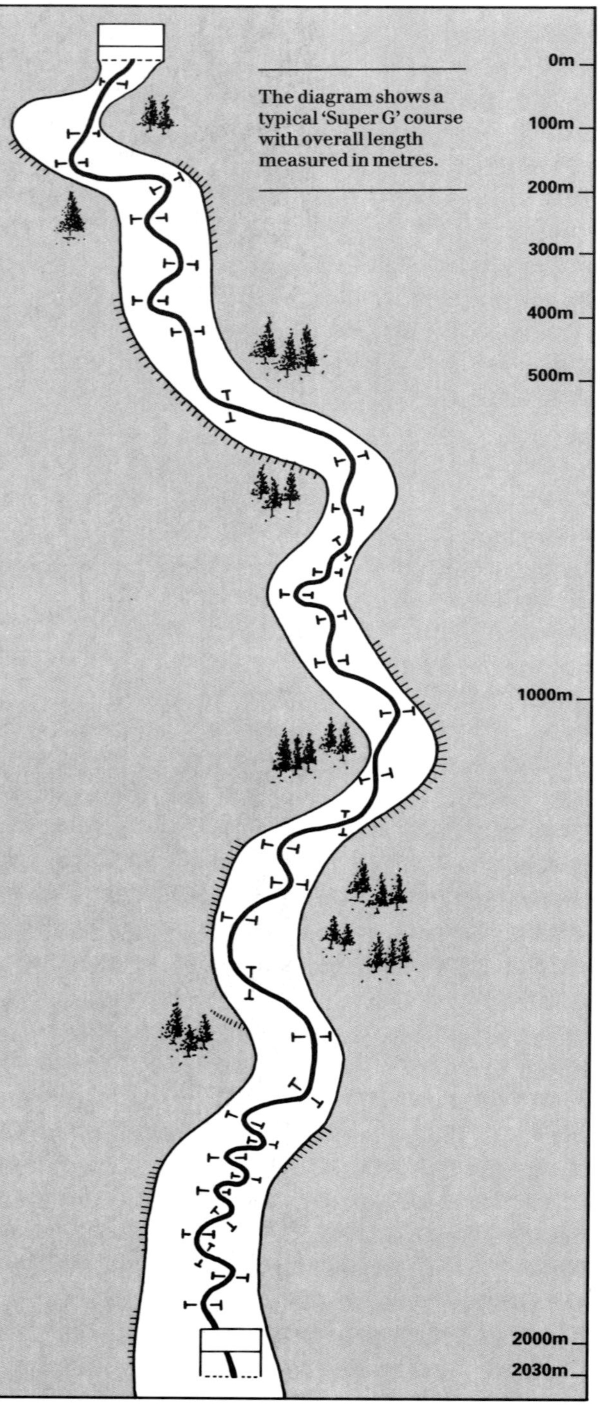

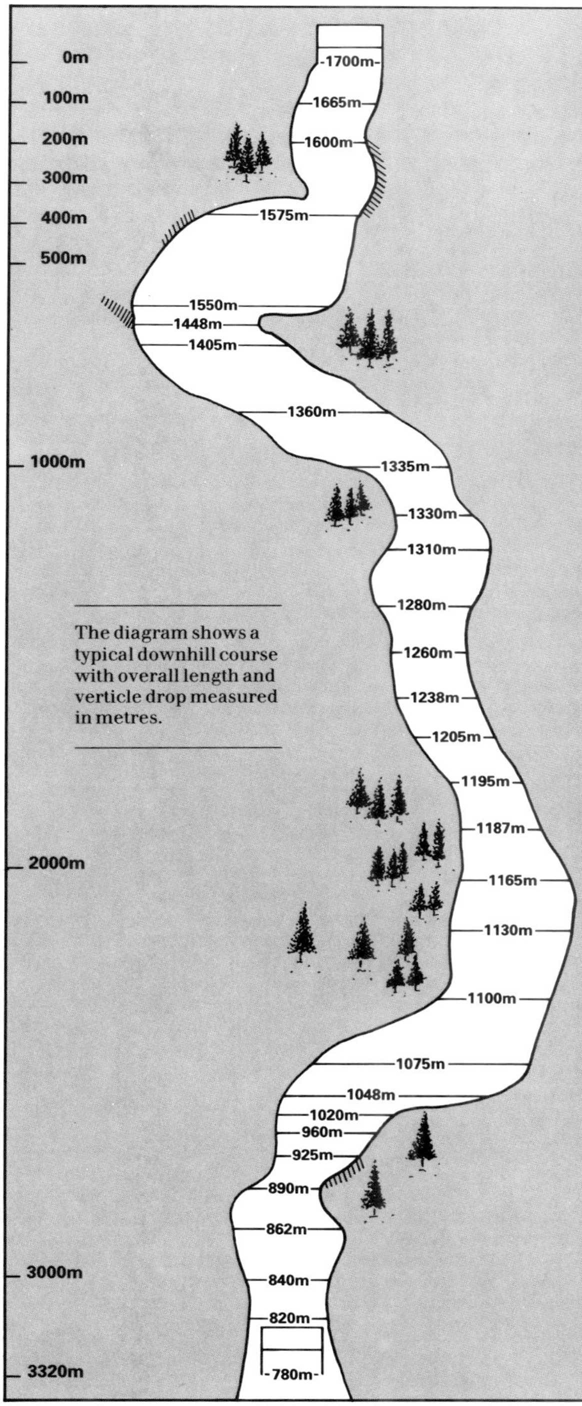


The diagram shows a typical downhill course with overall length and verticle drop measured in metres.

## DOWNHILL

All World Cup downhill courses must apply the following criteria and be approved by the FIS:

**Men**
Vertical drop: minimum 800m
maximum 1,000m
Width of gates: minimum 8m

**Women**
Vertical drop: minimum 500m
maximum 700m
Width of gates: minimum 8m

**General characteristics of the course:** The course must be completely cleared of stones, stumps and such obstacles, in order to eliminate all objective danger for the competitors, especially when snow is scarce. Very high speeds which may lead to the risk of dangerous falls, must be eliminated by setting sufficient gates to reduce the speed of the course, thus limiting average speed.

The course must not include steep ledges, which carry competitors through the air for long distances. The course must become wider with increasing speed. On the outside of medium or high speed curves there must be plenty of cleared space beside the course, so that a competitor who is falling and is thrown off the course cannot be injured by hitting obstacles.

Downhill gates are numbered from top to bottom, not counting the start and finish. Men's downhill courses are marked by red gates. Women's courses may be marked by alternating red and blue gates, or only red gates. A gate consists of two poles joined by a rectangle of cloth approximately 0.75m wide, 1.0m high.

mazda

# HOW TO WATCH SKI RACING

The major Alpine ski events began to be televised in the 1960s and the classics like the Lauberhorn at Wengen and the Hahnenkamm at Kitzbühel became great sporting events for the public at large.

When the World Cup competition imposed a structure on the season, the duels between the leading personalities attracted millions of new viewers each week and certain events like the parallel slalom at Val Gardena in 1975 broke all viewing records.

But however good television pictures may be, they cannot recreate the tension of the event viewed live. The standard of the competitors is now so high that it is becoming increasingly difficult to discern the almost imperceptible differences between them. And without the aid of the clock running at the bottom of the screen it would be virtually impossible to judge how a contestant was doing.

To the trained eye, though, all the vital information is there. The skiers themselves study their own videos in training. Each national team has a fully equipped video unit and every day contestants devote an hour or so to watching themselves on video and discussing how to improve their performance.

To help you appreciate what you are seeing, books and specialist ski magazines devote pages to photo-montages which are analysed by coaches and other experts. On the following pages, four skiers – Rok Petrovic, Michela Figina, Paul Frommelt and Silvano Meli – are shown performing the three principal disciplines: the slalom, the giant slalom and the downhill. The montages show clearly the differences between their techniques at the turn – short and sharp in the slalom, precise and controlled in the giant slalom, long and powerful in the downhill – their reflexes, the physical commitment and their choice of an "ideal" line which vary greatly from one speciality to another.

Alpine skiing is one of the most televised winter sports. The classics at Kitzbühel and Wengen are broadcast by between 20 and 30 TV stations from around the world. Television helps the organizers find big sponsors for their events and it makes the champions famous. Downhill is the most watched of the disciplines.

## THE SLALOM

Since the introduction of "rapid gates" – that is, articulated poles – the slalom has become a very spectacular discipline with few things in common with the slaloms of the mid-1960s. The racers now try to follow a straighter line without turning around the gates. They push the gates with their arms or their knees. Specialists such as Marc Girardelli, Ingemar Stenmark or Rok Petrovic ski with great power, dancing from one leg to the other as they pass the 60 to 70 gates of a run at around 50 miles an hour. Strong nerves, sharp eyes and fast reactions are necessary to find the fastest way through the forest of poles with the tips of their skis passing only centimetres away from them. Many slalomers wear a plastic helmet to protect their head from the plastic poles. Before the start of each season, the specialists pass through over 10,000 gates in training.

BASF
12
Wengen

BASF
SUISSE
DESCENTE
SUISSE
10

BASF
20

BASF
20
86
WORLD CUP FINALS

## THE GIANT SLALOM

Giant slalom is the most demanding discipline from the technical and physical point of view. Skill, determination, aggressiveness and power are all required to tackle a run. The best specialists are able to manoeuvre their skis under them with apparent lightness and follow the fastest line as if on invisible rails. In the giant slalom the turns are smoother and larger than those in the slalom. And, as in car racing, it is important to keep a constant speed around the curves and come out of them as fast as possible. In giant slalom racers must also keep strong control of their movements. They accelerate in the turns by standing up and crouching down. Some also lean back.

mazda
1
ST. ANTON
mazda
1
ANTON

## THE DOWNHILL

Downhill is not only the longest and the most dramatic, but also the most complete of the disciplines. To win on demanding courses like the Hahnenkamm at Kitzbühel, the Kandahar at St. Anton or the Cevedale at Bormio, a racer must be tough, aggressive, a fine glider, a good technician and have nerves of steel at the same time. It is impossible to win without all these qualities. The ability to keep the skis as flat as possible on the easier parts of the slope and to remain tucked in the most aerodynamic position is as decisive as being able to keep up as much speed as possible in the turns, where the pressure on the legs – which act as shock absorbers – is intense. Skiers show their courage when they are airborne in the great jumps, or when hurtling down a steep schuss at 90 miles an hour

# DOWNHILL'S GREATEST CHALLENGE

If there is one course that sums up what World Cup ski racing is all about it is the Hahnenkamm downhill at Kitzbühel. Each year only around 50 skiers take up its challenge even though there would be close to 100 on other runs. They prefer to watch it on television, or take part in other downhills – but secretly they dream of the day when they too, will also experience what must be one of the world's great sensations. So to appreciate something of what the top World Cup racers have felt, let's take a run down the legendary "Streif".

The starting point is a cabin at the top of a small hillock with a fantastic view of the Kitzbühel valley. Down there, all along the course, thousands of spectators are massed. The atmosphere is hushed, expectant. There you wait, the tips of your skis pointing into the abyss. The starter gives you the warning – "Ready" – "Attention" – and seconds later "Go!"

The shock awaiting those tackling the "Streif" for the first time is awe-inspiring. From the start you are plunged directly into freefall, a wide-open space that begins at the starting ramp and hurls you into a new dimension. Several seconds later there is an abrupt break. This is the famous "mousetrap". After a short turn to the left on a very technical slope you reach the sheer jump which must be judged precisely. By this time your speed is approaching 65 mph – the slightest loss of concentration would send you flying 50 yards, before crashing back onto the piste. Some skiers prefer to close their eyes.

Back on the icy surface, there is no time to draw breath. A curve to the left is followed by a short flat shelf, then a turn to the left and one to the right which leads to the sheer wall of the "Steilhang", a rock face that is as steep as it is icy. It has often been compared to the north face of the Eiger.

With its humps, two columns and an exit towards a forest, along a line of safety nets, the Steilhang is really quite terrible and just to cross it you need to be a top grade competitive skier. Often, it is nothing more than a wall of blue-tinged ice. For weeks on end, every evening, tons of water are poured over it to keep the snow in place. Then it can only be crossed on skis or crampons.

As you hurtle across the Steilhang your head rings with the noise of your skis. It is only the strongest and bravest that keep as high a line as possible, giving the maximum speed down the long track through the forest.

You scarcely have time to relax along this gliding path. Concentration here is of the essence. It is essential to hold the skis quite flat along the footpath and negiotate the turn to the left that leads to the centre of the forest. You must not think of the burning sensation in the muscles of your thighs which have remained tightly contracted for 20 seconds.

Then you arrive at a clearing and there is a small break in the slope – but not for long. It is followed by a long fast slope, a curve to the right, a ledge, a turn to the left, a new traverse forward, a small schuss and a long curve to the right followed by a long incline straight ahead.

This is a last brief moment of respite before the last major difficulty on the course, the "Hausberg". And there's still everything to play for. Here, the seconds count double, but by now your legs are aching and your concentration has gone. The slightest fault at the edge and there is an endless drop. Even the crash barriers will not be strong enough to contain you.

Then the terrain starts to dip again. An S-bend is followed by the Hausberg jump. There is another incline that levels out abruptly at the bottom, then the track swings left across a 65 mph traverse whose rutted surface has already been criss-crossed by the tracks of other racers. This brings you to the final launch ramp.

As you approach it, your speed is close to 85 mph. And at the bottom there's a savage compression where it is almost impossible to retain control. All you can think of is keeping as tucked as possible. You don't even hear the crowd roar as you hurtle past the finish. You hear nothing until you've stopped and taken your helmet off.

Then the first thing you do is look at the scoreboard. "Was I fast enough for a win and 25 more points?" There is not a skier on the World Cup circuit who has not dreamt of winning at Kitzbühel. A victory there is worth more than a gold medal. Many are happy just at having had the privilege of competing, and in their memories they will ski the course over and over again. It is classics like these that World Cup racing is all about.

Wool hat – many racers also wear a protective helmet in the slalom
Goggles have screens with different colours to suit various weather conditions
The gloves now look like boxing gloves
The skis are still the most important part of the skiers' equipment. The best carry a dozen pairs with them during the season
Slalom poles are metal or fibreglass Racing pants lend some protection against the slalom gates
Bindings are very sophisticated and can resist pressure of hundreds of kilograms
Boots are made of plastic with foam inside, formed to fit the feet

## EQUIPMENT EVOLUTION

The age of the wooden ski ended only seven years before the World Cup's inception. Adrien Duvillard heralded the new era in 1960, by winning the Hahnenkamm downhill on metal skis – "skis one does not need to wax," boasted Laurent Boix Vives, of Rossignol, the firm that had made Duvillard's Allais 60s.

Jean Vuarnet was to become Olympic champion at Squaw Valley a few weeks later on the same type of skis which were characterized as "clean and as black as night". This began sales of a thousand pairs a year in the US alone, and Rossignol were eventually to gain the allegiance of 20 million skiers world-wide.

Bindings went through a similar revolution. At the 1956 Cortina Games, Toni Sailer won his three gold medals with his boots bound to his skis with long thongs – the theory was that the ski would break during a bad fall, sparing the leg. But by 1958, Hannes Marker, a resourceful German engineer, designed a toe-piece with a mechanism that freed the foot in the event of an accident. A similar product was introduced in France by Georges Salomon and Bel who perfected a binding that released back and front.

The pressure of the World Cup forced manufacturers to use the races as a testing ground for improvement and innovation. Until then, the manufacturers' representatives only appeared at the prize-givings to drink champagne with the winner they had entrusted two or three pairs of skis to. But after 1967, the major manufacturers were putting together a real race service programme. Men from Rossignol, Dynastar and Dynamic in France; Atomic, Blizzard, Fischer, Kastle and Kneissel in Austria; Head in the US; Erbacher and Voekl in Germany and Spalding in Italy tuned and planed the skis they thought right for the conditions. Still there was only a limited number of skis involved. But as developments came thick and fast, the downhill racer became test pilot for new designs.

Dynamic's Michel Arpin, having ended his own racing career the year before, worked almost exclusively for Jean-Claude Killy in 1967. And a symbiotic relationship developed between the two. Both wore the same sized boots, so Arpin tested Killy's skis and they could discuss exactly what they felt under the bases.

Later, the services for the racers became more sophisticated, with various manufacturers feeding their computers masses of data determining – particularly in downhill – the appropriate choice of skis. Every snow condition, every course, was to be matched by a different pair of skis. The downhill racer, like the pilot or grand prix driver, now has to blindly trust his equipment to his serviceman.

In Franz Klammer's heyday on Fischers, the head of the race service was Dr. Gerold Krims, a man who meticulously kept every pair of skis on which Klammer had won. With each pair, there was an index card, detailing the snow temperature of various sections of the course, the maximum speed, even the run's compass direction. It was thanks to this background information

Slalom skiers attack the gates with such force that their equipment has to be reinforced. The ski edges must be razor sharp.

Karl Schranz

Bowed poles fit under the arms better when the racer is in the tuck position.

Strong helmets protect the racers from crashes at speeds up to 90 miles an hour.

Downhill boots are softer than slalom boots to help gliding.

Design of downhill skis is the result of high technology. Most research concentrates on the base of the ski and the control of vibration.

that Fischer's technicians could pick and tune winning skis some two or three years later. The method was all the better since run-in skis are incomparably faster than a pair just off the production line. Honore Bonnet, the French coach, was the first to detect that phenomenon in 1965.

The overall effect of this equipment evolution gave the technicians – the ski reps – working for the various manufacturers a crucial role. Jan Larsson, Rossignol's Swedish racing chief, says that skis must be chosen according to a racer's build and skiing style – whether it is aggressive or subtle. His height and weight will determine the amount of pressure put on various sections of the ski and his style will determine how their balance must be tuned. The most important factor, Larsson insists, remains the general and specific flex of any given part of skis – both in the shovel and the heel – and its torsion and camber which, together, give a ski its overall characteristics. But the final tuning must be done in the field, not in the factory.

For slalom and giant slalom, the ski must cut swiftly and grip with precision which requires a laterally flat base and a precisely filed edge along the whole length of the ski. For downhill, the skis are slightly longer – around 2.30 m as opposed to around 2.03 m for slalom. The skis must allow a downhiller to make high-speed turns without loss of momentum and – to avoid friction – the base must be as smooth as possible. Edges on downhill skis are sharpened along more or less of the ski's length, depending on snow conditions, steepness and the type and number of turns on the course.

Equipment progressed simultaneously on all fronts from 1967. For example, even the most trustworthy ski depends on the quality of the boot on it. Boots are harder and firmer in the slalom – downhill gliding requires softness and sensitivity. Downhillers like Peter Muller and Franz Klammer have often won in boots that were hardly tight. It is also the quality of the boot which allows the new multi-directional safety binding – designed to release in the greatest possible number of configurations – to function at its best.

Karl Schranz was the first to become aware of the advantages of properly modified ski clothing around 1965. He created quite a stir when he showed up for the 1965 Lauberhorn in a body-hugging one-piece silk suit, bought second-hand from an Italian speed skier who was achieving speeds of around 180 km/h (112.5 mph) on the slopes of the small Matterhorn, near the Theodul pass in Zermatt.

The French then took the lead in suit development, testing their outfits in wind tunnels in 1966. Their downhill suits, designed by Hans Hess, were plastified, a process until then forbidden. This revolutionized the look of the downhill skiers and allowed them to race under optimum aerodynamic conditions.

For the manufacturers, success in high-level competition is a way of keeping their brand in the public eye. But it also a way of testing and perfecting the mass-production equipment of tomorrow. The prototypes raced by today's champions are destined to enter tomorrow's public domain.

With cruising speeds today of 70mph compared with 50 to 60mph twenty years ago, top racers rely heavily on the preparation of their skis, particularly the base.

SH ARRIVO ZIEL
GUINNESS
LONGINES
CARIPLO
Valli & Colombo

# WHAT HAS CHANGED IN TWENTY ONE YEARS

The start of the 21st World Cup saw the competition returning home to the southern hemisphere. It was born there, in the Andes, far from the Alpine origins of skiing itself. The World Cup was created at Portillo in Chile in 1966. In August 1986, the World Cup began with two downhills at Las Leñas in Argentina.

The aim of the World Cup was always to broaden ski racing's horizons from the narrow confines of the Alps. True to that spirit, the World Cup has been staged in Japan, Alaska, the Vosges, the Pyrenees and at smaller resorts like Ebnat-Kappel in Switzerland and Todtnau in West Germany.

It has also taken place in more unlikely spots – the parallel slalom has been staged in Vienna. One day, perhaps, thanks to artificial snow, it will turn up in Berlin, Milan, Lucern or Basel, or even on Montmartre's famous Butte in Paris. The World Cup's goal has always been to be a truly international event and it is hoped that it will soon fulfil that destiny by including races in China, India, New Zealand, Australia and the Soviet Union.

Ski racing only fully developed when the World Cup helped it to expand beyond the home of the classics at Wengen, Kitzbühel, St. Anton, Garmisch, Val Gardena and Megêve. The Cup has also changed the sport out of all recognition. Downhill, slalom and giant slalom used to be the only events thought worth considering. The World Cup itself now includes parallel slalom and the Super-G. Cross-country skiing, jumping and relay competitions have their own separate World Cup competitions.

Alpine World Cup events were originally conceived for racers like Jean-Claude Killy, Marielle Goitschel, Karl Schranz and Guy Perillat who raced in everything and anything the schedule threw at them – slaloms, downhill and giant slaloms. The organizers did

Many things have changed in Alpine ski racing since the birth of the World Cup. It developed into a major sport which gets a lot of attention from the media from all over the world. The organizers of the classics hand out as many as 500 press accreditations.

not hesitate to substitute a downhill for a slalom, if conditions dictated. Nobody had grounds to complain as the champions could easily transfer from one event to another.

In 1967 and 1968, Killy set standards that many feared would never be matched. But comparing those early performances with those of today's champions like Pirmin Zurbriggen, Marc Girardelli or Ingemar Stenmark, is like comparing the Formula One performance of a driver like Fangio to that of Prost.

The needs of the national teams and their federations also increased ten-fold during the last 21 years. A team's success, and wins by at least one of its stars, became more essential than ever. Specialization became the order of the day. Skiers were trained more or less exclusively for a single event: downhill, slalom or giant slalom. However, the World Cup's real aim was to select the best overall skier and it soon faced its first crisis.

The problem began in the early 1970s with the long domination of the competition by the Italian slalom and giant slalom champions Gustavo Thoeni and Piero Gros. To counter this, the method used to establish overall placings in the World Cup was changed several times, while the points system for individual events, and for the Nations Cup (the World Cup's overall team championship) remained unchanged until 1979. From 1967 to 1978, the ten top skiers in each race scored points from a maximum of 25 for the winner to 1 for tenth place. In 1979, this was changed to include the top 25 skiers. Since December 1980, the first 15 have been allocated between 25 and 1 points.

For the last six years, the World Cup has returned to a less artificial formula in which the number of events counting towards the various classifications are determined by the number of races on the schedule. In 1986, for example, the five best results in the downhill, slalom, giant slalom and the three best in the Super-G

*Below:* The World Cup has been designed for skiers who can compete in all specialities. Henri Duvillard was one of the few who could win races in any discipline. The Frenchman was a great Cup star from 1969 to 1973 but never managed to clinch the overall title.

*Right:* Karl Schranz and Jean-Claude Killy, two greats of Alpine skiing and early World Cup winners. It wasn't until 1985 that another skier, Pirmin Zurbriggen, reached their standard.

and combined all counted towards the overall men's standing.

A number of changes were imposed on the World Cup and the International Ski Federation (FIS) committees by pressure from within the sport as national teams fought for advantage. Some of these changes were detrimental both to the Cup's spirit and its image. In 1971, while the Frenchmen Jean-Noel Augert, Patrick Russel and Alain Penz accumulated slalom and giant slalom wins, the French coaches proposed that the number of results counting towards the overall placings be increased from three to four. In the end, the racers' five best finishes in each discipline were included. This allowed skiers who specialized in the technical disciplines of slalom and giant slalom to clock up more points towards the overall title by virtue of the greater number of these races in the season.

The fact that the Frenchmen failed to win the World Cup despite this rule change shows what master tacticians the Italians were. They realized immediately that under the new formula their own slalom specialist Gustavo Thoeni could win the overall World

Italy's Gustavo Thoeni was the first of the slalom specialists to win the overall World Cup. His ability to surpass himself at moments of great pressure allowed him to take the trophy four times. 1975 was his best year. It was then that he finished second at Kitzbühel only three-hundredths of a second behind Franz Klammer.

The achievements of the champions always created excitement. In the 1970s, Switzerland's Russi and Collombin, Italy's Thoeni and Gros, Sweden's Stenmark and Austria's Klammer attracted a lot of fans.

Cup with good results in only the slalom and giant slalom. This was much easier than fighting it out on the downhills which require gruelling weekly training sessions. He could accumulate enough points in events in his own specialist disciplines without having to be a good all-rounder.

The formula was changed again before the 1972-73 season to counter the effects of this Italian specialization and to make the competition more balanced. The winter was divided into segments for the purposes of calculating overall placings. A limited number of the competitors' best finishes from any discipline were then counted towards the final result from each segment. In 1975, thanks to this system Franz Klammer, who won nine out of ten downhills (only failing in Megêve which cost him the final victory), stayed in the running with Thoeni and Stenmark right up to the very end of the season. All three reached the first final with the same number of points: 240, and all was decided during the most dramatic and exciting confrontation in World Cup history.

Klammer even had a considerable advantage over Thoeni and Stenmark. He had only to reach the quarter finals and he would have had too many points for his rivals to catch him. But on the eve of the race, the Italian organizers in Ortisei, Val Gardena, sprayed the course with water so that it was covered with a thin film of ice – more difficult to negotiate for the downhiller than the slalom specialists who regularly race on icy courses. This denied the Austrian downhiller any chance of winning the World Cup, although, including the points he gained in the combined, and in one of the giant slaloms (he nearly won at Whistler Mountain in Canada), he could have become the first great downhiller to take the World title, thereby taking revenge on the slalom and giant slalom specialists who refused to wear the downhillers' helmet. That winter, Thoeni won the famous final against Stenmark and his brilliant record-breaking fourth World Cup title. It was also that year that the slalomer from Stelvio swore to himself that he would become a great downhiller. He was as good as his word in a way that elicited admiration from his opponents, especially the

downhillers. He finished second in the legendary Hahnenkamm. This was a triumph in itself – but the slalom-specialist was only one-hundreth of a second behind "Kaiser" Klammer himself.

In 1978, the World Cup reverted to the 1967 to 1970 formula, devised at Portillo in an effort to encourage all-rounders again. This counted only a racer's three best results in each discipline.

The effects of this step back were disastrous because even before mid-January, after a series of wins, Stenmark, the arch slalom specialist found himself virtually crowned overall World Cup winner. So it was then decided that, to give an advantage to racers who made the effort to compete in all the disciplines, points should be awarded down to 15th place. In 1974, another modification was tested to encourage all-rounders. Any racer who was placed in the top ten in a contest such as the Lauberhorn, Hahnenkamm or Arlberg-Kandahar – which by definition included both downhill and slalom events – would see their points doubled. A year later, the combined downhill-slalom titles were reinstated in the points structure instead, as the World Cup itself was a kind of combined event. The combined solution was simpler, but it always had the disadvantage of giving cheap points to racers who simply managed to finish a downhill or a slalom.

These changes have sometimes meant that the World Cup has missed an overall dominating personality, an all-round champion like Killy or Schranz. This has, fortunately, happened infrequently and eventually the World Cup again found the kind of racers it was

Franz Klammer was the best downhiller of the World Cup. He won 24 downhills from 1973 to 1985 and lost the overall World Cup title in 1975 only in the last race, a parallel slalom in Val Gardena.

created for. Scoring on all fronts, Peter Luescher – in 1979 – and Andreas Wenzel – in 1980 – found themselves capable of beating the specialist Stenmark, despite his brilliance in the slalom and giant slalom. Before becoming Olympic champion in the 1984 Sarajevo slalom, American Phil Mahre – overall Cup winner from 1981 to 1983 – also realized that he had no real chance of beating Stenmark without competing in the downhills and picking up combined points. He chose Kitzbühel in 1981 to prove himself, to show that even the fierce Hahnenkamm course did not frighten him. Mahre came ninth, taking World Cup points while Stenmark was left with the field. This clinched the overall title for Mahre and, after that, Stenmark lost all interest in the World Cup rankings after racing in this, the only downhill of his career.

Since 1984, the World Cup has at least two new champions who are able to win in all the disciplines: Pirmin Zurbriggen and Marc Girardelli. And there are more waiting in the wings.

A fourth event was added to the original three principal Alpine disciplines in 1983: the Super-G. This is a hybrid conceived as a meeting place for the best technical skiers among the downhillers and the most daring of the giant slalomers. The International Olympic Committee immediately adopted the Super-G for the 1988 Calgary games after the US television company ABC offered a firm $305 million for the broadcasting rights.

In the last few years, sponsors – without whom the big competitions would not exist – have become partners in the World Cup itself and in its various events. Back in 1967, sponsorship brought

America's Phil Mahre was Ingemar Stenmark's greatest rival from 1977 to 1984. Their fight for supremacy brought a lot of attention to Alpine racing. Second in 1978, third in 1979, Mahre won the overall title from 1981 to 1983 after becoming a good downhiller.

in only a few hundred thousand dollars to all the races, men's and women's, those in the US as well as those in Europe. Today the race organizers alone receive roughly 15 million dollars a year from sponsorship, TV rights and gate money. Add to that the money generated by the World Cup – travel expenses, coaches' and technicians' salaries, the cost of ski equipment given to the racers by manufacturers – and you have a massive, and growing, multi-million-dollar industry. So it is not surprising that, since 1984, the skiers themselves have been clamouring for cash prizes.

The evolution of the World Cup has been swift. Back in Portillo in 1966, no-one imagined that from such a modest beginning an event of such universal appeal would arise.

As long as a native of the country where a World Cup event is being held has a chance of victory, the crowds flock to line the courses. The arrival of a number of superstar skiers like Maria Walliser, Pirmin Zurbriggen, Marc Girardelli, Erika Hess and Ingemar Stenmark is eagerly awaited around the world.

In some quarters, though, the World Cup has not received the attention that is its due. In March 1986, during the World Cup's stay at Aspen, Colorado, an American broadcaster said: "Let's remember that in the US, skiing is ranked 26th of all sports, even behind water polo." But all the swimming pools around the world where water polo is played would not be large enough to hold the tens of thousands of spectators who crowd around the Hahnenkamm downhill's finish.

The World Cup has accelerated the evolution of Alpine skiing. Pre-World Cup there were only four or five major competitions, among them the great 'classics' in Wengen, Kitzbühel, Megêve and the Arlberg-Kandahar. The present racing calendar includes 30-odd World Cup competitions on four different continents.

The season used to begin in January and last just a few weeks. In 1986 it started in August in Las Leñas, Argentina, and continued in Europe and North America from December to end late in March.

The increase in the number of races has had two direct consequences on the racers' lifestyles. They have had to increase training time and they have, for the most part, specialized in one or two events to give themselves a better shot at victory.

A single win in a World Cup event is now the primary goal of most athletes on the circuit. Only four or five champions can realistically hope to win the overall title, while no more than fifteen racers stand a real chance of taking the season's honours in the downhill, slalom, giant slalom or Super-G.

Ingemar Stenmark won 83 World Cup events from 1974 to 1986, but he only clinched three overall titles, in 1976, 1977 and 1978. His refusal to race in the downhill certainly cost him more. He took part in only one, at Kitzbühel, in January 1981. He came in ten seconds behind the winner, but was third in the combined.

The most spectacular changes have been in the equipment. Downhillers now have a choice of six pairs of skis, each designed for different snow and weather conditions. Boots, poles and suits are also different for different specialities. The ski industry invests millions of dollars in ski racing and provides the best equipment and expert service for the World Cup's leading skiers.

The various national ski federations and the manufacturers devised a system of more or less official bonuses given to athletes according to their performance. The top racers can also expect payment from equipment manufacturers, on a year-to-year, contract-by-contract basis, while all members of the national team are given official salaries in the form of broken-time payments which vary according to a racer's standing.

This broken-time payment system, controlled by the national and international team managers, was set up in the 1960s by the FIS when it was forced to accept that Alpine ski racing, at world class level, was essentially a full time occupation. The payments were also accepted by the often reactionary International Olympic Committee which long defended the ideal of amateur sports.

Since 1985, the FIS has allowed skiers to sign individual contracts with commercial companies and to wear such companies' logos on their helmets or ski hats. The individual national federations – which approve such contracts – take a percentage of the skiers' earnings, varying from 15 per cent in Switzerland to 50 per cent in Austria.

Top racers can command up to $50,000 a season from such deals, added to their already lucrative contracts with their equipment suppliers. Big stars now earn something between $300,000 and half-a-million dollars a year – impressive sums compared to 1967, when they earned perhaps a 20th of that, but still substantially less than the earnings of top tennis players, golfers or racing drivers. Ski racers still receive no cash prizes. The ski resorts hosting the races do absorb the bed and board costs of the various national teams – as long as the racers ski at world class levels according to the FIS rankings. Turkish, Senegalese and Brazilian skiers – for example – have, so far, had to pay their own way.

The cost of staging a World Cup race varies from resort to resort. Michael Horn, a member of the Hahnenkamm's organizing committee in Kitzbühel, estimates the cost of the race to be seven million Austrian schillings, or roughly $400,000. The racers' room and board, and the course preparation take the lion's share of the budget. Austrian soldiers working the Streif course cost the organizers $30 a day and they often have to turn out in force, numbering up to 120 depending on snow conditions.

Spectators each pay over 100 Austrian schillings and there is a capacity crowd of 35,000. Over 25 television networks broadcast worldwide from the town and over 500 journalists seek accreditation each year. The 20,000 beds in and around Kitzbühel are never enough to meet demand and local shopkeepers say the race weekend is like Christmas and Easter combined.

But Kitzbühel is an exceptional case. One-day races like those at Madonna di Campiglio in Italy, or Adelboden in the Bernese Oberland are far less expensive, with shorter race courses and fewer participants. Roughly $50,000 covers their budget, if local hoteliers pitch in with promotional prices.

The World Cup circuit includes a large number of traditional ports of call where races are held every, or almost every, year. This is the case with Val d'Isère in France, Madonna di Campiglio in Italy, Kitzbühel and Badgastein in Austria, Garmisch-Partenkirchen and Pronten in West Germany, Kranjska Gora and Maribor in Yugoslavia, Wengen and Adelboden in Switzerland, Åre in Sweden, Furano in Japan, Aspen and Waterville Valley in the US, and Whistler Mountain, Lake Louise and Sunshine in Canada.

Through their national federations, countries with proper skiing facilities propose their resorts as a venue for a World Cup fixture. The World Cup committee then opts to allocate one or more races to, say, Spain, Bulgaria, Czechoslovakia, Norway, Poland or Argentina. Around 127 resorts in 15 countries have so far played host to World Cup races.

The 1967 schedule was for 17 races. But by 1986, the number had grown to 38, not including another seven for the combined downhill-slalom title.

Only a handful of racers ski in all the races, and those who do are mainly athletes with a realistic chance of winning the overall Cup. The price they have to pay is a winter-long trek – by car, bus, train and aeroplane. It is not uncommon for racers – especially those from North America, Japan, Scandinavia and the Eastern Block – to spend months away from home.

In the early 1980s, the American Mahre brothers were so fed up

Pirmin Zurbriggen, World Cup title-holder in 1984, opened a new era in modern ski racing in 1985 by winning all disciplines and becoming downhill World Champion in Bormio without summer training in that event.

Racers spend more time travelling than racing during a season. They often visit more than 25 resorts during the whole winter and fly around the world – to Scandinavia, Japan, North and South America. Journeys of 20 hours are not rare, leaving racers tired even before major events.

with being away from their families for months on end, they decided to bring their wives and children to Europe with them, turning the cars they toured in into hotel porters' nightmares.

Some racers travel with their ski technicians – or reps – or other competitors, as do Pirmin Zurbriggen and Max Julian who both come from the southeastern Valais region of Switzerland. Others travel with their coaches, as do Marc Girardelli – whose coach is his father – and Ingemar Stenmark, whose coach is Ermano Nogler.

Communal life in hotels demands organization and discipline. Team members often eat together at long tables. Times are set by the coaches who penalize persistent latecomers.

On the circuit, everyone's life is dictated by his job and the race at hand. As a rule everyone rises early to tune their equipment and check the course. On race mornings, while the racers loosen up and sharpen their reflexes with free-skiing, the coaching staff review the course, check snow, air temperature and humidity readings. The data is then analysed and compared to recordings taken during training sessions.

It is only at the last moment that the ski rep chooses among the racer's many pairs of racing skis. This decision is crucial. A win in the downhill depends increasingly on the equipment, its suitability for the conditions and the fine tuning and waxing.

In 1978, Franz Klammer may well have lost the world title because of an error of judgment by the rep assigned to him by the ski company. And in 1985, the Austrian star was so surprised by the unexpected speed of the skis which he used for the first time at Bormio that he made a series of uncharacteristic errors halfway down the course and had to settle for fifth place when a medal was easily within his reach. In 1984, Helmut Hoflehner got the wrong pair of skis at the start of the downhill, after his rep misunderstood a colleague's radio message. The Austrian's skis were utterly wrong for that morning's temperature and Hoflehner finished fifth while America's Bill Johnson – racing on the same brand of skis – won. But Johnson's skis had been meticulously tuned by Blake Lewis, a former racer with eight years of technical experience behind him, including working with world champion speed skier Franz Weber. Lewis was not one to share his secrets, even with other reps working for the same company. One night before the Sarajevo Olympic downhill, he even hid Johnson's skis under his bed, he was so fearful of spies or sabotage.

Each year, downhill skis reputed to be particularly fast in certain snow conditions, mysteriously disappear. The guess is that they have been "salvaged" by laboratories of rival ski manufacturers hoping to discover their secret.

Some teams are blessed with particularly good ski technicians, as were the Italians whose reps came up with a notably fast wax in 1984. When one of the team's servicemen gave some of it to a friend working for an Austrian firm in the hope of securing a full-time job, it was immediately put to good use. Anton Steiner's bronze medal performance in the Olympic downhill was certainly not hampered by the Italian wax. The rep was not hired by the Austrians though, nor by anyone else. And he was fired by the Italians.

As Alpine racing competition progressed and as the general public's interest increased, technical rivalries between teams and their equipment suppliers reached fever pitch. With wins and losses decided by tenths – and sometimes hundredths – of seconds and the average downhiller reaching speeds of over 90 miles an hour, equipment must be as near-perfect as humanly possible, to be safe, reliable and competitive.

While the makers of skis, bindings and racing suits invest more and more money in research, the athletes find they must spend more and more time in physical and technical training. Before the advent of the World Cup, racers rarely trained as a team, usually regrouping at most a month before the onset of winter. The rest of the time they worked – if they held jobs – as mountain guides, farmers and civil servants. Staying in shape was a matter of taste and personal preference and their fitness was usually maintained by cycling, jogging, trekking or soccer. Occasionally they would spend a few days up on glaciers in summer, to test new skis, or to race in Summer Grand Prix at Val d'Isère, Alpe d'Huez, Zermatt, Kaprun or Stelvio.

The birth of the World Cup was to dramatically alter the rhythm of a ski racer's life. Now with a longer season, racers have to stay in shape, and produce results, for longer periods of time.

After Portillo in 1966 it also became evident that summer training on skis was most useful if it took place under winter conditions. So resorts in the southern hemisphere became a regular training ground from 1966 on.

The top skiers today devote themselves almost entirely to their sport. For over four months a year they race and for another five they train.

The Austrian national team skiers regroup as early as April for

While European skiers can often go home during the Alpine season, the North Americans have to stay away from home for months. For ten years, the Mahre brothers spent every winter in Europe.

Skiers dedicate almost ten months a year to their sport. They race for four months and train for five. They also spend a lot of time testing their equipment. Nowadays, a race can be decided by hundredths of a second and skis, boots, poles, bindings and even ski suits can mean the difference between victory and defeat.

their first on-snow sessions, which are used by the coaches to correct any technical flaws discerned during the previous season not yet a month behind them. For the rest of the spring, the racers work on their physical stamina out-of-doors or in weight-lifting gyms. By July they are back on skis.

The old Alpine glacier training camps – often located above 9000 feet – were hard going. To benefit from good snow conditions, racers had to rise very early. And many found it difficult to find the motivation to ski while everyone else was sunning themselves on the beach. So coaches now take their teams to South America, Australia or New Zealand – where it is mid-winter and the skiing season is in full flood.

Whether training in Las Leñas in Argentina, Thredbo in Australia or Mount Hutt in New Zealand, technical refinement is the main goal. The coaches set courses which sharpen their racers' reflexes and expose their weaknesses. But the rhythm of these early camps is carefully controlled to prevent the athletes from going stale. The activities are as varied as possible and include rest periods, trekking and games like soccer, bicycle races, jogging, golf and tennis.

A battery of physical and medical tests are also administered to help coaches follow the racers' progress. Some coaches like Switzerland's Karl Frehsner and Austria's Dieter Bartsch feed all the data into a computer.

Coaching is equally important at junior level. And in Alpine countries, there are often regional, national and even international competitions for younger skiers. Each federation has its own "farm" system to bring the young talent on. Some are backed by local government or sports ministries like those in Austria, France,

Italy and Yugoslavia, while others rely on donations, like those in Switzerland, the US and Scandinavia.

Countries with great Alpine traditions are blessed by massive popular support. In Austria and Switzerland, skiing is not only a national pastime, but a major tourist industry.

Thousands of youngsters impressed by the feats of the champions, dream of making the national team. Parents help and support them as much as possible. The price of failure is not as high as it used to be as many young Austrians, Swiss and Italians hedge their bets by learning a practical trade as a carpenter, mason, draughtsman or accountant at the same time. In countries like France and the US though, parents are more insistent on the need to finish high school or college – a course of action often incompatible with world class ski racing.

The apprentice champions have to decide before the age of 15 whether they want to take the gamble on ski racing as a way of life. It is then that, in Europe, youngsters are chosen for the junior national teams which are already engaged in international competition. Two or three years later, the teenagers can make their debut in the Europa Cup and, if successful, graduate to the World Cup.

In theory, only ten skiers from each team can make the start of a World Cup race. If, however, they are ranked high enough by their FIS points, an exception can be made in races counting towards combined downhill-slalom titles.

*Below left:* In the 1950s, champions like Christian Pravda used to look after their own skis. *Below:* Today highly trained technicians prepare and check the champions' skis. They work in the basements of hotels and sometimes spend as much as three hours on one pair.

Every national team member's goal is to make it into the first seed. This is the select group in each of the disciplines comprising the best 15 skiers in downhill, slalom, giant slalom or Super-G. Members of the first seed have all the advantages: better pay, less rutted courses to race on, lower starting numbers and international prestige. But to get into the first seed – and to stay there – a racer must have consistently good results throughout the season, with the time differences between the racer and the winner becoming much more important than how far down he may be in the place rankings.

The length of the great champions' racing careers has noticeably increased in the course of the last 20 years. Jean-Claude Killy was not yet 25 when he retired in 1968 after skiing for the French team for nearly eight years. Guy Perillat, crowned combined 1960 downhill-slalom World Champion on his 20th birthday, was already considered old when he stopped racing in 1969.

In those days there was a lot more money to be made outside, rather than inside, ski racing. Things have greatly changed in this respect which explains why athletes continue their careers as long as possible, and with success, when one considers the performances of men like Stenmark, Wirnsberg, Frommelt and Muller who are all over 25.

But the most spectacular changes concern the number and the quality of skiers who raced in the 1967 World Cup and those making a name for themselves on the circuit 20 years later. Less than 50 skiers were world-ranked in 1967. There were 120 of them by 1986. That the number of races has doubled, and the first 15 – instead of just the first 10 – are now awarded points can partially explain this change.

The status and the financial incentive of a win have for their part directly influenced the way champions now race. While in the past most of them skied in all the races now only a minority choose to do so.

In 1967 or 1968 the leaders in the overall standing all scored points in downhill, slalom and giant slalom, the three traditional events. By 1986 only three racers – Girardelli, Zurbriggen and Wasmaier – had done the same, in order to top the overall rankings. But Marc Girardelli was nonetheless alone at the beginning of 1986 to start in the first seed in all four disciplines.

The excess of specialization has had two consequences. First it has spurred the evolution of each event. And, second, it has created two parallel circuits – one for the downhill and one for the

slalom, giant slalom and Super-G. These two circuits only converge on the weekends of the great classics.

Each circuit highlights its separate stars and only Girardelli and Zurbriggen – today's big draws – are among the leaders in all of skiing's four disciplines.

In specializing, most racers have considerably narrowed their scope, as well as the length of their performance. A quick bit of mental arithmetic will reveal that downhillers actually race for less than 30 minutes a year. Needless to say, there is no margin for error in that half-hour if they hope to reach the top. A single mistake or a fraction of a second can easily lose a race or cost a favourite his title.

World class Alpine ski racing now demands nerves of steel, outstanding physical shape, excellent fundamental technique and – above all – powerful motivation.

Ski racing is faster these days, but demonstrably less fun. Competitors used to hold big parties after major events, but these no longer take place. Skiers now have to stay in peak condition and they have to keep up with the circuit's exacting schedule. An hour or two after the end of a race, most of the athletes are already heading home or towards the next race.

If the amusements have changed, the joy and the deep passion which fire the winners have not. Winning a race by one-hundredth of a second is – it seems – even more exciting than winning by a full second.

Since 1966, summer training has become a major part of the skiers' preparation. In July or August, the teams practise on the Alpine glaciers or travel south to Australia, New Zealand or Argentina. Since 1983, the new resort of Las Leñas in Argentina has become the capital of summer training. World Cup events were held there in 1985 and 1986.

DYNASTAR
DYNASTAR
DYNASTAR
DYNASTAR

# OVERALL WORLD CUP WINNERS

Among the elements that give a sport international appeal, there can be no doubt that the quality of its champions is paramount. They provide the show and draw the crowds. It is their skills that are emulated, their courage that is admired, their personalities that attract the attention of the press worldwide.

In this, Alpine ski racing is no different from any other sport. Throughout its brief history it has been dominated by people of outstanding human qualities, physical stamina and technical ability.

Until 1966, the great heroes of the sport came to light in the Olympic Games and World Championships. They were judged by the number of gold medals in the various disciplines they had won. A victory on the "Streif" at Kitzbühel stood alone. And the number of wins in the Arlberg-Kandahar events were recognized by the coveted Diamond "K" awarded by the select Kandahar Club.

This produced super champions like James Couttet, Rudi Rominger, Emile Allais, Christl Cranz and Toni Sailer. But there was no forum in which the all-round skier, like speed ace Anderl Molterer who won a large number of classics in the 1950s, could shine.

Since 1966 though, Alpine skiing's most outstanding challenge has been the World Cup. The qualities required to win this marathon competition, which runs for four months of the winter season, mean that only the most outstanding athletes stand any chance.

Only complete all-rounders like Jean-Claude Killy, Karl Schranz, Pirmin Zurbriggen, Marc Girardelli, Nancy Greene, Annemarie Moser-Proell or Hanni Wenzel, or a brilliant performer in at least two specialities, like Piero Gros, Ingemar Stenmark, Lise-Marie Morerod or Tamara McKinney, join the select club of World Cup holders.

But each victory has its own history and each champion their own legend. These are the stories of those who have won Alpine ski racing's most demanding competition.

The scene is set. The contenders are out of the starting box. The crowd is expectant and ready for the thrills of Kitzbühel's great classic.

WINNER 1967/1968

# JEAN-CLAUDE KILLY

Even at first they said that, alongside Toni Sailer, Jean-Claude Killy was the best skier of all time. The proof was already in the 1964 record books. But he went on to win the very first World Cup with a massive 225 points – the maximum possible under the rules at that time – and to take three gold medals in the 1968 Winter Olympics at Grenoble.

"King" Killy (left) and "Kaiser" Klammer were two of the greatest heroes of modern ski racing: Killy winning 12 races out of 17 in 1967 and Franz Klammer taking 10 downhills in a row in 1976-77.

During those four years the Val d'Isère skier won all the major races, including the Arlberg-Kandahar (1964/65/67), the Hahnenkamm (1965-67) and the Lauberhorn (1967).

Born in August 1943 in a Parisian suburb, the son of an Alsatian hotel-keeper, Killy became the ski hero of the 1960s. At his best under pressure, he is thought of by his entourage as "a man of challenges".

His skiing career was multi-faceted. From its beginnings in

1959, he never limited himself to one discipline. He won the 1961 *Criterium de la Première Neige* giant slalom in 1961 and came second in the difficult Chamonix Kandahar in 1963. But his first big international win came at the 1964 Garmisch-Partenkirchen Kandahar giant slalom, eight days after finishing fifth in the Innsbruck Winter Olympic's giant slalom.

During the next winters, he skied into the slalom record books of the Megêve, Kitzbühel and Mürren classics, brilliantly demonstrating his *ski total* approach to these events and to the sport.

But it was in August 1966, during the Portillo World Championships, that Killy's epic period began with the downhill and combined downhill-slalom title. This outstanding performance inspired the French team as a whole. They flew home with 16 of the 24 medals at stake.

These early gold medals not only bolstered Killy's confidence, they made him hungry for more. In January 1967 he clocked up six consecutive wins – three downhills, two slaloms and one giant slalom at Wengen, Kitzbühel and Megêve. He followed that with his uncontested victory in the first World Cup. In those days a skier's nine best results counted towards the total, three each in downhill, slalom and giant slalom.

Killy won twelve of the first World Cup's seventeen races: all five downhills, four out of five giant slaloms – ranking third in the only one he did not win – and three of the seven slaloms. That gave him maximum points in each section and not even a look-in for any other contestant.

He repeated his victory in 1967 with a staggering 111-point lead over his nearest rival, Heini Messner of Austria.

During the American circuit in March 1967, Killy further demoralized his rivals by winning eight out of the nine races (some of which counted towards the Skiing World Series) failing to finish in only one, the last slalom at Jackson Hole.

These outstanding victories captured the American imagination – the American press dubbed him "King Killy" – and did much to popularize Alpine ski racing in the US. American audiences were glued to the ABC's broadcasts of the Grenoble winter Olympics which showed Killy taking three gold medals, two of them – the downhill and the slalom – under particularly difficult conditions.

A few minutes before sliding into the downhill's starting shack, he skied over a patch of ice, scraping almost all of the wax off his racing skis. Despite this huge handicap, he put in a superhuman effort and managed to beat his friend Guy Perillat by eight hun-

Killy became the second skier after Toni Sailer to take three Olympic gold medals. This achievement was the springboard for his second career.

*Above:* One of the successes of Killy's post-racing career was the line of sports clothing he started in the mid-1970s.

*Opposite:* Killy had to wait until 1966 to win his first downhill, at Portillo. But in 1967, nobody could beat him at that event during the first World Cup season.

dredths of a second, leaving the highly touted Austrian favourites deep in his wake.

Then he had to race the slalom in a dense fog, only beating Austria's Herbert Huber by the infinitesimal margin of twelve hundredths of a second over the two runs. Karl Schranz who clocked up the best overall time was disqualified, as was Norway's Hakon Mjoen.

His giant slalom victory was undisputed though. He beat Switzerland's Bernard Favre by over two seconds.

That year the Olympic Games counted towards the World Cup and Killy's triple-win at Grenoble gave him an impressive lead. He won the overall Cup title yet again, this time with 200 points and a massive 81-points ahead of the runner-up, Switzerland's Dumeng Giovanoli.

At the age of 24 – convinced he had nothing left to prove in the world of Alpine skiing – Killy retired to enjoy the fruits of his unparalleled victories. Advised by American business lawyer, Mark McCormack – specialist in marketing great sports champions – Killy, an ex-customs officer, headed for the United States where a number of lucrative contracts awaited him.

He adapted well to life after his skiing career. He started as a promotional figure for some of America's most important companies. Then, after a brief comeback in the 1973 World Professional Ski Championships, he accepted an even more daring business challenge. He created his own line of sportswear. It was a huge success and Killy – along with his friend Michel Barnier, a deputy from the Albertville area – is now the driving force behind a committee that aims to bring the Winter Olympics to the Savoie region in the 1990s.

Though in his mid-forties, Killy is still an athlete. After only a year's training, he managed to run the 1982 New York Marathon in under four hours. He is a cycling and golfing addict – and he is a racing driver. With his co-driver, journalist, Robert Cahier he has chalked up a number of fine results in the Monza 1000-kilometre endurance race and the Targa Florio.

In 1973 he married Danielle Gaubet, a former actress who he had starred with in the movie "Snowjob". He has a daughter and two adopted sons.

Now a successful businessman in his own right and a consultant to a number of well-known companies, Killy complains of spending more time on aeroplanes than at home. But his real problem is constantly finding himself new challenges.

15

WINNER 1969/1970

# KARL SCHRANZ

Not only one of Alpine ski racing's greatest champions and most controversial characters, Karl Schranz was also a privileged witness to the evolution of the sport. When he began racing, downhillers used wooden skis and averaged 38 mph. By the time he retired skis were metal or fibreglass and skiers hit speeds of over 80 mph.

Ex-director of the famous Arlberg ski school, Schranz won all the major races and was holder of all the important titles, with one single exception. He was world downhill and combined downhill and slalom champion in 1962 at Chamonix, giant slalom champion in 1970 at Val Gardena and overall World Cup winner in both 1969 and 1970. "Karli" also won several times at Kitzbühel, Wengen and Megêve, and the famous Arlberg-Kandahar events. But he never won an Olympic gold medal.

Born in St. Anton, the birthplace of the Kandahar, on the eve of the Second World War, Schranz's international racing debut took place in the 1950s when Italian Olympic champion Zeno Colo and the legendary Stein Eriksen were still in competition. By the time he ended his career in February 1972, when he was 33, he was sharing the circuit with skiing's most prestigious athletes – fellow Austrians Christian Pravda, Anderl Molterer, Toni Sailer, Egon Zimmer, Franz Klammer, Ernst Hinterseer and his son Hansi; the Frenchmen Adrien Duvillard, François Bonlieu, Guy Perillat, Jean-Claude Killy, Patrick Russel, Henri Duvillard and Jean-Noel Augert; the Italians Carlo Senoner and Gustavo Thoeni; and Switzerland's Roger Staub, Dumeng Giovanoli, Bernhard Russi, Roland Collombin and Heini Hemmi.

No other skier raced as long as Karl Schranz. His first victory was in 1957, his last in 1971. He won 20 of the greatest downhills at Chamonix, St. Anton, Kitzbühel, Wengen, Garmisch, Megêve and Val d'Isère.

In 1968 Schranz came close to beating his Olympic jinx. He set the best overall time but was later disqualified. It was suspected that he had missed a gate in the fog. Still, he was Olympic champion for half-an-hour!

In all, Schranz won 19 world class downhills between February 1957, at Chamonix, and January 1972, at Kitzbühel. His only real failure was in the arena of the Winter Olympics. He participated in four Olympiads but his best result was a second place finish in the 1964 Innsbruck games.

He seemed set to win a medal at the Sapporo Olympics in 1972. The rather technical Mount Eniwa downhill course was suited to his style and he had just won the three preceding downhills – one at Val d'Isère and two at Kitzbühel. But the outspoken Schranz found himself out of favour with the Olympic authorities. Before the games he spoke out on the subject of shamateurism and openly and repeatedly criticised the Olympics' millionaire president Avery Brundage.

Schranz found himself disqualified by the International Olympic Committee's executive body – by a vote of 28 to 14 – though it was widely held that the Austrian's status was no different than that of other stars who certainly earned as much money as he did.

In the end the banning of Schranz backfired. It caused such a scandal that new executives were brought in to replace Brundage and his team and provoked a gradual recasting of the Olympic qualifying rules.

The Sapporo crisis and the martyred Schranz's triumphant return to Austria were the last episode in a long and variable career. Seasons of particular brilliance often followed fallow spells.

He completely flubbed the 1959-60 and 1960-61 seasons, after some notable successes in earlier years. But he was back on top in 1962 and 1963. In 1964 he slumped again but made a fine comeback in 1965 and 1966 with wins at Kitzbühel and Wengen. He then seemed set for the World Championships at Portillo. But in the Andes he finally had to make do with a modest bronze.

After two more years marred by disappointment, the thinking was that Schranz, then aged 30, would retire. But that was not to know the stuff Schranz is made of. He wanted to get even – with fate and with the particularly brilliant French squad that followed in the wake of Jean-Claude Killy and Guy Perillat.

Schranz's will power, his prodigious physical strength, his huge amount of experience and his strong motivation finally put him back on the road to success. His 1968-69 season was astonishing. Unbeatable in the great classics at Wengen, Kitzbühel and St. Anton – home of the Kandahar that year – the Austrian team's veteran also won two giant slaloms and closed on the top slalomers as well.

Jean-Claude Killy was one of the man from Arlberg's toughest rivals in the mid-1960s. Killy, like Schranz in his heyday, could compete in all disciplines.

Scoring 182 points against the second-placed Frenchman, 20-year-old Jean-Noel Augert's 123, Karl Schranz became the second skier to have his name placed in the overall World Cup winners' column. And he was to win the Cup's fourth overall winner's title in 1970, under even more difficult conditions. His rivals – Patrick Russel, Gustavo Thoeni and Jean-Noel Augert – were all younger men. All three accumulated wins and top-three finishes in slalom and giant slalom events. But happily for Schranz, none of them did well in the downhill.

In the end, the Tyrolean Schranz – who had won the Val Gardena World Championship giant slalom – seized the overall title from Thoeni's grasp, with 145 points to the Italian's 140.

But nothing could stop the leaders of the new generation. The following winter was marked by the coming of age of a new brood of Italians, French and Swiss. And yet another lacklustre season convinced Schranz to specialize in the downhill, a decision which allowed his career to shine one last time in the winter of 1971-72. His terrific duel with Henri Duvillard during the two Kitzbühel downhills are now one of the legends of the "white circus."

Schranz was faithful throughout his whole career to one ski maker, Franz Kneissl – another of the pioneers in the history of Alpine skiing. And he was the complete athlete. But it was his will power that marked him out and put his name in the record books, time and time again, right up to the end of his career.

Gustavo Thoeni (left) holds the record for victories in the World Cup. In his last win, he had to beat Ingemar Stenmark in the last race to clinch the Cup.

WINNER 1971/1972/1973/1975

# GUSTAVO THOENI

Four-time overall winner of the World Cup (1971-73 and 1975), Gustavo Thoeni was the biggest hero of Italian sports fans in the 1970s. Around the world he was bathed in gold and glory, totting up wins in all the most prestigious races during his long career – including 24 wins in races that counted towards the World Cup and five Olympic and World Championship gold medals.

Born in 1951, Thoeni was coached by his father on the slopes above the Stelvio Pass where both Italians and Swiss ski in summer. There he became the undisputed master of the slalom and giant slalom until the advent of the Swede Ingemar Stenmark in 1975. The Italian was blessed with perfect technique, but what he is best remembered for was his remarkable coolness under the pressure of Olympic events and the final races of the World Cup.

His greatest victory was, perhaps, his daring slalom and giant slalom wins in the 1974 St. Moritz World Championships. Placed fifth after the slalom's first run, nearly a second-and-a-half behind his friend and team-mate Piero Gros, Thoeni refused to concede defeat. Taking every imaginable risk in the second heat, he skied the race of a lifetime and finished more than two seconds ahead of his nearest rival, while Gros missed a gate and was disqualified.

His coolness in adversity was again evident during the 1975 parallel slalom finals. He needed an outright win – over Stenmark, then his young rival – to secure the overall crown. The race, witnessed by 20,000 spectators, remains one of the World Cup's most exciting moments.

Thoeni was particularly brilliant that winter, even coming within one hundredth of a second of beating Austria's "Kaiser Franz" Klammer down the 3,850 metres of the legendary "Streif" at Kitzbühel.

It is sometimes said that Thoeni – who is by nature shy and self-effacing – did not fully develop his own potential and that, if he had wanted to, he could have become one of the best all-round skiers ever. But what Thoeni may sometimes have lacked in daring, he made up for in steadiness. Up to 1977, he accumulated 69 top-three placings in World Cup races including four individual wins in 1971, one in 1972, three in 1973 and six in 1975.

His great success contributed enormously to the forging of the strong Italian team, nicknamed the *"Azzura Avalanche"*, which played the dominant role in international ski racing between 1972

Thoeni's strength was staying quiet and concentrating in tense situations – his best races were often won under great pressure. Now he has more time to relax with his wife and three daughters.

In the early 1970s, Thoeni could sometimes clock the best time on the giant slalom without touching a gate.

and 1976. In 1974, the Italians made history by being the only team to have two racers finish first and second in the overall Cup standings, having dominated the slalom and the giant slalom and setting a memorable record in the Berchtesgaden giant slalom by grabbing the first five places.

Married in 1975 and the father of three daughters, Thoeni retired after the 1980 Winter Olympics to go into business. Recently, he's come back into the Italian squad as a technical advisor to the slalom racers.

*Right:* Piero Gros was only 19 when he won the overall World Cup in front of Gustavo Thoeni in 1974. *Below:* After giving up competition, "Pierino" opened a sports shop in his home town of Sauze d'Oulx in the west of Torini. He is now also the town's mayor.

WINNER 1974

# PIERO GROS

Among all the great champions who left their mark on the World Cup, Piero Gros was without a doubt both one of the most spectacular and endearing. For ten years between 1972 and 1982, the Piedmontese skier ranked with the very best in the slalom and giant slalom to become a central figure in Italian skiing. He became overall World Cup winner in 1974 – ahead of Gustavo Thoeni – and Olympic slalom gold medallist in Innsbruck in 1976.

Born in Sauze d'Oulx in October 1954, "Pierino" won twelve races in his first three international seasons. Starting from the third seed, he was barely eighteen when he won his first World Cup race, the giant slalom at Val d'Isère. A week later he confirmed his reputation as a child prodigy by beating Thoeni in the difficult Madonna di Campiglio slalom. The next year he became the youngest ever World Cup winner. He was not quite 19½ when he accepted the crystal trophy in Vysoke Tatry in 1974.

In Kitzbühel, the following season, he was to win his last World Cup race. Though he often finished among the top three, subsequently victory was to prove maddeningly elusive.

Like the rest of the famous *"Azzurra Avalanche"*– Italy's formidable armada of talent in the mid-1970s – he could not stave off Ingemar Stenmark's attack. The Swede was undisputed king of the slalom and giant slalom from 1975 to 1981.

Part of the blame for the sudden slump in the fortunes of the *"Squadra"* can be laid at the door of the Italian coaches. From 1976 onwards they kept changing routines and training methods. Gros, whose *ski total* style of racing made for extremely exciting television and live performances, could not and did not make full use of his great talent and scale the heights that were undoubtedly within his reach. He retired from racing in 1982, after finishing sixth in the Schladming World Championship's slalom, to run a ski store with his wife.

**With his flamboyant, aggressive style, Piero Gros was a great star of the technical events. But he was only 20 when he celebrated his last World Cup victory. For seven years he tried to regain that success.**

WINNER 1976/1977/1978

# INGEMAR STENMARK

"Once upon a time there was a little boy who lived in the wilderness of northern Sweden..." That's how the story of Ingemar Stenmark, the man who has dominated the world of Alpine skiing for the last ten years, should start out. It is practically a fairy tale come true. There is even a fairy godmother – or godfather at least.

Born just outside the Arctic Circle in the north of Sweden, Ingemar Stenmark became one of the most consistent winners in World Cup history. For over a decade he has set records, each more impressive than the last.

Of course, it was utterly normal that a Swedish child should learn to ski. And there were not many other distractions in Stenmark's home village of Tarnaby where the winter nights seem endless and the local children can ski well into the late spring on a 4,500-foot hill nearby.

The village ski club, endearingly named the Fjakkenwinden Club after the wind that blows through the nearby mountains had already produced several members of the Swedish national team. One of them, Eric Stenmark, was Ingemar's father. He raced in the Olympics and in the 1956 and 1958 World Championships.

It was the elder Stenmark's advice, and long-running rivalries with his young schoolmates, among them Stig Strand and Bengt Fjaelberg, that made Stenmark into the most promising newcomer of the early 1970s. Strand and Fjaelberg themselves came to prominence on the international scene in the early 1980s.

Stenmark's fairy godfather came in the form of Ermano Nogler,

Stenmark was the greatest skier of the World Cup's second decade. He won three overall and 15 slalom and giant slalom titles. In 1979 he won 13 out of 20 races.

Extremely powerful and very talented, Stenmark set impressive records in the giant slalom where he seeks perfection. He won 15 giant slaloms in a row from March 1978 to February 1980.

the ex-Italian champion from Val Gardena who had coached Carlo Senoner to his 1966 Portillo World Championship slalom win. He was hired as team coach by the Swedish Ski Federation. As soon as he set eyes on Stenmark, Nogler realized that he had found a truly great talent.

"I was immediately struck by his perfect co-ordination, his instinct and his will power," he was later to say. "He didn't talk much, but one could feel he was determined."

The two men understood and respected each other immediately. And in Nogler's hands, Stenmark quickly polished his technique and rapidly came to dominate the junior Swedish races.

Described as a natural talent by his trainers, Stenmark excels at all kinds of sport which require determination, strength and balance.

Stenmark scored his first World Cup points in December 1973, finishing ninth in the Saalback giant slalom which was won by Austria's Hubert Berchold. He was not yet eighteen. But few people appreciated the feat that had been accomplished on that cold stormy day by a young man who had started from the very last seed, wearing number 73.

In the last slalom and giant slalom races of the 1973-74 season at Vysoke Tatry in the Czech mountains, Stenmark impressed World Cup racers, coaches and observers alike by fighting into contention from still very poor starting numbers and racing on the same pair of skis in both the slalom and giant slalom. The era's seasoned favourites, confirmed champions like Italy's Gustavo Thoeni and Piero Gros, Austria's Hansi Hinterseer and David Zwilling, and Spain's Francisco Fernandez-Ochoa, had to outdo themselves to beat the young Swede. The evidence was soon to become irrefutable. Stenmark was of a different stature. He was one of the superchamp breed, produced so rarely in any sport.

In the course of the next five winters, this six-foot 12-stone athlete was to win 83 races, five Olympic and World Championship gold medals, 15 slalom or giant slalom World Cup titles and to be crowned overall World Cup winner in 1976, 1977 and 1978. And he almost won it in 1975, but fell in the Val Gardena parallel slalom, going all out to win the title and just lost to Gustavo Thoeni.

The record's set by Stenmark will be hard to beat. In 1979, he won all of the season's ten giant slaloms and was to remain unbeaten in the event from March 1978 to February 1980 – a period that included the Lake Placid Winter Olympics – chalking up 15 consecutive wins.

At 18, Stenmark was shy and unknown. But in March 1974 he finished among the top four, five times despite high number starts.

In February 1979, he beat Bojan Krizaj by a staggering 4.06 seconds in the Jassna giant slalom in Czechoslovakia and in 1982 he blazed down Kitzbühel's tough slalom course to beat a stunned Phil Mahre by a massive 3.19 seconds.

A great many skiers sought to discover the secret of Stenmark's extraordinary success, to understand the reasons for the unparalleled longevity of his career and to uncover his weaknesses.

"Ingemar's major strong point is his attitude – his exemplary behaviour during and after the race," says Marc Girardelli who many see as Stenmark's heir. "He is a perfectionist and leaves nothing to chance in his physical and technical training."

But one cannot disregard the Swede's impressive psychological advantages, his ability in moments of enormous stress to keep his concentration and his coolness.

Practically untouchable in the slalom and giant slalom between 1975 and 1981, Stenmark's winning streak was challenged during the World Cup and at the Schladming World Championships by the American Mahre brothers.

In 1986, Stenmark celebrated his 30th birthday at Lake Placid by winning his 83rd World Cup race. And he intends to go on racing as long as he enjoys it.

Stenmark, it is true, did have other things on his mind. A girl had stormed into his life in March 1980 during the Saalbach finals, shaking his concentration on the sport. But this did not stop him winning the 1982 Schladming World Championship slalom, or nearly a dozen World Cup races in 1984.

When he was excluded from the Sarajevo Winter Olympics by the FIS qualifications committee – Stenmark had opted for a semi-professional "B-licence" in 1980 so that he could sign some highly lucrative contracts – it was feared that he might abandon his career. But his passion for skiing outweighed even his desire to spend more time at home following the birth of his daughter Nathalie in March 1984.

In the course of the next two seasons, Stenmark showed what he was made of. He refused to be discouraged by repeated failures in his winless 1984-85 season and his determination was quickly rewarded. He scored an 80th World Cup victory in December 1985 in the giant slalom at La Villa, Italy.

Relaxed after this sensational comeback, Stenmark soon found his old form and in 1986 won four races at St. Anton, Hemsedal and Lake Placid. Elsewhere he often finished among the top three and nearly took the Cup's giant slalom title which was eventually won by Joel Gaspoz after a fine finish in the last race at Lake Placid.

Had Stenmark even finished third in that race, he would have taken the season's overall giant slalom honours. But, as always, he was generous in defeat.

"I'm happy for Joel," he said. "He'd never won that title despite being one of the best giant slalomers for a long time. Of course, I'd have been happy to win another World Cup, but my happiness does not depend on it. I'm already very happy with my season and I've already won so much in the past. Now I race for the fun of it."

The great Swedish skier entered only one World Cup downhill in his entire career. In 1981 he raced in Kitzbühel to score points in the combined.

WINNER 1979

# PETER LUESCHER

Though the redoubtable Swede Ingemar Stenmark won 13 individual races during the 1978-79 season, it was Switzerland's Peter Luescher who took the overall World Cup title with a single outright slalom victory at Garmisch-Partenkirchen and two combined downhill-slalom first places. The Swede did not race in a single downhill or combined downhill-slalom event–so he could not be credited with more than a maximum of 150 points. Luescher, who was also a brilliant giant slalomer, beat Stenmark with 186 points, 65 of which came from combined events.

Under these conditions, it is not hard to understand why Luescher's victory did not get the international attention it deserved. Nonetheless the Swiss had an excellent season with seven top-three finishes in either slaloms or giant slaloms, including five second places in the wake of the seemingly unbeatable Stenmark, earning himself the number two place in the giant slalom ranking into the bargain.

A city-bred native of Romanshorn, a small industrial town near St. Gallen in northeast Switzerland, he came into ski racing almost

Peter Luescher won only one race in 1979, but his all-round performance in all the disciplines was enough to make him the first Swiss holder of the overall World Cup title.

Luescher's career was marked by a series of ups and downs – his falls were as spectacular as his comebacks.

by chance. In his youth he suffered from anaemia and was sent to recuperate in Arosa. There he discovered the sport. But it was not his only pastime. Ever-conscious of the need to stay in shape, he also took up water-skiing with considerable success. He won the European Junior championships several times.

But later he decided to concentrate on Alpine skiing. After dominating the Swiss junior national championships he first made the Swiss national team in 1975, when he was 18. That year he also scored his first World Cup points and rose to 25th place in the overall ranking in 1976 with a fourth place in the Aspen downhill. By 1978, he had risen to 16th overall. So in 1979, when he won the crystal trophy, there was every reason to believe that this businessman's son had all the makings of a big-time international skiing champion.

But then things began to turn sour. He only finished among the top ten three times during 1980 and a combined downhill-slalom title was his only victory. Then, after making some of the best intermediate times, he fell in the Lake Placid giant slalom.

The following year was to prove even worse. With a seventh place downhill finish his best result, his future as an all-round skier was in serious jeopardy. Wisely opting to specialize in the downhill, he quickly rose up the list of favourites again. He came second in the 1982 combined downhill-slalom World Championships. Then he won the 1983 St. Anton downhill and the Garmisch-Partenkirchen Super-G. At the end of the season he led the Swiss team with his overall fifth place ranking.

But in 1984 he tumbled to 55th, then launched a new comeback in 1985 with a strong second place finish in the Wengen downhill.

Further bad luck plagued him following a fine performance in the Lauberhorn. And a terrible fall on Bad Kleinkirchheim's downhill course tore ligaments in his knee and ended his career.

WINNER 1980

# ANDREAS WENZEL

Only 15 years old when he raced in his first World Championships at St. Moritz in 1974, Andreas Wenzel had an inauspicious debut. As his older sister Hanni was winning the slalom gold medal, young Andy trailed Gustavo Thoeni by more than 20 seconds to come in 37th in the giant slalom. But to look on the bright side, he came in nearly two minutes ahead of Formosa's Yeh Yung-Hsing who was 68th and last.

At the time both Wenzels still held German passports, though

they were racing for the Liechtenstein Ski Federation. Their father, who had been their first coach, had moved his family to the principality in the 1950s, following a visit to the tiny country on a cycling tour. He found work as an avalanche and torrent-control expert. His interest in skiing was, later, to give him an influential role in creating Liechtenstein's strong national team in which his children were to star, alongside the Frommelt brothers and the Konzett siblings. Between 1974 and 1985, the Liechtenstein skiing squad was to bring home no less than 24 gold, silver and bronze medals.

A few weeks after Hanni's St. Moritz victory, the authorities in Liechtenstein approved Wenzel's long-standing request for naturalization. They were not sorry. Hanni and Andreas were to win and win in the following years.

Andreas Wenzel has been able to achieve some of the highest goals over the last ten years. Along with his overall World Cup win, he has five Olympic and World Championship medals.

In 1978, Andreas took the combined downhill-slalom title at the Garmisch-Partenkirchen World Championships after a fine second place slalom finish behind Ingemar Stenmark. Two years later, he beat the Swede to the top of the World Cup's overall rankings, having excelled in all three disciplines, winning the Kitzbühel slalom, for example, 24 hours after a strong fourth place finish in the brutal Hahnenkamm downhill. In March he won a World Cup giant slalom, after his February Lake Placid Olympic silver medal in the same event.

The years to come proved more difficult though. It was another three seasons before he finally won another slalom, in Tarnaby. Then, in 1984, he managed a bronze medal in Sarajevo's Olympic giant slalom.

Meanwhile his life had been shaken by family problems, among them his parents' separation. Ski racing which had, for so long, united the Wenzel racing clan – which had come to include Andreas' younger sisters Petra and Monika – finally caused an explosion. The strain of the competitive World Cup circuit and everyone in the family being constantly on the move proved too much to endure.

His domestic situation has improved now though. He was married three years ago and has recently become the father of a little girl. At 28, Andreas Wenzel remains one of the strongest personalities on the Cup circuit. And despite taking time off to complete his secondary education at Austria's ski-studies high school in Stams, Wenzel has regularly ranked in the World Cup's overall standings' top ten since 1978.

WINNER 1981/1982/1983

# PHIL MAHRE

Like former American greats, Phil Mahre was an outstanding slalom specialist. From 1977 to 1983 he was one of Stenmark's toughest rivals and ended his career with a slalom victory at Sarajevo.

Among all the World Cup's overall winners, Phil Mahre is surely the most enigmatic. The American from White Pass in the state of Washington is, in fact, impossible to label as this or that kind of champion. During an international ski racing career spanning nearly a decade, Mahre has always followed one code – his own!

That attitude made him one of the World Cup's great personalities between 1976 and 1984. And it did not stop him fashioning an extremely brilliant record either. Three times overall World Cup champion from 1981 to 1983, he won 27 individual races, a total only bettered by Ingemar Stenmark. He came second in the 1980 Lake Placid slalom, where he captured the overall combined downhill-slalom crown. Then he retired in March 1984 after an extraordinary Olympic win in which he just edged out his twin brother, the 1982 Schladming world giant slalom champion, for the Sarajevo slalom gold medal.

Mahre first impressed the international racing world with a fifth-place finish in the 1976 Innsbruck Olympic giant slalom, which was won by Switzerland's diminutive Heini Hemmi. He was then to become one of the circuit's best slalom and giant slalomers during the 1976-77 season with two clean wins. He was in contention for the overall World Cup honours in 1979, but his hopes were dashed when he broke an ankle at Lake Placid in early March.

His impressive racing style and his vaunting ambition quickly made him Ingemar Stenmark's great rival. But the Swede kept the upper hand until February 1981 when, in the Åre slalom, Mahre beat him by four hundredths of a second. It was to be a turning point in both men's careers. While the Scandinavian began a long, difficult, doubt-filled period, the American blossomed.

Though some 60 points behind Stenmark before the decisive Åre race, Mahre nonetheless beat the Swede to that year's overall World Cup title after a struggle that was fascinating to the end. Mahre only took the overall lead in the season's last giant slalom in Laax in 1981.

In 1982, it was easier. Mahre quickly raced into an unbeatable lead, regularly finishing among the top-three in the slalom and giant slalom – some 15 times in all – and accumulating the maximum number of points in the combined events. By the end of January 1982, Mahre was already assured of this second overall World Cup title, even his losses at the Schladming World Championships could not affect his decisive superiority – brilliantly re-

Phil and Steve Mahre were more than twins. They were a two-man team, training together and giving each other encouragement and tips even when they were direct rivals.

Phil Mahre concentrated on the slalom and giant slalom until 1978, but made fast progress in the downhill once he realized its World Cup advantages.

confirmed at the end of the season by beating Stenmark in the overall individual slalom and giant slalom rankings as well.

After making their mark as athletes, Phil and Steve Mahre – born to a family of seven sisters and brothers – then gave a display of a kind of truculence until then little known on the ski racing circuit. In 1983 and 1984, they travelled the circuit in the company of their wives and children, shocking and annoying other racers, officials and European journalists by their behaviour and their statements.

Never shy about expressing their opinions, they strongly criticized FIS officials when the latter decided to introduce a new event to the international schedule – the Super-G, a hybrid race somewhere between the downhill and the giant slalom. The Mahre twins believed that Alpine racing did not need a fourth event, so they simply boycotted it.

In 1982, during the Schladming World Championships, they had also refused to enter the Alpine Combined races newly introduced by the FIS. As far as they were concerned the old formula, with only three events counting towards the points, was good enough.

They further surprised the Europeans by suddenly flying home after only a few races in December 1983. Lack of snow, poor training conditions and disappointing results were probably the cause of their unusual decision.

The rest of the season, however, proved the two top Americans right. Having regenerated reflexes and motivation during the January races, they turned in their fabulous one-two performance in the Sarajevo Olympic slalom. In a marvellous example of family spirit and good sportsmanship, which even the gold medal at stake could not shake, they traded advice and encouragement before the start of each heat.

Respectively first and third after the first run, Steve and Phil, as usual, compared notes during the crucial wait before the second heat, which Phil was to start first. At the finish – with his brother potentially poised to beat him – Phil was to radio up his impressions of the course and its conditions. Trying again for the fastest time, Steve raced all-out but could not avoid making too many mistakes towards the end of his run. The scoreboard blinked out the verdict: third in the final heat. And Phil had beaten his twin brother by a few tenths of a seconds in the two runs' aggregated time to win the gold medal.

A few weeks later, after the Vail giant slalom, the Mahres bid their friends and rivals farewell. Half-a-dozen races still remained on the World Cup schedule but the brothers knew when to quit.

With their futures assured by solid promotional contracts with most of the manufacturers of the equipment they had used throughout their careers, there is little chance that they will be bored. Both are particularly enterprising men having, for example, read dozens of "how-to" books, they built their own houses.

"The Mahres were stubborn, and they almost always did what they wanted to do," says Harald Schoenhaar, the 1985 American head coach who had been their first trainer. "It wasn't always easy working with them because they followed their instincts and had developed their own technical and physical programme. But when they started something, they always finished it."

The only regret one could have about Phil Mahre's career is that – despite having become a fine downhiller – he was never able to win a downhill race. Faithful to his credo, he never spent more time training on long skis than he believed absolutely necessary. This meant that he only rarely tested his equipment which, in the event, proved to be less competitive than his rivals'.

The Mahres' retirement leaves a big hole among the "white circus" ranks, not to mention a gap in the American team which will have to wait a long time before having such a dynamic duo again.

The Mahres' careers lasted extremely long by American standards. They travelled the World Cup circuit for almost ten years, part of it with their wives and children.

WINNER 1984

# PIRMIN ZURBRIGGEN

The hero of modern Alpine ski racing is a young man with curly blonde hair and blue eyes called Pirmin Zurbriggen. He is Swiss and lives in a village called Saas-Almagell. He has raced on the World Cup circuit since December 1980 when he was 17. Since then he has come on fast and strong, winning his first points in January 1981, his first race in March 1982 and his first overall World Cup in March 1984.

But it was in 1985 that Zurbriggen became the idol of Swiss ski racing, despite the fact that he was beaten in the World Cup by Marc Girardelli. The young hotel-owner's son became World

Zurbriggen became the hero of the Swiss team when he won two gold medals in the World Championships at Bormio only three weeks after badly injuring his knee.

After he won his first overall World Cup title in 1984, Zurbriggen became the first skier since Jean-Claude Killy to celebrate victory in all specialities.

Champion by winning all of the different Alpine events, the first to achieve that feat since Jean-Claude Killy.

After taking the Super-G, a long one-heat giant slalom and a slalom in December 1984, Zurbriggen won the difficult Kitzbühel downhill in January. And he did it two days in a row – his second Hahnenkamm made all the more difficult after severely injuring his knee a few hundred yards from the finishing line.

He was rushed back to Switzerland after the race and underwent surgery the next day in a special clinic near Basel. The injury dismayed Alpine fans who admired Zurbriggen's charm, exemplary behaviour and sense of fair play. And with the Bormio World

Zurbriggen is a family man. He finds being at home with his family the best way to recharge his batteries. But his 1985-86 season was affected by the illness of his sister Heidi.

Championships only two weeks away, many of Switzerland's hopes were resting on Zurbriggen's shoulders.

But there was no need to worry. From his first day in hospital the champion from the eastern Valais fought to get well. Convinced that he could be fit again in time, he spent his convalescence working out on an exercise machine. He even managed to maintain and tune his concentration by racing downhills in his imagination each day and by studying the videos of his previous runs.

Two weeks after his accident, he was back on skis again. This greatly delighted his fans who were convinced that Bormio's downhill run would suit their hero to perfection. A week later Zurbriggen's childhood dream came true. He won the gold medal in the downhill ahead of team-mate Peter Muller and American Doug Lewis.

As though that was not enough, "Zubie" also took the gold in the combined and a silver medal in the slalom, a mere five hundredths of a second behind West Germany's Marcus Wasmaier.

But the effort of his rapid comeback was to take its toll later in the season. During the last races in America, Zurbriggen was not up to form, while Marc Girardelli – who was second and third respectively in Bormio's slalom and giant slalom – was by then unbeatable.

In the end only 17 points separated the two men in the overall standings, a slim margin considering Zurbriggen had missed a total of ten races after his accident.

The following year Girardelli again edged Zurbriggen out of the overall title, this time by 10 points. In contention until the very last slalom at Bromont in Quebec, Zurbriggen's third place was only half-a-second off Girardelli's winning time; half-a-second which cost Zurbriggen the season's overall honours.

In fact, Zurbriggen's whole 1986 season was short of wins. A bad fall kept him out of a series of December races. In February, while favoured to win the Morzine downhill, he took another spill. It was only in the slalom at Åre, in Sweden, that he finally celebrated his first win. Oddly, slalom was to prove to have been his best event that season, while he turned in lack-lustre performances in his chosen specialities of downhill and giant slalom.

A devout Catholic, Zurbriggen has made numerous pilgrimages to Lourdes and it is a safe bet that he is far from having used up his full potential. When he starts to, it is in Jean-Claude Killy's tracks he will be racing again.

Zurbriggen is very aggressive on skis and trains at all kinds of sports to remain in good shape. He likes to run in the mountains or climb them with his bike.

Excelling first in giant slalom, then becoming an all-rounder, Zurbriggen was 19 when he won his first World Cup race, the giant slalom in Piancavello.

Marc Girardelli celebrated an impressive total of 11 victories in the 1984-85 season to win his first overall World Cup title.

WINNER 1985/1986

# MARC GIRARDELLI

Two-time overall World Cup winner, Marc Girardelli is one of the "white circus's" star performers, but not just because he has recently added a remarkable downhill talent to his already proven slalom and giant slalom abilities. The fame surrounding this surprising and exceptional champion is partly due to the fact that, though born in Austria in July 1963, he has been racing for the Luxembourg Ski Federation since 1976.

Girardelli was barely 14 when he first raced on the World Cup circuit in the Madonna di Campiglio slalom. His performance went unnoticed, but not the fact that – although Austrian – he was racing under the colours of the Grand Duchy of Luxembourg.

His father and sole coach, former racer at local level Helmut Girardelli later explained why he had made this surprising choice for his son. He believed that it would allow Girardelli junior the best psychological and technical conditions under which to develop. The atmosphere in the local Voralberg regional racing framework, he felt, was too tense, if not downright hostile.

The local talent scouts and coaches – and the other young racers' doting parents – soon became rather irritated that the young Girardelli, coached solely by his father from the start, kept winning without recourse to the official techniques recommended by the Austrian coaches and manuals.

Helmut journeyed to Luxembourg in the spring of 1976 to meet with the Grand Duchy's Ski Federation officials and ask them to give his son Marc an international ski racing licence. The Austrian ski authorities applied a lot of pressure to prevent this, but finally it

*Opposite:* The slalom was Girardelli's best event at the beginning of his career. From January 1984 to March 1985, he won 12 of the 13 slaloms he finished. Girardelli did not start the downhill until 1983. But despite a terrible crash in March 1983, he became one of the best downhill specialists by 1986, finishing three times among the top three.

mazda
12
ST. ANTON

Since 1977 Marc Girardelli has been competing in World Cup races although he did not start his first downhill until January 1983. Despite a terrible fall in March of that year, he had become one of the best downhillers in the "white circus" by 1986.

was to no avail. Marc eventually got his Luxembourg licence and has raced for the Grand Duchy in World Cup events ever since.

But that was not the end of his nationality problems. Only the last-minute presentation of a petition for naturalization persuaded the officials in Bormio to allow Girardelli to race in the 1985 World Championships. And he will need a weightier document – a Luxembourg passport – if he is going to race for his adopted country in the 1988 Winter Olympics in Calgary.

Girardelli has pursued his education by correspondence courses since the age of 16, but it has not noticeably slowed down his career. He made his much-acclaimed entry into the ranks of the world's best in 1981, with a second place in the Wengen slalom, behind Yugoslavia's Bojan Krizaj but ahead of Ingemar Stenmark who he greatly admires.

In February 1983, he won a prestigious victory in the Gaellivare slalom in Sweden, beating all the favourites including Sweden's Stig Strand, Stenmark, the American Phil Mahre, Yugoslavia's Krizaj and the Italian Paolo de Chiesa.

But Girardelli's career almost ended a few weeks later. A bad fall on the Lake Louise downhill course in Canada tore all the ligaments in one knee – a particularly serious injury for a top-class skier. Luckily he was operated on by one of the best knee specialists in the world, Dr. Richard Steadman, who had already performed miracles on America's top racers, the Mahre brothers, Cindy Nelson and Christine Cooper.

"It was one of the most serious injuries of that kind I've ever had to operate on," Steadman admitted later. "I wasn't even sure that Marc would be able to ski, period."

But the champion from Bodele – who had not truly grasped the seriousness of his injury – was sure that he would not only ski again, but he would also race. His iron will and great courage helped him convalesce in the most energetic way possible. Disdaining pain, he followed a brutal regimen to speed healing. Three months later he was skiing on one leg – the injured one.

His comeback was impressive. Winning five individual races, he took the overall World Cup slalom honours in 1984. A year later, after 11 wins, he won not only the slalom and giant slalom titles, he took the overall World Cup as well. And in 1986, he won the overall World Cup again with many more fine performances in all the disciplines.

*Left:* Girardelli seems set to break some of Ingemar Stenmark's records. He has won 20 World Cup events since 1983 and has always been an admirer of the Swede who has won 83 races in 12 years. *Above:* Girardelli is strongly supported by his parents who have invested time and money in his career. His father, Helmut, is also his trainer.

WINNER 1967/68

# NANCY GREENE

Jean-Claude Killy and Nancy Greene dominated the 1967-68 season. They both won the overall World Cup, as well as Olympic medals at Grenoble. Like Killy, Greene retired from racing and became successful in business.

European women, particularly the French who had dominated previous seasons, were shocked by their unexpected defeat in the first two World Cups. They lost out to Nancy Greene, a freckle faced Canadian upstart whose friends called her the "Tiger".

One of the youngest competitors at the 1960 Squaw Valley Olympics, Greene had to wait until she was 22 to burst into international stardom with four wins in the first five races of 1967. But those four races – the downhill and the giant slalom at Oberstaufen and the downhill and the giant slalom at Grindelwald – put her among the best in the world. But only six months earlier Nancy had barely managed a fourth place in the World Championships' giant slalom at Portillo.

By the end of January 1967, she still led the overall standings when she was forced to fly home to race in the Canadian National Championships, then under the patronage of two of the Canadian ski team's main sponsors. The World Cup had yet to gain wide recognition in Canada and there was no-one there who would have understood Greene's absence from the Nationals.

In her absence, France's Marielle Goitschel, then women's skiing's powerhouse, took over the World Cup lead thanks to a series of wins and top-place finishes.

Greene did not rejoin the circuit until the American leg in March, but wasted no time in making her presence felt again. After a third-place finish in the Franconia giant slalom, she won the last two giant slaloms of the season, in Vail and Jackson Hole – the latter under particular pressure. With Goitschel still nursing more than a 20-point lead in the overall standings, Greene had to win the final slalom cleanly to beat the French girl. And that is exactly what she did. In an impressive display of cold-blooded aggressiveness, she beat Goitschel by seven hundredths of a second over two runs, while Florence Steurer – who had won the first heat – was pushed down into third place.

That dramatic finale, followed by a no-less memorable party in Jackson Hole's Cowboy Bar, greatly contributed to the popularity of Alpine skiing throughout Canada. It was also to make Nancy a national heroine, a status she made good use of when she retired in 1968 after winning a second overall World Cup – with a 32-point

lead over France's Isabelle Mir – and an Olympic giant slalom gold medal. Those victories coupled with 14 wins in World Cup events ensured a plethora of promotional contracts from major North American manufacturers when she retired. Hard-working, well organized and ambitious, Greene knew how best to capitalize on her name and fame and is still today one of the best-known athletes in Canada.

Few of her successors have been able to reach the same heights. But business commitments have not stopped Greene from success in her private endeavours. A wife and a mother, she is also the driving force behind Nancy Greene Lodge which she built at Whistler Mountain, a big ski resort north of Vancouver, and one of the World Cup's venues.

Still involved in Alpine competition, through the Canadian Ski Federation, she's undoubtedly been a solid influence in Canada's development of big-time national team skiers such as Innsbruck giant slalom gold medalist Kathy Kreiner, 1970 Val Gardena giant slalom winner Betsy Clifford and 1982 Haus downhill winner Gerry Sorensen. Laurie Graham, one of today's best downhillers, is now on track to succeed them.

Nancy Greene was only 16 when she started her career at the Squaw Valley Olympic games in 1960. But she had to wait until 1966 for her first victory in an international event. Then in 1967 she won seven races, seizing the World Cup with the last slalom of the season.

WINNER 1969

# GERTRUD GABL

Gertrud Gabl was by far the leading slalom specialist, winning four races in 1969. Later she became a close friend of Annemarie Moser-Proell.

In 1969, St. Anton was to celebrate a prestigious World Cup double. Both the women's and the men's overall winners – Gertrud Gabl and Karl Schranz – were members of the famous Arlberg Ski Club. Earlier in the season the two had also distinguished themselves in front of their home-town audience, Schranz by winning the Kandahar downhill and Gabl by dominating her fear of speed to come eighth in the women's event, after the favourite, France's Annie Famose fell and tore her Achilles' tendon.

Gabl, the smiling daughter of a local ski teacher who spent his winters in Stowe, Vermont, was above all a brilliant slalom specialist. In 1968 and 1969, she won five slaloms as well as two giant slaloms.

Short on wins in the following season, she was to finish fourth and fifth respectively in the 1970 Val Gardena World Championship's slalom and giant slalom and make the top three only four times in 1971. Gertrud, who had become the close friend and confidante of Annemarie Moser-Proell, was to stop racing in 1972 after a relatively disappointing season. By then, never finishing in the top three, she had fallen to 18th in the overall World Cup standings.

She was later to marry a wealthy British businessman and ski buff. They were skiing together in the Arlberg range in 1976 when an avalanche broke loose above them. Gertrud was not able to ski out of its way.

Only 27 at the time of her death, Gertrud Gabl was not the first Alpine ski champion to meet such a tragic end. American Buddy Werner, Hahnenkamm downhill winner in 1959, and France's Charles Bozon, 1962 world slalom champion, were also the mountains' victims while on skis.

French women's teams dominated the first decade of the World Cup, but they produced only one overall winner, the graceful slalom specialist Michèle Jacot.

WINNER 1970

# MICHELE JACOT

Since 1967, 17 French women racers have won a total of 91 events counting towards the World Cup. But only one, the graceful Michèle Jacot, has managed to take the overall title.

It happened in 1970, as she led a French trio to the top of the standings. Two other French skiers finished that season in ninth and tenth place overall, to round out a season in which the French women's team won 17 out of 26 races. That winter, 18-year-old Michèle and her team-mates were also to head the overall rankings in the various individual disciplines.

Picked for the French squad in 1968, Michele won her first international race during the 1969 Vipiteno giant slalom. Only five foot four inches tall and weighing eight stone, her frail physique hides great determination. That, and her technical mastery, has allowed the skier from Chamonix to win all of ski racing's events. Particularly strong on hard or icy snow, Michèle won three races in a row in 1971, each in a different discipline. But towards the end of the season she was unable to rise to the level of her greatest opponent, Austria's Annemarie Moser-Proell who won five of the season's last nine races and the overall World Cup title.

World Champion at the 1970 Val Gardena combined downhill-slalom, her last feat was to be a silver giant slalom medal in the 1974 St. Moritz championship race, won by Hanni Wenzel.

Jacot retired after the 1976 Innsbruck Winter Olympics.

Furano

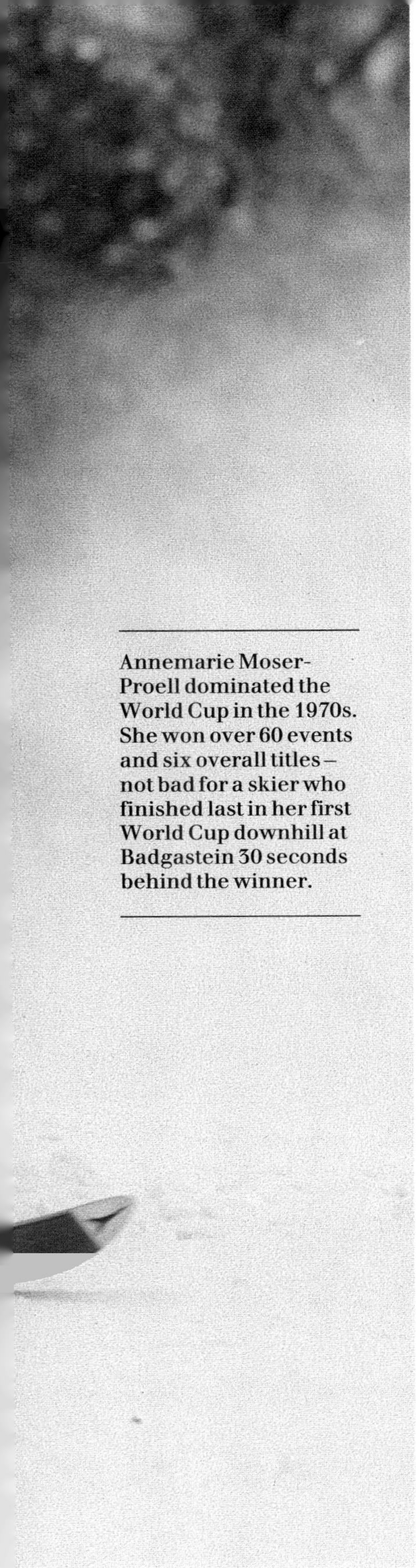

Annemarie Moser-Proell dominated the World Cup in the 1970s. She won over 60 events and six overall titles – not bad for a skier who finished last in her first World Cup downhill at Badgastein 30 seconds behind the winner.

WINNER 1971/1972/1973/1974/1975/1979

# ANNEMARIE MOSER-PROELL

Records are made to be beaten, but it is unlikely that any woman skier will overturn those set by the extraordinary Annemarie Moser-Proell who is considered the greatest woman skier of modern times.

Born in the small village of Kleinarl near Salzburg in 1953, she has won every trophy of any importance in the course of her long career. First making the grade in 1969 with a second-place finish in the St. Gervais downhill – won by France's Isabelle Mir – she did not retire until 1980, after a splendid victory in the Lake Placid Olympic downhill.

In between the Austrian had won 62 races – 36 downhills, 16 giant slaloms, three slaloms and seven combined downhill-slaloms – three World Championships and one Olympic gold medal, at Garmisch-Partenkirchen, St. Moritz and Sapporo. But most important of all, she won 16 World Cups – six overall, seven downhill and three giant slalom titles.

Her ferocious will to win, her courage and her impressive strength allowed her to dominate the downhill. From 1972 to 1975, "La Proell" – as the French called her – won 19 of the 28 World Cup downhills, often by margins as big as two and even three seconds.

It was very rare for her to be beaten on key days. But among the few who occasionally beat her were Marie-Thérèse Nadig in Sapporo, Lise-Marie Morerod in the 1977 World Cup and Hanni Wenzel in the 1978 and 1980 Cup competitions.

Moser-Proell's major defeats – along with her great victories – are the stuff epics are made of. Racing in her first World Cup downhill – after a bitter fight with the coaches who, afraid of the course's particularly difficult conditions, did not want to let her ski – Moser-Proell, then known only as Annemarie Proell, finished some 30 seconds behind the winner, in 78th place and in last place in the strong field.

She was not yet 15 years old and had fallen three times. But she had finished.

By 1972, she was the big favourite to win the Sapporo Olympic downhill, having just won the five previous races. Yet this young woman with muscles of steel and the determination of a born fighter was badly shaken by the unfair banning from the games of team-mate Karl Schranz and by the tension the International Olympic Committee's decision had bred among the athletes in the Olympic village.

Annemarie Moser-Proell was beaten in both the downhill and the giant slalom by Switzerland's Marie-Thérèse Nadig, a daring but blithe spirit who had never won a major race until then.

Moser-Proell won some of her biggest races in the second phase of the career she interrupted in 1976 to enjoy life, get married, then take care of her father who was gravely ill.

She lived at home in Kleinarl during this hiatus and built up a cafe-bar whose pastry enjoyed a well deserved reputation. At first, she did not seem to miss her former life of tension and travel around the globe. But after four months of rambling inactivity she decided – on her own account– to rejoin the "white circus" of the World Cup.

Moser-Proell stopped racing from March 1975 to December 1976. During the break she relaxed at home with husband Herbert and took care of her father who was ill.

Though she had trained only lightly before the season, it did not take Moser-Proell long to slide back into form. By mid-December she had already won the difficult Cortina d'Ampezzo downhill, ahead of the Italian Elena Matous, (then racing under Iranian colours despite her Czech origins and having formerly raced for the small republic of San Marino.)

Moser-Proell's comeback was to prove particularly successful. It included two World Championship gold medals in the downhill and combined downhill-slalom and, finally, her sixth overall World Cup title, a mere three points ahead of adopted Liechtensteiner Hanni Wenzel.

She had come to the season's last two races at Furano, Japan, trailing Wenzel by seven points. But 50 points were at stake. In the slalom, Wenzel increased her advantage, finishing second to Moser-Proell's third. But Wenzel was decisively beaten in the giant slalom. She came in fifth to the Austrian's second to lose the overall title.

This was doubly disappointing for Wenzel. That year the scoring formula had been changed to award points to the first 25 finishers in the season's last three races in each event. Under the previous system – which was re-adopted shortly after – Wenzel would have won overall.

Moser-Proell's final season was equally memorable. It began with a slalom win, more than eight years after her first victory in that event, and ended with an Olympic gold medal in the Lake Placid downhill, eight years after her bitter defeat in the same event at Sapporo.

Ironically, Nadig was by then the big favourite at the 1980 Lake Placid Winter Olympics, but, slowed by gusting winds, she had to make do with an Olympic bronze medal.

"La Proell" retired a few days after her 27th birthday. She has a daughter named Marion. Unlike other international skiing stars, Annemarie Moser-Proell has not tried to capitalize on her name or her fame. Instead, she shares her life between caring for her family and running her cafe.

If there is a name that could be said to epitomize all that is best in World Cup ski racing, it would be " Annemarie Moser-Proell" – the Salzburg flyer.

At 27, Moser-Proell celebrated her last triumph at Lake Placid where she won the 1980 Olympic downhill, eight years after her bitter defeat at Sapporo.

WINNER 1976

# ROSI MITTERMAIER

From 1967 to 1975, Rosi Mittermaier wanted to enjoy life first and race second. But in 1976 she became ambitious and aggressive, although everyone remembers her for her nice smile.

The year 1976 was like a fairytale come true for West Germany's Rosi Mittermaier. At 26, the ever-smiling Bavarian from Reit im Winkl, a small resort near Austria's Tyrol, was the doyenne of the "white circus", though she had only won five races in the nine previous World Cup seasons. Then suddenly, in one winter, she scaled all the highest peaks of Alpine ski racing, dominating both the 10th World Cup and the Innsbruck Winter Olympics.

Her four wins and nine top-three finishes, spread across all of racing's disciplines, earned her the overall title with a 67-point lead over runner-up, the Swiss Lise-Marie Morerod. She also earned herself the nickname "Gold Rosi" – and a red-carpeted entrée into the ski-business world – with Olympic gold medals in the downhill and slalom and a silver in the giant slalom, after a surprise win by Canada's Kathy Kreiner.

Rosi Mittermaier had been born into a skiing family. Her two sisters also raced for West Germany at one time. But neither Heidi nor Evi looked upon ski racing as an end in itself and Rosi adopted much of their casual attitude.

Between 1967 and 1975, she raced mainly for fun, taking each day as it came and not training any harder than it was necessary to stay in shape. She was also attending school in hotel-keeping at the time. But her relaxed attitude made the Bavarian girl very popular on the circuit. Even the racers from other teams cheered on her occasional successes.

It was only towards the end of her career that Mittermaier began to become truly ambitious. But she was frustrated by a series of missed opportunities and bad luck. A surfing accident in Hawaii in 1973 probably cost her the overall slalom title in the World Cup. And she injured herself badly when she collided with a day skier practising downhill on Innsbruck's future Olympic course.

But these misfortunes only served to stiffen her resolve. As the German women's team veteran she trained long and hard during the summer of 1975. And her determination at the beginning of the 1975-76 season was unshakeable.

The combination of this aggressive frame of mind and the real pleasure she took in skiing – a joy she never lost – bore immediate fruit. By the time she got to the games at Innsbruck, she had a commanding overall World Cup lead but was still relaxed enough to take a confident approach to the tough Lizum courses.

A perfect race won her the Olympic downhill, ahead of the great Austrian favourite Brigitte Totschnig and America's Cindy Nelson. This was an unexpected victory. It was her first win in the downhill. It so boosted Mittermaier's confidence that she easily beat Italy's Claudia Giordani and Liechtenstein's Hanni Wenzel in the slalom. And it was only a bare twelve-hundredths of a second that deprived Mittermaier of the Olympic grand slam, as Kathy Kreiner just edged her out of the giant slalom gold.

Any other skier would have been bitterly disappointed. But not Rosi Mittermaier. She took it with a smile.

"It's not serious," she said. "I had one of my best giant slalom races ever."

She took her revenge within a few days in the Copper Mountains of Colorado with back-to-back slalom and giant slalom wins and a third-place finish in the Aspen downhill.

Her wins, her joie de vivre and her beguiling smile charmed not only her fans, but also the advertising executives who beat a path to her door with lucrative promotional contracts.

In Innsbruck, Mittermaier amazed her rivals by winning her first downhill. She remained out of reach in the slalom and lost the giant slalom by a mere twelve-hundredths of a second.

WINNER 1977

# LISE-MARIE MOREROD

Five Swiss skiers were to win the overall title, but Lise-Marie Morerod was the first to get the crystal globe. She was also the first to beat the legendary Annemarie Moser-Proell in the general classification.

Had Lise-Marie Morerod been able to ski out her destiny, racers like Marielle Goitschel and Perrine Pelen, or Hanni Wenzel and Erika Hess – who clocked up some 20 wins between 1981 and 1986 – would probably not even be mentioned as possible candidates for the all-time best slalom or giant slalom champion. But a terrible car crash in the first weeks of the 1978-79 season was to forever alter Morerod's life and leave blank pages in her personal record book.

Morerod was born in the small Swiss village of Vers-l'Eglise, near Gstaad and Les Diablerets. And between 1975 and 1978 she won 24 World Cup races and took the women's overall World Cup title in 1977 after a great rivalry with Austria's champion Annemarie Moser-Proell.

It was in March 1972, at the Swiss National Championships in the Valais's Haute-Nendaz, that Morerod first made a name for herself. She beat Marie-Thérèse Nadig who, only a few months earlier, had won two Olympic gold medals. Morerod's feat was all the more surprising since, in the previous Swiss Nationals when she was only fourteen, she had finished last in the giant slalom and the downhill and next to last in the slalom.

After a disappointing performance in the Innsbruck Olympics – with a fourth in the giant slalom and a fall in the slalom – she made rapid progress on the World Cup circuit, finishing the season second in the overall rankings and first in the giant slalom in 1976. And by 1977 she finally celebrated total success with eight wins and five top-three finishes in the slalom and giant slalom, and the overall World Cup title.

In 1978 she was to fall back to third place in the World Cup rankings, but consoled herself with a silver medal in the Garmisch-Partenkirchen World Championship giant slalom. She had to make do with a seventh-place finish in the slalom.

On the day of her accident, Morerod was only 22, with her best racing years still ahead of her. But fate decided otherwise. That she survived at all was a miracle. The accident, which was caused by a British tourist driving too fast on narrow mountain roads, left her unconscious. She was taken to a small local clinic, but at first the seriousness of her injuries was not apparent. When the extent

of the damage was realized, she was rushed to Lausanne where a team of surgeons fought to save her life.

It took her months to recover from shock and she was never able to regain the extraordinary form which – in her best years – allowed her to play cat and mouse with the finest skiers in the world. She gave up ski racing in 1980. But she had, by then, been able to influence the budding hopeful Erika Hess who had, like Morerod herself, come to light in the Swiss National Championships.

Morerod excelled on difficult technical courses. Blessed with an aggressive technique, she was not one to play it safe, nursing a first-run lead with cautious second-run tactics. And close scrutiny of the record books reveals that she finished in the top three in more than half of her races.

Only speed and utter perfection of style were of interest to her. Though some found her carefree attitude unsettling, it only served to conceal a skier who was deeply committed and sensitive. She also fought for women's rights in the world of Alpine ski racing, demanding in 1977 that the women's overall World Cup winner be awarded a crystal trophy the same size as the men's.

Now a ski teacher, Morerod has remained in the world of ski racing by coaching young racers in the French-speaking part of Switzerland. She was married in the spring of 1986.

Morerod was the best slalom and giant slalom specialist from 1975 to 1978. She knew only one tactic – to go for it from start to finish. This won her 24 events until a car accident finished her career.

Hanni Wenzel scored her first World Cup points in 1972 and remained at the top until 1984. She won two overall titles and a total of 33 events, plus four gold medals in the Olympics and World Championships.

WINNER 1978/1980

# HANNI WENZEL

Along with Annemarie Moser-Proell, Marie-Thérèse Nadig and Rosi Mittermaier, Hanni Wenzel is one of the World Cup's biggest stars. Winning the overall Cup twice during the course of her long and distinguished career, she was also a four-time World Championship and Olympic gold medalist in 1974 and 1980.

Between 1972 and 1984, Wenzel won a total of 33 events – two downhills, 12 giant slaloms, 11 slaloms and eight combined downhill-slaloms. From 1973, except for a single year, she was never out of the top ten overall rankings. That one exception was 1982, when she injured her knee ligaments in a serious fall in the downhill and was unable to compete in anything but the season's early races and the Schladming World Championships.

Born in 1956 in Straubirn, West Germany, Hanni was the oldest child of the Wenzel family. She came to prominence on the international skiing scene in 1972 and scored her first World Cup points in the Heavenly Valley slalom.

She refused to ski for West Germany in the Sapporo Winter Olympics, opting to stay with the Liechtenstein team. Her parents and younger brother Andreas had emigrated to the principality and she did not want to compromise her chances of citizenship by competing for another country. The Wenzel family's naturalization request was approved in 1974 a few weeks after she won the World slalom title at St. Moritz.

Coached by her father – who was one of the 1950s best international four-event specialists – Hanni quickly showed promise as a junior. And she was able to train with the Swiss team.

Her international career was erratic, to say the least. Brilliant in 1974 and 1975, she had to wait until December 1977 to win again, in the Madonna di Campiglio slalom. But in 1978, though she dominated the World Cup with six individual wins, she was unable to score at all in the World Championships.

Pipped at the post by Austria's Annemarie Moser-Proell in 1979, Hanni Wenzel got even in style the following year, winning not only two gold medals at the Lake Placid Winter Olympics, but – finally – the overall World Cup title as well.

Her following seasons were largely ruined by serious injuries and she had to wait from December 1981 to March 1983 for another win, this time at Furano, Japan.

This return to form gave her every reason to pin her hopes on the Sarajevo Winter Olympics. But the FIS committee did not allow her to race. Like Stenmark who was also excluded from the games, she had taken out a semi-professional "B-Licence" in 1980 which allowed her to sign individual contracts with companies.

The FIS's regrettable decision did not discourage her. Winning races in each discipline during the 1985 season – a feat unparalleled since 1971 when Michèle Jacot and Annemarie Moser-Proell were the first to do so – Hanni hoped for a third overall World Cup title until the very end. Finally, after the Oslo slalom, she came up only nine points short of beating Erika Hess.

That was to be her last race. After 12 years of international competition, the Liechtenstein racer decided to concentrate on her personal affairs. In the spring of 1986, she married the Austrian Harti Weirather, the 1982 downhill World Champion.

Able to train with the Swiss team she was soon confronted by Erika Hess, the outstanding slalom specialist who beat her by nine points in 1984.

WINNER 1981

# MARIE-THERESE NADIG

Winner of two Olympic gold medals in 1972, Nadig had to wait until 1981 to win the overall World Cup title.

Marie-Thérèse Nadig had to wait until she was 27 before she finally succeeded in winning the overall World Cup title. That was in the 1980-81 season which she dominated from the beginning. Ultimately taking the title with a 30-point lead over team-mate Erika Hess, Nadig's winning performance included four downhill wins and two each in the slalom and giant slalom.

This fine victory was to end a long and full career, during which "Maite" became one of the big stars of the women's circuit. Since then she has taken to a more leisurely and gentler sport – soccer!

As relaxed as she was aggressive on skis, the Swiss champion's first international victories came during the Sapporo Winter Olympics where she beat the great Austrian favourite Annemarie Moser-Proell in both the downhill and the giant slalom.

Nadig then took three years to match her performance in those two brilliant races, accumulating top-three World Cup finishes but not winning again until the eve of the 1976 pre-Olympic Lizum downhill which she won ahead of "La Proell".

Nadig was to win another Olympic medal – this time a bronze – at Lake Placid. She had gone into the downhill there as the big favourite. She had already won six of the season's seven downhills and the Olympic course was perfectly suited to her style. But a violent gust of wind upset her performance.

Her bitter Lake Placid defeat added to her feeling that she still had untapped potential. This convinced her that she should continue her career – a wise decision as it turned out. It was in that season – her tenth – that she took the overall World Cup title.

Nadig not only played a major individual role on the international skiing scene but – by her spirit and her example – she contributed to the flowering of the Swiss women's team which now holds the record for individual races and overall World Cup titles won. In the first 20 World Cups, the overall title has been won by five Swiss women, two Austrian women and by one Canadian, one French, one German and one American woman.

World Ski Teacher's Woman Champion in 1986, Marie-Thérèse Nadig now shares her time between running a sports shop in Flums, organizing private ski race clinics and women's soccer, a sport she has played for the last ten years.

Nadig was favourite for the Olympic downhill at Lake Placid in 1980 after winning the six preceding races. But a violent gust of wind cost her a lot of time on her way down Whiteface mountain.

*Left:* Downhill is not Erika Hess's best event, yet she is able to finish among the specialists when she has to – scoring the combined points that helped her to the Cup.

WINNER 1982/1984

# ERIKA HESS

Erika Hess won her first World Cup race – a slalom in Schruns, Austria – at 13 hours (1 pm) on 13 January 1981, wearing bib number 13. Despite these ill-omens, the win itself was not unexpected. Then 19, she had already achieved a spate of top three finishes and all the experts agreed she was bursting with ski racing talent.

Hess was born in the Canton of Obwalden in central Switzerland and first came to prominence when she came second in the 1977 Swiss National Championships. Then only 14, she made rapid progress. She finished ninth in the 1978 Garmisch-Partenkirchen giant slalom, then took a bronze in the Olympic slalom at the 1980 Lake Placid games.

This graceful Alpine ballerina then soared from mere success to ultimate triumph over the next few years, setting some of World Cup skiing's most impressive records in the process.

Winning six slaloms in row, her superb 1981 season's end giant slalom victory propelled her into the overall ranking's second slot, behind team-mate Marie-Thérèse Nadig.

The winter of 1981-82 was to prove even more brilliant – with seven new wins she dominated the World Cup circuit. And for good measure she won no less than three gold medals – in the slalom, giant slalom and combined – in the Schladming/Haus World Championships.

*Opposite:* 1982 was by far Hess's best year. She won three gold medals in the World Championships as well as her first World Cup.

Coupled with her charm and modesty, these performances turned Erika into the new star of women's Alpine ski racing. A number of European publications nicknamed her "Heidi" – after the unspoilt mountain girl. After all, her father did have a farm above the small village of Grafenort.

But the fact that Erika became one of the best skiers in the world was no accident. Her aunt, Annemarie Waser, had been an excellent slalomer in the 1950s, winning a bronze medal at the Badgastein World Championships in 1958. And one of her cousins, Monika, has also raced for Switzerland since 1982.

On many occasions Erika has shown not just her talent but her strength of character and willingness to work, notably when she has been plagued with bad luck. Injuring her knee so seriously that she had to undergo surgery at Christmas 1982, she refused to be discouraged. She still put up a fine fight against America's Tamara McKinney who only beat her by 30-odd points in that winter's overall standings.

Despite a disastrous spell at the Sarajevo Olympics – fifth in the slalom, seventh in the giant slalom – she came back to take the overall World Cup title a second time.

1985 was to prove a year of great disappointments, but also of great joy. She fell in the second heat of the Bormio World Championship slalom, after winning the first leg. But she was still able to

Erika Hess's parents own a farm in the mountains near Lucern where the Swiss ski champion likes to relax in summer. That is why the foreign papers dubbed her "Heidi".

find the motivation to win the winter's last two slaloms, taking in the process, the overall ranking in that event.

A long talk with Jacques Ramont, the Swiss women's team coach and a friend, helped her to regenerate her drive and her love for the sport.

"We realized that I was too tense as I raced," she explained. "I was thinking too much of winning. From then on I tried to forget the pressure the fans were putting on me and to only think about skiing as fast and as relaxed as possible."

That method proved successful. Consistent again in 1986, she won two races and was runner up in another four. Only Maria Walliser, her brilliant downhill team-mate, was able to beat her in the overall World Cup ranking, while Austria's Roswitha Steiner, who won four individual races, just managed to edge Erika out of the other slalom honours.

But there is still great hope for Erika Hess. Her coaches and friends are pressing her to continue racing until the Calgary Winter Olympics. After all, she will only be 26 years old in 1988 and at the peak of her career.

Hess won more slaloms than any other skier on the women's circuit – 18 from 1981 to 1986. She also set a record with six consecutive wins in 1981.

WINNER 1983

# TAMARA McKINNEY

There was a 15-year gap before another North American woman racer was to repeat Nancy Greene's winning performance in the World Cup. But after a 1983 season filled with surprises, America's Tamara McKinney finally managed to hold the Europeans at bay and walk off with the crystal trophy.

Leading the final standings by more than 30 points, McKinney had beaten the two big favourites, Hanni Wenzel and Erika Hess who had, between them, won the overall World Cup title four times.

But the diminutive Tamara's success came as no real surprise to her rivals. Since 1981 she had been among the world's best giant slalomers. With 16 wins – seven of them in 1983 – McKinney ranks third in the World Cup list of slalom and giant slalom specialists of all time. And the only medal now missing from her collection is a gold one.

McKinney is a Californian from Olympic Valley – formerly Squaw Valley where the 1960 Winter Olympics were held. Her mother, former ski teacher Frances McKinney, played a crucial role in the future champion's development. Wanting to raise her eight children in the mountains where she could practise her profession, Mrs McKinney spent long months apart from her husband Rigan, a former steeple-chase jockey who now breeds thoroughbred horses in Kentucky.

Tamara McKinney was the first US woman skier to win the overall World Cup. She did it in 1983 with truly outstanding performances at the end of the season. She won four out of five races in North America and came second in the fifth.

With 18 victories and three giant slalom and slalom World Cups, McKinney is by far the best American skier for 20 years. She has less luck with medals though, with no golds in the World Championships or the Olympics from 1982 to 1985.

So, apart from a brief period in Lexington, Kentucky, Tamara grew up in the great Californian outdoors around the shores of Lake Tahoe. She never even went to school and completed her education by taking correspondence courses under her mother's watchful eye.

The ski slopes were the McKinney children's playground and all of them raced in one form or another. Tamara's brother Steve was later to gain fame for his speed skiing records and he and her elder sister Sheila were the first family members to make the American team. Tamara herself was not yet 15 when she took part in her first World Cup event.

In the 1977 Heavenly Valley downhill, Sheila had a terrible fall and was in a coma for week. Although she recovered completely, Tamara was badly shaken by the event and specialized in the slalom and giant slalom afterwards. Only much later did she race in the downhill again in an effort to earn points in the combined downhill-slalom events.

Third in the 1978 Piancavallo slalom, this ambitious young woman was to head the World Cup's overall giant slalom ranking in 1981, to general surprise, after having won three individual races in that event.

A broken hand hampered her in 1982, but while still skiing in a cast that February she managed to come in sixth in the World Championship giant slalom.

A fine horsewoman and a free-spirit, Tamara convalesced in summer by going off into the wilderness alone. And in 1983 she was to come into her own. With her confidence restored by a first win in the Limone slalom, she quickly regained her first-seed ranking.

By March the overall World Cup title was still up for grabs. Only some 15 points separated Tamara from Erika Hess and Hanni Wenzel and there were nearly ten events still to be raced. Going for broke, the young American was able to outdo herself at crucial moments. She won four of the last six races and finished second in a fifth to clinch the title.

Unfortunately, she did not recapture her total concentration and wonderful feel for the snow during the next few winters. While managing to win six races in 1984 and 1985, she was noticeably missing from the medals at the 1984 Sarajevo Winter Olympics and the 1985 Bormio World Championships.

And in 1986 she was never among the top three, a truly disappointing result for such a gracious champion.

WINNER 1985

# MICHELA FIGINI

Michela Figini was not yet 19-years-old when, in 1985, she became the 11th woman racer to win the overall World Cup title. This was not a record in itself – Austria's Annemarie Moser-Proell was also 18 when she took the title for the first time. But not even Proell, or any of the other great women racers of earlier years, had amassed a record of wins to match Figini's at such a young age.

A year earlier the girl from the Italian-speaking Swiss canton of Ticcino had become the youngest ever Olympic champion, winning the Sarajevo women's downhill – a taste of things to come. In Bormio the next year, she was to win the World Championship downhill gold medal as well.

In short, the astonishing "Michi" had – within two years – reaped Alpine skiing's highest honours, each time showing outstanding determination and grace under pressure.

This extraordinary champion learned to ski at the age of five on the little slope of Prato-Leventina, her native village, and her coming of age was as swift as it was irresistible. Spurred by the example of another Ticcinese racer, Doris de Agostini – one of the best downhillers from 1976 to 1981 – Michela was already, at the age of

Michela Figini's international career began in 1983. A year later she won her first race, was world downhill champion in 1985 and took the World Cup one month before turning 19.

*Right:* Figini is a great downhiller and excels at the giant slalom and the Super-G too. In January 1985, she won six races out of seven in these disciplines.

*Below:* Since 1984, the Swiss women's team has won more than half the World Cup events. They stay in shape by taking part in all kinds of sports.

12, considered to be one of the great Swiss hopes. Her first coaches – and her rivals – were already strongly impressed by her power and her will to win which, more than once, helped her beat boys of her own age.

She made her debut on the World Cup circuit in 1983 before even being nominated to the Swiss national team and when she only ranked 128th on the international FIS downhill listings. Early in the season though, she managed a third-place finish in the Mont-Tremblant downhill in Canada and, a year later, celebrated her first win in Megêve before her Sarajevo triumph, five hundredths of a second ahead of team-mate Maria Walliser.

In 1985, she buried her opponents: In January, she won seven races, in the downhill, giant slalom, Super-G and the combined.

At the Bormio World Championships, she again showed great control under pressure, winning the downhill despite the public's and the media's clamorous expectations.

Remarkably calm and well-balanced for her age, she managed to keep her attention firmly focused on her goal, even though the race was delayed for 24 hours because of stormy weather. The delay – in Sarajevo – actually won her the race. At the point the event was called off, to be run the next day, her time was not the fastest down the hill.

Fluent in French, German and English as well as her native Italian, Figini is a sports interviewer's dream, a young lady who is both frank and amusing. Her openness knows only one limit – that of her private life. Fiercely protective of her family, she tolerates few intrusions, for it is in the midst of her family, playing with her spaniel Pipa or walking in the hills, that she recovers from her hectic competitive life.

She should not be short of motivation in the winters to come. In the 1985-86 season she first learned what it is to lose. It was a bitter lesson. Often labelled easy-going, Figini progressively lost drive and faith in herself as the poor results accumulated. By the end of the season she had not chalked up a single win.

What is more, she could not find a reason or even a rational excuse for this slump. It is true that she had trained a little less than usual in the summer of 1985, due to minor surgery on her knee. And her fastest pair of racing skis had gone missing towards the end of the 1984-85 season, perhaps "borrowed" by a rival manufacturer's test laboratory. But she could not accept these as the cause of her failure.

In the spring of 1986 she decided to ski on a different type of ski anyway, hoping that a new product would bring her renewed success. Not the type of person to accept second-best, Michela Figini is anxious to recoup lost ground.

The men's season starts in August with the downhills at Las Leñas, Argentina. The women start in November, training in summer on the European glaciers.

WINNER 1986

# MARIA WALLISER

In winning the 1986 overall World Cup title, Maria Walliser finally achieved the recognition that had escaped her in the 1982 Schladming and 1985 Bormio World Championships and the 1984 Sarajevo Olympics.

One of the big downhill favourites on those occasions and among the circuit's best downhillers since 1981, she fell short of her goal each time.

In 1982 at Schladming she finished only 12th, having earlier won the downhill which counted towards the combined medal. In 1985, the Bormio scenario was almost an exact replay, only with a sixth-place finish in the main downhill.

In 1984, she missed the Sarajevo downhill gold medal – won by teammate Michela Figini – by five-hundredths of a second or the length of a ski tip.

All these consecutive defeats made Maria re-evaluate her skiing and determine to outdo herself in 1986. Concentrating and motivated as never before, the beautiful Maria had a brilliant season, winning in downhill, giant slalom and combined events more than making up for former disappointments. She was finally to take the overall World Cup title with a 40-point lead over her team-mate Erika Hess, three years after her first big win in Megêve.

But her Swiss fans adored her even before her World Cup win for other talents than her ability on skis. Born near St. Gallen, the intelligent and vivacious champion was often invited to host Swiss television talk shows.

An outspoken young lady, she never hesitates to tell the international racing officials exactly what she and her fellow skiers have on their minds when discussing the rules or the make-up of the season's schedule.

Yet this dynamic Swiss athlete does not want to be thought of as the spokeswoman for the world's best skiers.

"All I do is to speak my mind," she says. "A lot of things can be bettered on our circuit, but it isn't my business to do it. For the time being, I've first got to take care of my own career. This already takes a lot of energy and I've got a lot of goals to attain."

Whether World Cup, World Championships, or the 1988 Olympics, Maria Walliser is certain to be in contention for honours.

The Swiss ski racing team use all kinds of sports in their training. But one of the best exercises for a world-beating ski racer is rollerskating. It helps the skier develop balance and suppleness.

*Left:* Maria Walliser had to fight hard to become the 12th skier to win the women's overall Cup. She was fifth in 1983, eighth in 1984 and third in 1985.

*Above:* Maria is not only a well-known skier, she has also made a name for herself as a model and a popular chat show hostess on Swiss television.

mazDa
DESCENTE

The downhill is not only a matter of skill and endurance it requires great concentration. Note the rapt attention of Maria Walliser as she gauges her exact moment of landing.

uvex
COLMAR
3
NATI DEL MONDO
CATERINA 1985

# CHAMPIONS AND PERSONALITIES

Among the thousands of men and women who have competed in at least one World Cup ski race, less than two hundred have tasted the thrill of victory. Many more have had to be content simply with the satisfaction of scoring one or two championship points.

Some racers have even become personalities in the World Cup "white circus" simply because victory has always eluded them - like Italy's Paolo de Chiesa, who notched up 13 second and third places in the top slaloms of the international circuit, but never managed a first.

Established champions – like Werner Grissmann of Austria, Erwin Stricker of Italy, Poland's Andrzej Bachleda, Malcolm Milne of Australia, the Americans Wladimir "Spider" Sabich, Bill Kidd, Tyler Palmer and Andy Mill, and Canadian Jim Hunter – were in the limelight of the Alpine scene for various reasons other than their skiing talents. Each brought with them to the Alpine world a touch of mystery, an exotic flavour and, above all, eccentricity.

Bachleda, winner of a slalom in Banff, Canada, in 1972, was one of the top slalom and giant slalom specialists from 1968 to 1974 and finished sixth in the overall World Cup standings in 1972. He studied architecture in Krakow but went on to become the trainer at a French ski club. He was also a refined and cultured man and used to entertain his fellow racers with long piano recitals.

He left the World Cup scene in 1975 to pick up a few dollars on the American professional circuit. And it was there that he met the Australian Malcolm Milne, who was perhaps the forerunner of the *ski total* approach to downhills later made famous by Roland Colombin, Franz Klammer and the Canadians Read, Irwin, Podborski and Murray. Milne, a daring downhiller, was adopted by the French team in 1965, a year after his brother Ross was killed on the Olympic run at Innsbruck during a training session. He later made his reputation as a specialist in 1970. He won the bronze medal in the World Championships at Val Gardena, two months after victory at Val d'Isère. Malcolm Milne was from, of all unlikely spots, Thredo in Victoria.

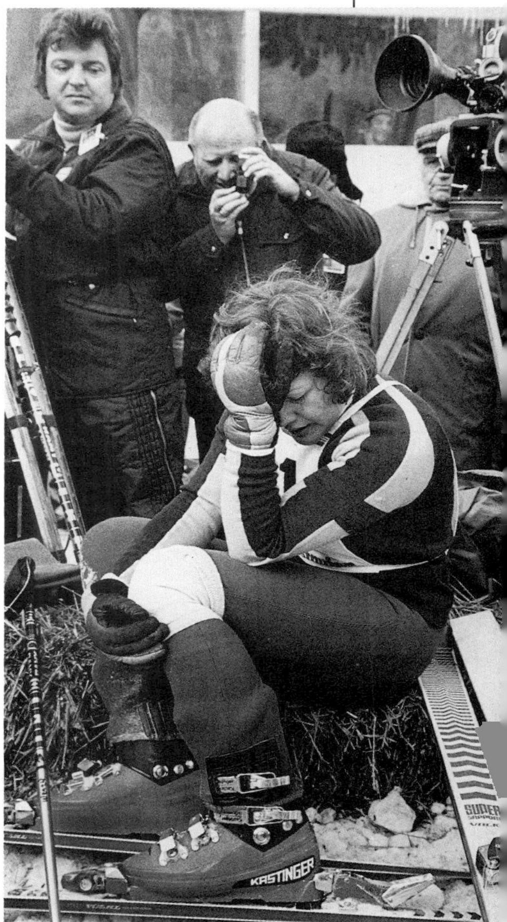


The agony and ecstasy of ski racing, summed up perfectly by Hanni Wenzel *above* and Marcus Wasmaier *left*

Opposite top: Some of the great characters of the World Cup were not always the winners. Men like Italy's Paolo de Chiesa who finished ten times second or third. *Opposite middle:* Austria's Werner Grissmann, who has a remarkable sense of humour, was as fast with his tongue as with his skis. *Opposite bottom:* The Italian Erwin Stricker invented many gadgets – including the slalom helmet – to make skiing safer.

Werner Grissmann and Erwin Stricker were known as the clowns of the World Cup in the 1970s. They were the source of a stream of jokes, banter and daft ideas that amused some and irritated others. But their pranks did not prevent them from achieving some fine racing performances. Grissmann was third in the world downhill at Garmisch-Partenkirchen in 1978 and swept into the top three on such varied courses as Kitzbuhel, St Moritz, Lake Louise and Val Gardena.

He also established a kind of record in losing ten races after having had the best intermediate time in each one. This led, logically enough, to the creation of a special prize, the "Grizzly" Trophy, which was presented to skiers who were beaten after leading at the halfway mark. He then wrote a spicy book about his skiing career which had spanned more than a decade. The book was full of incident and disputes with trainers who used to reproach him for not taking enough care of his fitness. A chimney sweep by profession, Grissmann went on to become one of the top drivers in the Austrian rally.

Stricker also came into conflict with his coaches, whom he accused of favouring the stars like Gustavo Thoeni and Piero Gros. It must be said that Stricker, who was born in Austria, was not easy to live with and constantly created consternation in the ranks of the *Squadra Azzurra.* But he was popular among the journalists with whom he shared his numerous technical innovations in the field of aerodynamics and shock absorption. And he was one of the rare Italian skiers to shine in all events.

He could have won the World Cup in 1974 had he not been badly concussed by a heavy fall in the Kitzbühel downhill. That did not stop him from setting the third best time in the first leg of the slalom the next day without taking the time for a thorough medical examination. And he was still holding that position in the second leg when he fell within sight of the finish.

*Above:* Australian Malcolm Milne was the first non-European to win a World Cup race. *Right:* Poland's Andrzej Bachleda was the best skier from Eastern Europe in the 1970s.

During the St. Moritz World Championships, he deliberately gave up a chance of victory in the combined event because he wanted, above all, to beat his team-mates in the slalom, the last event in the championships. He "blew up" at the start of the course, allowing the Austrian Franz Klammer to win his first title. Stricker stopped racing in 1980 but stayed in the ski world as a representative and consultant for major ski-wear manufacturers.

Like him, Billy Kidd and Andy Mill never realized their full potential. Kidd was Olympic slalom silver medallist in 1964 and world combined champion in 1970 before becoming one of the stars of the professional circuit. But he did not have the success he deserved as a result of several serious accidents in the 1960s.

He has, however, succeeded in a new venture. Working for a US television channel and Colorado's Steamboat ski station, he has become a leading figure in the American ski business.

Jim Hunter, third in the world combined during the Sapporo Olympic Games in 1972, was one of the great personalities of the World Cup until 1977. He was a highly committed skier and played a major role in the formation of the group of great downhill champions, the "Crazy Canucks", who competed on a level with the Swiss and the Austrians from 1976 to 1984.

Hunter's friends called him "Jungle Jim" because of his powerful physique and passion for training as well as various Tarzan antics like swinging in the trees and walking on his hands. On skis he set the pace for Ken Read, Dave Irwin, Dave Murray and Steve Podborski at the start of the 1970s. Distinguishing himself in all events, Hunter served as a kind of benchmark for his friends who eventually surpassed him in the winter of 1975-76. That season

*Bottom:* Downhill racing had an intense and fascinating era from 1975 to 1984 when four Canadian racers called the "Crazy Canucks" challenged the Europeans. They were Ken Read, Dave Irwin, Dave Murray and Steve Podborski (*below*) who won the downhill World Cup in 1982.

Read became the first Canadian to win a World Cup race when he captured the Val d'Isère downhill. Two weeks later, at Schladming, it was Irwin who triumphed. Skiing with remarkable aggression, the two men both became victims of their boldness in the second downhill at Wengen when they fell in mid-course – but Hunter came through to take third place.

Irwin never fully recovered from the serious concussion he suffered in that accident, but Read regained his place among the best specialists in 1979. Winner in 1980 at Kitzbühel and Wengen, he fell at the start of the Olympic downhill at Lake Placid after being among the favourites. He ended the season only nine points short of victory in the final World Cup downhill rankings.

It was Steve Podborski who became the first North American skier to triumph in that title. In 1982, this athlete from Ontario won with 115 points. The previous year only Austria's Harti Weirather had been able to edge him out in the last race by five points.

"Pod", who had become a big star in Canada with his bronze medal in the Olympic downhill at Lake Placid, triumphed on the most demanding courses from 1981 to 1984 – St. Moritz, Kitzbühel and Garmisch-Partenkirchen.

But, like all his team-mates, he was a victim of serious ligament and knee injuries – though Todd Brooker holds the record with eight separate operations. The condition forced Podborski to retire in 1984 after being placed eighth in the Sarajevo Olympic downhill. And like his friends Read, Murray and Irwin, Podborski assured himself a secure future in the business side of the sport.

The world of the downhill, synonymous in the public eye with speed and danger, has without any doubt produced some of the great heroes of the "white circus." The best known of them all is Franz Klammer, the "Kaiser" of Austrian skiing, who stamped his authority on the event on courses throughout the world from 1973

Ken Read was the first of the Crazy Canucks to win a World Cup race – in 1975 in Val d'Isère. Bad luck prevented him from crowning his career with a gold medal or a crystal trophy. But he was as famous in the Alps as in the Rockies.

to 1985. The list of his exploits and records is too long to set out in detail, but among the most memorable was his incredible display of daring in his victory in the 1976 Olympic downhill at Innsbruck. Driving himself to the limit, risking a dramatic fall every metre of the way, this son of a cattle breeder became the unforgettable hero of Austrian sport by edging out his friend and rival in the Swiss team Bernhard Russi by just half a second.

It was in March 1972 that the man who later became known as "The Klammer Express" made his international debut at Val Gardena. In December 1973, a few days after his 20th birthday, he swept ahead of all the favourites on the course at Schaldming, which was notorious at the time for average speeds of more than 70 miles an hour on a surface that was often icy.

Second in the World Championship downhill in 1974 – he was beaten unexpectedly by David Zwilling who had finished second in the World Cup the previous year – Klammer reigned supreme on the downhill courses from December 1974 to March 1977. During this period, he won 19 out of 27 World Cup downhills, sometimes by margins of more than three seconds – as at Wengen in 1975 – and once, in Kitzbühel the same year, *Cont. on page 146*

Franz Klammer, sometimes described as the "Klammer Express", was the great hero of Alpine skiing from 1973 to 1985. His impressive victories and his numerous records made him famous in skiing and non-skiing countries alike. His 1975 victories in eight downhills out of nine, his Olympic run in 1976 and his comeback in 1982/83 are some of his most famous achievements.

16
Bundes

by just three- thousandths of a second ahead of the runner-up.

A bit of luck could have helped him win the World Cup in his best season. At the end of the winter of 1974-75, Klammer had amassed 240 points – the same as Gustavo Thoeni and Ingemar Stenmark – as they prepared for the parallel slalom at Val Gardena. With eight victories and other leading positions in giant slalom and combined events, the idol of the Austrian public had been the most brilliant of the three, that year. Even a fourth place would have been enough to assure him victory.

Unfortunately the course selected by the Italian organizers, which was too steep and icy for a parallel slalom, put him at a clear disadvantage to the other two slalom specialists. His elimination in the first round of the event against Helmut Schmalzl certainly influenced the remainder of his career. Preferring to concentrate on the downhill, the Blue Riband event of Alpine skiing, he gradually neglected other events.

Clearly Klammer never realized his full potential after his fabulous Olympic success at Innsbruck. Most trainers at the time believed that to win you had to specialize totally in a particular event, a theory whose shortcomings only became evident in the 1980s.

David Zwilling was Gustavo Thoeni's strongest rival in the fight for the overall World Cup in 1973. A dramatic fall in the Kitzbühel downhill cost him the title. But he took his revenge in 1974 with a gold medal in the World Championship downhill at St. Moritz, beating Franz Klammer.

From March 1978 to December 1981, Klammer went through a barren period in which he never managed to break into the top three placings. He wasn't even selected for the Lake Placid Olympics in 1980.

He decided to change equipment in 1978 after having inexplicably lost the Garmisch-Partenkirchen world downhill – he was placed fifth, 0.65 seconds after the winner Sepp Walcher. But this was not in itself responsible for his sudden loss of form. Some people believe he lost the will to win after his much loved younger brother Klaus was paralysed by a fall during a race at Lienz in February 1977.

Winner of the downhill in the 1978 Garmisch-Partenkirchen World Championships, Sepp Walcher was one of the best Austrian specialists from 1973 to 1982, celebrating a double victory in Kitzbühel in 1978. He died in 1984 in an accident in a ski race near his home.

The "Kaiser" finally stormed back in December 198l by winning at Val d'Isère. He could have won again at Schladming but for a bad fall in a final training run. Even so he finished seventh after recording one of the fastest intermediate times.

He celebrated two more prestigious victories in 1983 and 1984. First he took the World Cup downhill championship for the fifth time after edging out his great rival, the Swiss Conradin Cathomen by two-hundredths of a second in the last race at Lake Louise in Alberta, Canada. Then he notched up his fourth victory on the formidable "Streif" at Kitzbühel, even though it was covered that day with a layer of hard-packed icy snow.

Klammer ended his illustrious career in March 1985, after having narrowly failed to win the World Championship title again when he finished fifth in the Bormio downhill. But he was well prepared for an alternative career. With his wife Eva, who he married in 1979, he launched a range of upmarket clothing called the "Klammer Line" which is well known for its lively and original colour combinations.

Klammer had been doubly fortunate. His great years coincided with a golden age for world skiing, which gained in popularity in the 1970s and sparked renewed passion in the Alpine countries and Scandinavia. In North America, his widespread popularity following his Innsbruck triumph led to innumerable appearances on US and Canadian TV from 1975 to 1985. But Klammer had fans in every country. He even had some in Switzerland who were also his greatest rivals.

Among the Swiss specialists who had dominated the downhill events at the start of the 1970s, two men in particular took up Klammer's challenge and fought to depose the Kaiser in a series of dramatic duels – Roland Collombin and Bernhard Russi.

Collombin, dubbed "Collombe-the-bomb" by supporters as a

tribute to his aggressive style, was the best downhiller in 1973 and 1974, winning several times in succession at Val Gardena, Garmisch-Partenkirchen, Kitzbühel and Wengen.

In 1974, Klammer often finished just behind him and Collombin, who shot to fame with a silver medal at the 1972 Sapporo Olympics, could have challenged the Kaiser's supremacy in 1975 and 1976 – but bad tumbles at Val d'Isère at the start of the season curbed his performance. The second accident came close to leaving him paralysed.

At the time Switzerland was virtually divided into two camps – those who followed Collombin and those who followed Russi, a double gold medallist at the 1970 World Championships and the Olympics two years later. Against Collombin's explosive style, Russi displayed a technique that combined the utmost refinement and precision.

Always a smooth performer, the Andermatt skier was a model of elegance on the high-speed bends and jumps. But he ran into difficulties on winding or icy courses that demanded a more forceful approach. He never won at Kitzbühel or Garmisch-Partenkirchen. But he was the winner of nine World Cup downhills between 1970 and 1977 and finished second or third some seventeen times.

Russi's best race was in the 1976 Olympics at Innsbruck. Starting third, he raced brilliantly down the demanding Patscherkofel run, making only one slight error on the final right-hand bend.

Klammer, starting 15th, noted Russi's fast time and realized that he would need a perfect run to beat his Swiss rival – no faults and a maximum of speed and aggression.

*Right:* Bernhard Russi was World and Olympic Champion in 1970 and 1972. *Above:* Roland Collombin dominated the scene from 1973 to 1974, winning the greatest classics. He was seriously injured, falling twice in Val d'Isere in 1974 and 1975.

"I came close to my absolute limits today," said the Austrian at the finish. "I couldn't have skied any faster. I diced with falling from start to finish."

Russi, who had been ahead of Klammer at the halfway mark, was the first to congratulate him.

"I haven't lost the gold medal," Russi said after the race, "I've won the silver."

Two years later he retired, a few days after starting fastest in the Garmisch-Partenkirchen downhill but finishing a disappointing 13th. Illness during the preceding months had prevented him from competing in all but one race, at Cortina d'Ampezzo where he was second behind Italy's Herbert Plank. At 30, he decided to start a new life after devoting ten years to Alpine competition.

From the very beginning of Alpine racing, the downhill has been practically the exclusive domain of the Austrians and the Swiss who recorded 123 victories in the 166 World Cup races between 1967 and 1986. By contrast, they were less than outstanding in other events regarded as "technical". The Austrians Alfred Matt and Hansi Hinterseer, and the Swiss Dumeng Giovanoli, Heini Hemmi and Joel Gaspoz were the only ones to top the World Cup final standings in the slalom and giant slalom, which were dominated by the French, then the Italians, and finally by the legendary Swede Ingemar Stenmark.

Edy Bruggmann of Switzerland, and the Austrians Reinhart Tritscher, Klaus Heidegger, Herbert Hubert and Werner Bleiner were all prominent at various times.

Some of their exploits were more spectacular than others – like little Hemmi, who beat Stenmark for the giant slalom Olympic title in 1976 and won the World Cup championship in the same event the following year – but for the most part success eluded them at crucial moments.

Giovanoli, third in the World Championship giant slalom in 1970, was the top slalom specialist before the 1968 Olympics, winning both Wengen and Kitzbühel, but there was no place for him on the rostrum at Grenoble.

Heidegger took the honours at Wengen and Kitzbühel in 1978 and recorded the fastest first leg at Garmisch-Partenkirchen, but fell on the second leg. The previous year he had presented a determined and consistent challenge to Ingemar Stenmark in the World Cup series.

He could have beaten the Swede if he had competed in the downhill and combined events, but unfortunately the Tyrolean

Herbert Plank was by far the best Italian downhiller from 1974 to 1980 and took the 1974 Olympic downhill bronze medal. He excelled on fast, icy courses.

*Below:* Heini Hemmi was the surprising Olympic champion in Innsbruck beating the favourites Stenmark and Thoeni. He won the giant slalom World Cup title in 1977, the only title in the technical events that Stenmark lost from 1975 to 1981. *Bottom:* Joel Gaspoz won the giant slalom World Cup in 1986, only one point ahead of Stenmark.

lacked sufficient confidence to take the risk – and was strongly advised against doing so by his slalom coach.

Tritscher, who was outstanding in all events from 1968 to 1973, had the cruel misfortune to break a leg in 1969 when a promising career lay before him. It took him several years to recover fully from the injury. The same bad luck befell Matt, while Bleiner and Hubert never succeeded in emerging from the long shadow cast by their captain Karl Schranz.

Hubert, one of the most gifted skiers of his generation, was particularly sensitive: he later hanged himself.

Hansi Hinterseer, son of 1960 Olympic slalom champion Ernst Hinterseer, was another who did not achieve the success he deserved. Both the tension that constantly surrounded this charming young man and the fact that he never gained the full support of the Austrian public prevented him from exploiting his immense talent to the full.

This was also the case for one of the great rivals of Gustavo Thoeni at the start of the 1970s, the Frenchman Henri Duvillard. Alpine ski racing is a great tradition in the family of Clovis Duvillard. Henri's father managed the family farm in the hills above Megêve.

Henri's brother Adrien was an unhappy hero of the 1960 Olympic downhill. He was on the point of winning when a momentary lapse of concentration brought him crashing off course near the finish. A few weeks before the Squaw Valley games, Adrien had won brilliantly on the classic course at Kitzbühel.

Henri Duvillard, who first drew attention to himself in December 1968 by beating all the favourites in the Val d'Isère downhill before it became part of the World Cup calendar, was never rewarded with a champion's crown. Runner-up in the World Cup in

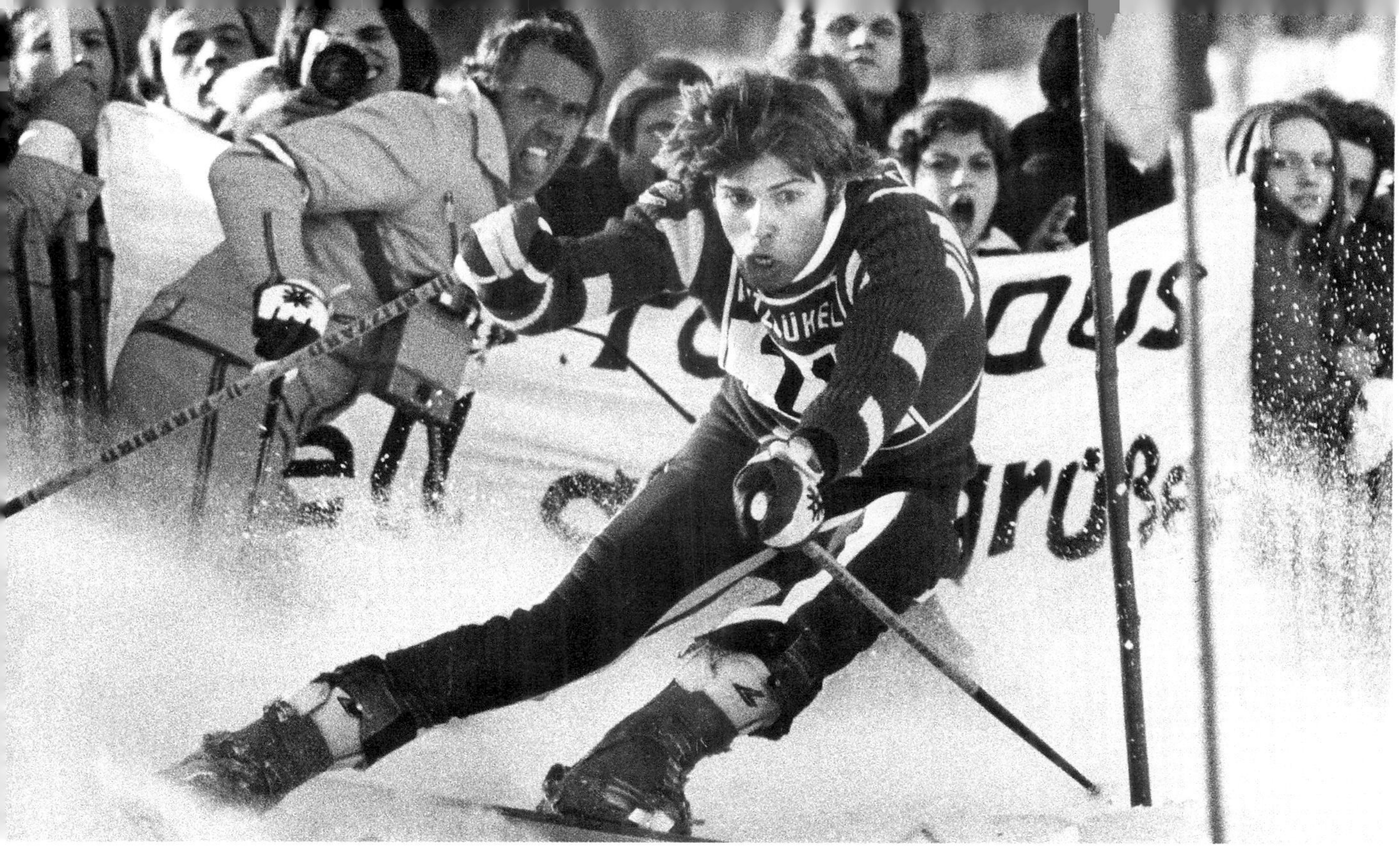

1971 and 1972, he gained no World Championship or Olympic medals in 1970 and 1972 and was even further from the rostrum two years later.

That year he was not even able to compete at St. Moritz as he had been dropped from the French team along with Jean-Noel Augert, Patrick Russel, Roger Rossat-Mignod and the Lafforgue sisters, Ingrid and Britt.

These racers, the best in France at the time, had been outstanding on the international circuit for several years with 49 World Cup wins to their credit. Ingrid Lafforgue and Augert had won the world slalom titles in 1970 while Russel was second in this championship in 1970 and finished second and third in the World Cup in 1970 and 1971 before breaking a leg the following year.

Unfortunately these champions, who had formed the backbone of the French team for several years, had been sharply critical of their trainers whose methods they considered ineffective. In February 1973, Augert and Duvillard were suspended for two weeks for "indiscipline", before being pardoned and cleared to resume competition in the World Cup.

Augert, 24 at the time, promptly won the final two slaloms at Naeba and Heavenly Valley. But in 1974 there were no further pardons. The six rebels were forced to stay at home during the World Championships at St. Moritz and a black period began for French men's skiing which continued until January 1986 and the World Cup victory of Didier Bouvet in the Parpan slalom –

*Top:* The talented Hansi Hinterseer was Olympic slalom champion in 1960. *Above:* Klaus Heidegger was by far the best Austrian slalomer in the mid 1970s.

Guy Périllat was one of the great stars of the French team from 1960 to 1969. He became combined World Champion in 1960, the day of his 20th birthday, and won several major classics in 1961. He won another gold medal in 1966 and was third in the overall World Cup standings in 1967.

although he had already gained a bronze medal two years previously in the Olympics.

With the banning of these athletes, a glorious era in French skiing came to an end: since 1959, their country had played a major role in the international scene with a string of outstanding individual and team performances. At the start of the 1960s, skiers like Adrien Duvillard, Guy Perillat – who dominated the downhills in 1961, won the giant slalom World Championship in 1966 and a silver in the 1968 Olympic downhill – Leo Lacroix, Francois Bonlieu and all of what were known as Jean-Claude "Killy's Merry Men" had thrilled a French public that was only beginning to discover winter sports.

Tales like those of Henri Duvillard, whose dramatic battles against Gustavo Thoeni and also with the unpredictable Karl Schranz at Kitzbühel in 1972, form part of the legend of the World Cup. Each team produced one or two stars whose exploits may have been forgotten by the general public, although this does not diminish their contributions. For example, there were the German pair Christian Neureuther and Sepp Ferstl.

Neureuther, a doctor's son who developed a passion for competitive skiing before marrying the delightful World Cup champion Rosi Mittermaier, was almost 30 before achieving the sixth success of his career in the Kitzbühel slalom, some six years after his first win at Wengen. He figured among the best slalom racers in the world for six years, but never gained a World Championship or Olympic medal or a World Cup trophy.

Ferstl was one of the rare skiers to gain two consecutive victories at Kitzbühel – in 1978 and 1979. But he was pipped for the bronze medal in the 1978 World Championship downhill by just hundredths of a second. Ferstl's simplicity, good humour and courage earned him the lasting affection of his companions on the international circuit.

In 1978, Ferstl had shared victory at Kitzbühel with another classic champion, the sadly missed Sepp Walcher. An Austrian and downhill World Champion in 1978, he struggled against misfortune throughout his career, suffering injury at least once every year. Yet accidents never diminished his passion for skiing or his good humour.

But it was this enthusiasm for the sport and for enjoying himself that led to his downfall. He was taking part in a competition

*Below left:* Jean Noel Augert and (*below*) Henri Duvillard were two of the four Musketeers – along with Patrick Russel and Alain Penz – who led the French domination of the World Cup from 1969 to 1973, even if they couldn't win the coverted overall title. *Bottom:* After they were fired by their trainers, France had to wait until 1986 for another victory.

*Below:* Sepp Ferstl and (*right*) Christian Neureuther were the best German racers in the 1970s. They tied first place in the 1978 downhill at Kitzbühel where Neureuther won the slalom in 1979.

organized for tourists at his home resort of Schladming when a fall in one of the races ended in tragedy when he crashed into a metal pole and died from his injuries.

Equally tragic was the loss of Italy's affable and talented Leonardo David. Winner of the European Cup in 1978, he was considered the brightest prospect in the *Squadra Azzurra,* and even as a potential rival to the great Stenmark.

After confirming his early promise by winning the slalom at Oslo in 1979, he fell twice in downhills, first during his national championships and then, just ten days later, during the Olympic trial at Lake Placid. After the second crash he went into a coma, from which he never recovered. A few years later, he died.

Fortunately, such fatal incidents remain exceptionally rare. Road accidents have been a greater killer that have deprived the World Cup competition of a string of brilliant and popular skiers. Italy mourned the deaths of Bruno Noeckler, Illario Pegorari, Roberto Burini and Adams in the late 1970s and early 1980s. The same fate befell the remarkable Alexandre Zhirov as he was driving in a Moscow suburb in the autumn of 1983.

Zhirov – "Sacha" to his friends – was one of the Soviet Union's finest slalom racers and matched the best in the world in 1981, the year his comrade Valery Tsyganov won the Aspen downhill.

Big and powerful, with a remarkably direct technique, he beat such stars as the Mahre brothers and Stenmark at Furano in Japan, Borovetz in Bulgaria and Laax in Switzerland in 1983.

These successes lifted Zhirov third overall in the World Cup standings that year, but recurring knee injuries kept him out of the World Cup honours the following season.

The Soviet skiers emerged to challenge the established stars in 1978. Vladimir Makeev was ninth that year in the Garmisch-

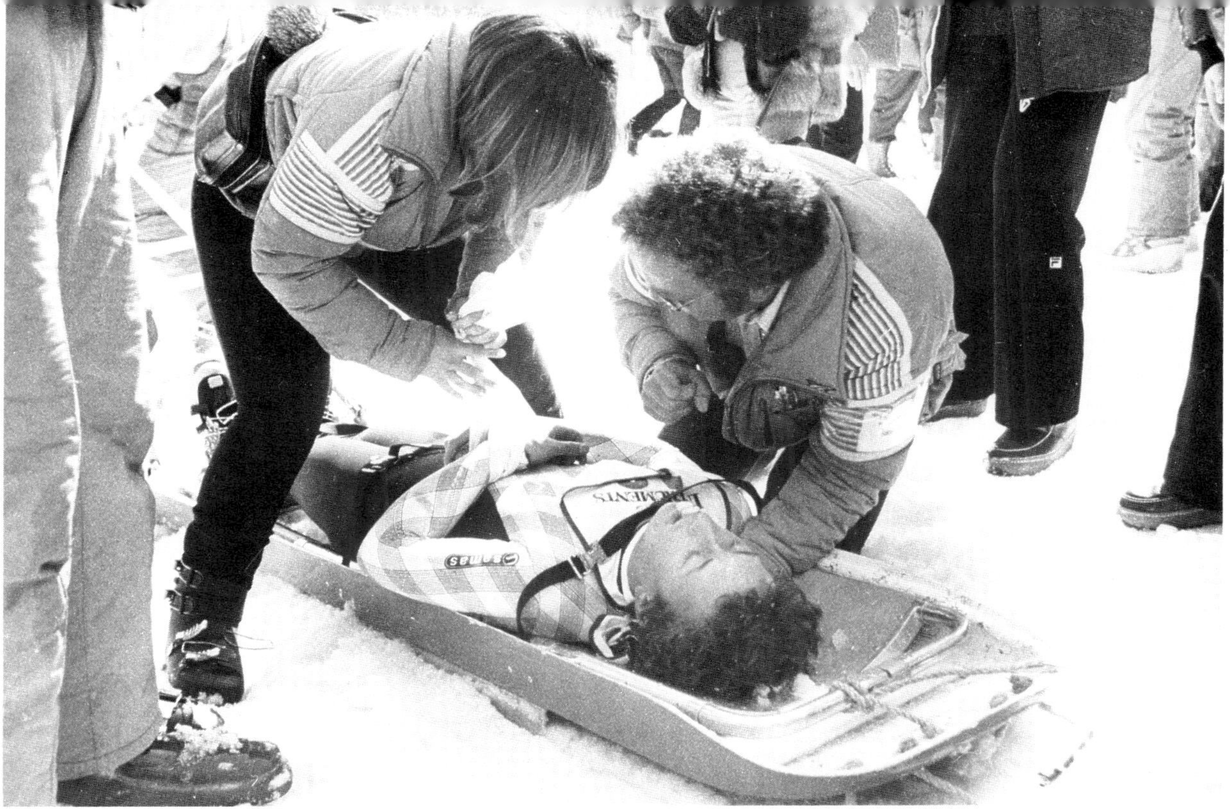

Partenkirchen world downhill. But they did not remain long among the world elite. Worn out by extremely tough summer training schedules, involving 100 days of skiing and 50 days of physical training, they vanished as suddenly as they had appeared. During their brief season, bad luck had denied them the medals that were within their grasp at Lake Placid, for Tsyganov in the giant slalom, and at Schladming, for Makeev in the downhill.

There were no medals either for the Norwegian Erik Haker, who recorded the fastest first leg of the 1972 Olympic giant slalom before falling on the second run. The Scandinavian was winner of four giant slaloms at the start of his career and later became one of the world's best downhillers. His finest achievement was beating his rivals twice in succession in the 1979 Val Gardena downhill. The two races were held on the same day – the first was annulled due to problems with the automatic timing.

*Top and above:* Italy's Leonardo David and (*third from left*) Russia's Alexandre Zhirov did not realize their potential. Both died tragically: one in a 1979 downhill, the other in 1983 in a car crash.

# THE WOMEN

Marielle Goitschel and Françoise Macchi of France figure prominently among the great stars of women's skiing who richly deserved World Cup trophies, but who failed to win the crucial races.

Goitschel, one of the top personalities of the 1960s, came desperately close to triumph in 1967. She was finally beaten by Canada's Nancy Greene after losing the last slalom of the season at Jackson Hole, Wyoming, by seven-hundredths of a second.

The World Cup was the only official award missing from the trophy cabinet of this great skier from Val d'Isère. She was World Champion of the combined events at Chamonix in 1962 shortly before her 17th birthday – though the youngest world champion in women's Alpine skiing was Betsy Clifford, who won the giant slalom title in 1970 at the age of 16 and four months. Goitschel then edged out her sister Christine to win the Olympic giant slalom in 1964. The two sisters also dominated the slalom, but this time Christine won ahead of Marielle.

In 1966, Marielle won two gold and two silver medals at Portillo. Annie Famose, who could have won the overall World Cup title in 1969 if she had not torn an Achilles' tendon in a fall in the St. Anton downhill, won the slalom while the downhill went to Austria's Erika Schinegger.

Perhaps the most bizarre tale from Portillo was that the Austrian should never have competed in that event. Subsequent medical tests revealed that she was a man. She changed her name to Erike and a surgical operation later allowed her to become a father.

Meanwhile Marielle Goitschel won the affection of the French public with an effervescent personality and natural charm that allowed her to mix happily with government leaders of the day and VIPs like the Shah of Iran. She retired in 1968 after winning a final Olympic title at Grenoble, but never really tried to make use of her immense popularity in the commercial world. Instead she aimed for a political career in the hope of becoming a member of parliament or government. So far these dreams have not been fulfilled.

Françoise Macchi, one of six women skiers to have tasted victory

*Opposite:* The French sisters Marielle and Christine Goitschel were winners of 12 gold and silver medals from 1962 to 1968. But despite their great talent they could not win the overall World Cup titles they deserved. *Above:* Francoise Macchi was second in the overall standings in 1972. *Right:* Canada's Betsy Clifford was giant slalom World Champion in 1970.

in the three traditional Alpine events, was only 20 points behind Annemarie Moser-Proell at the start of January 1972, just before the Sapporo Olympics. She was thought to have a good chance of beating the Austrian champion – many of the technical races were still to be held. But unhappily she was injured in a fall in a training session in Japan. That accident led her to an early retirement at the age of just 21.

France has produced some of the greatest stars of women's skiing, who dominated the international circuit for many years. They included Isabelle Mir, one of the best downhill specialists from 1966 to 1972. The Lafforgue sisters, Ingrid and Britt whose Swedish mother May Nilsson had been third in the world slalom at Zakopane in 1939, between them won the World Cup slalom championships from 1970 to 1972 as well as the 1970 world title. Danielle Debernard was Olympic slalom silver medallist in 1972 and third in the Innsbruck giant slalom in 1976. Patricia Emonet was the best slalom racer of 1973. Fabienne Serrat was a graceful double World Champion in 1985 after an impressive string of 15 World Cup victories.

If Annemarie Moser-Proell was by far the most brilliant Austrian woman of the World Cup – the Salzburg flyer accounted for almost half of all the victories achieved by Austrian teams since 1967 – some of her colleagues nevertheless produced great performances from under her shadow.

Monika Kaserer, who excelled in giant slalom from 1972 to 1978 with eight wins to her credit, finished three times among the top three in the overall standings, while Brigitte Totschnig-Habersatter won the World Cup downhill championship in both

*Above:* Isabelle Mir, the best French downhiller from 1968 to 1972 and runner up in the overall classification in 1969, and (*right*) the charming Fabienne Serrat, double World Champion in 1974. They were two of the most popular French skiers on the World Cup circuit.

1976 and 1977. Olga Pall, the downhill Olympic champion in 1968, and Wiltrud Drexel, third in the 1972 Olympic giant slalom and the 1974 St. Moritz downhill, shared eight victories and two World Cup titles between them.

Bernadette Zurbriggen, a distant cousin of Pirmin Zurbriggen, was only 16 when she finished seventh in the Sapporo Olympic downhill. She never fulfilled her early promise, but a series of defeats in the classic World Cup races did nothing to diminish her popularity in Switzerland.

Another greatly admired Swiss star, Doris de Agostini from Airolo at the foot of the Gothard Pass, changed radically during the seven years she devoted to the World Cup competition. Soft and gentle at the start of her career, she gradually became a tough and determined athlete in her bid to reach the top.

Her uncompromising personality, imposing physique and humble origins did nothing to endear her to her rivals who made no secret of their dislike for her. She was most notably out of favour in 1976 when she won the Badgastein downhill in appalling weather conditions that wrecked the hopes of less determined competitors. De Agostini retired in 1983 after a well deserved triumph in the World Cup downhill championship.

Although it has achieved only one success in the World Cup overall championships, the West German team has been one of the prominent forces in women's skiing since 1974. That year the lovely Christa Zechmeister won four successive slaloms, thereby hastening the end of the career of her team-mate Rosi Mittermaier who fiercely contested each event.

Zechmeister failed to produce the same form when chasing medals, though. But her namesake Christa Kinshofer meanwhile captured the Olympic silver medal in the 1980 slalom, after having

*Above:* Perrine Pelen, World Champion in 1985 and winner of 15 World Cup slaloms, clinched the slalom World Cup in 1980. *Below:* Austria's Monika Kaserer, one of the best giant slalom skiers from 1973 to 1978, was also a tough rival of Annemarie Moser-Proell. Kaserer finished five times among the best three in the overall World Cup.

*Above:* Bernadette Zurbriggen – pictured here with 1977 World Cup champion Lise Marie Morerod – and (*above right*) Doris de Agostini were, with Olympic champion Marie Thérèse Nadig, the best Swiss downhillers from 1975 to 1983. The Swiss team won six downhill World Cup titles out of seven from 1980 to 1986.
*Below right:* For years the Epple sisters led the strong German team. Irene, with trophy, who stopped racing in 1985 to study medicine, won the giant slalom World Cup in 1982, four years after Maria won the World Championships in Garmisch-Partenkirchen. Maria left the World Cup in 1986.

achieved the unique feat of winning five consecutive giant slaloms the previous year. Kinshofer never reached such heights again, though when she was finally dropped from her national team she promptly decided to race for the Netherlands.

The Epple sisters, Irene and Maria, had differing fortunes. Irene, the elder, never achieved the success she richly deserved after a second place in the 1978 World Championship downhill, the 1980 Olympic giant slalom and the overall World Cup standings in 1982. Maria meanwhile won an unexpected gold in the 1978 giant slalom World Championships. The younger sister then had to wait until February 1981 to repeat this success in the World Cup, at Zwiesel in the southeast of West Germany. Irene had also had to be patient – seven years separated her debut in World Cup competition and her first success at Saalbach in March 1980. She finished among the top three in downhills on 16 occasions, but celebrated victory only once at Val d'Isère in December 1983.

The Americans, who won almost 50 races in the first 20 World Cup series, enlivened the women's circuit during their runs of success, notably from 1967 to 1972 and then again from 1981 to 1985.

The sisters Nagel and Christine Cutter and then the Cochran sisters, all of them excellent specialists in the technical events,

were serious rivals of the Europeans in the first period. Between them they won 14 World Cup races and, at Sapporo, Barbara Cochran snatched Olympic gold from Danielle Debernard by two-hundredths of a second.

In the intervening period, only the blonde Cindy Nelson was able to challenge the Alpine stars. The skier from Lutsen, Minnesota, competed with honour for 14 years in the World Cup – from December 1971 to March 1985 – but perhaps her greatest victory was at the expense of the extraordinary Annemarie Moser-Proell in the Grindelwald downhill in 1974, after the Austrian had won the previous 11 races.

Nelson had mixed fortunes in various competitions. Third in the 1976 Olympic downhill and second in the 1982 World Championships, her best result in the World Cup overall standings was fourth in 1979. But she did play a major role in the formation of an outstanding American team at the start of the 1980s. Her experience, generosity and competitive spirit inspired her team-mates who grew from success to success from 1981.

Tamara McKinney, the attractive Christine Cooper, Holly Flanders, Debbie Armstrong, Diane Roffe and Eva Twardokens skied brilliantly everywhere they went – the World Cup, Olympic Games, World Championships.

Cooper, second in the slalom and giant slalom at Schladming in 1982, was well placed to become the first American to lift the World Cup in 1983 when she suffered a bad ankle injury in January. Though her career seemed threatened, she made a brilliant comeback in 1984 when she won silver in the Sarajevo Olympic giant slalom despite two dramatic falls. Although only 24, she decided to retire after having competed at the highest level for seven years.

The US team dominated women's ski racing from 1981 to 1985. *Left:* Christine Cooper and (*above*) Cindy Nelson were its leaders. In 1983, Tamara McKinney became the first US woman skier to win the overall World Cup title.

Downhill racing remains the most popular Alpine discipline and the battles between the favourites are watched by millions of TV viewers. In 1986, (*below*) Canada's Laurie Graham, (*opposite*) Austria's Katrin Gutensohn and Switzerland's Maria Walliser dominated the women's downhill, while (*below right*) Austrian Peter Wirnsberger took the title on the men's circuit with four victories in a row, ten years after his international debut.

# TODAY'S STARS

More than 200 skiers scored points in the course of the 20th World Cup series that was marked not only by the victories of Maria Walliser and Marc Girardelli, but equally by the exploits of some 20 other racers who staged thrilling duels on courses throughout the world.

Outstanding among the women were the specialists in the technical events like Roswitha Steiner of Austria, who notched up four slalom victories, and Vreni Schneider of Switzerland who dominated a giant slalom series and finished third overall despite an ankle injury that kept her out of competition for several weeks.

Schneider's closest rivals included the Yugoslav Mateka Svet, who was only 15 when she won at Vysoke Tatry in Czechoslovakia and Bromont in Quebec, and West Germany's Traudl Hächer who displayed a remarkable blend of grace and determination.

Traudl and her team-mates Marina Kiehl and Michela Gerg formed a formidable trio that may well mount a strong challenge for an overall World Cup title.

Meanwhile another talented pair, Katrin Gutensohn of Austria and Laurie Graham of Canada, fought Maria Walliser every inch of the way in the downhills and forced the Swiss star to excel

CARRERA
mazda
mazda

herself in the final races of the season to take the World Cup title.

Gutensohn, whose shy smile and apparent fragility conceal a strong will to win, is only 20 and has a promising future. Graham, third in the 1982 World downhill, celebrated her 26th birthday in March 1986 but is aiming for Olympic honours in Calgary, Alberta in 1988.

Others achieved unexpected successes – like Peter Wirnsberger, at 28 one of the "old men" of the Austrian team. Olympic downhill silver medallist back in 1980, he first came to the fore in December 1976 when he was placed twice in the first ten races at Val Gardena which were dominated by the great Franz Klammer. A brilliant career seemed assured for the charming 18-year-old. But he had to wait almost 10 years to confirm his early promise – after three wins in 1979 he did not taste victory again until January 1985 in Wengen.

Wirnsberger swept to four consecutive victories in the winter of 1985-86, a feat nobody had achieved since the reign of Klammer. Several other leading placings helped him become the sixth Austrian to win the World Cup downhill championship, though he had to battle to the end to overcome Peter Muller, the 29-year-old from Zurich who has been competing on the international circuit since 1977.

Muller is one of those rare city-dwellers who has risen to the summit of Alpine competition. It cost him an enormous effort – proud and self-willed, Muller always punishes himself in training to beat the men from the mountains who mocked him at the start of his career.

Only a gold medal and an elusive victory at Kitzbühel are missing from his list of honours. With 13 individual and three cham-

Peter Muller is the best Swiss downhiller of the last decade. A native of Zurich, he is known for his very aggressive style.

Marcus Wasmaier could become the first West German skier to take the overall World Cup. The giant slalom World Champion in 1985, he finished third in 1986. He was the best Super-G specialist of that winter.

pionship wins in the World Cup, as a champion in the competition he runs second behind Klammer. His other achievements include second placings in Sarajevo in 1984 and Bormio the following year. But two bad crashes at Åre in Sweden and at Whistler Mountain in British Columbia denied a fourth World Cup downhill championship to this athlete renowned for his aggressive style on the pistes and his peaceful nature in daily life. In contrast to ski racing, his favourite pastimes are fishing and cultivating mushrooms.

With foresight Muller has already prepared for the future by investing in gymnasiums where he goes himself for training. He is also an accomplished performer in other sports such as motocross, tennis and windsurfing – the latter is a particular favourite with skiers including Andy Wenzel, Ingemar Stenmark, Australia's Steven Lee and the West German Marcus Wasmaier.

Marcus Wasmaier surprised everyone in 1985 by becoming the first German skier since 1939 to win a World Championship event when he outclassed two great specialists, Pirmin Zurbriggen and Marc Girardelli, in the giant slalom at Bormio. He confirmed his brilliant form later that season by winning two Super-G races, topping the 1986 World Cup final standings in this new event, and a third placing in the overall championship.

It has been a spectacular rise for this 23-year-old athlete who only came to the fore in March 1984 when he came fifth in a Super-G at Opdal in Norway. He may well have the potential to

The Australian Steven Lee won a Super-G in 1985 at Furano and has scored many points in the downhill. Didier Bouvet (*below*) was able to end France's long run of failure when he won a slalom in January 1986, 13 years after the last World Cup victory.

become the first German to win the coveted World Cup.

Wasmaier has the good fortune to live by the shores of a large lake in southern Bavaria. Like many skiers, notably from France, Italy and Austria, he is currently doing a five-year stint in the army, but he still has enough free time to devote himself completely to ski racing.

Even more astonishing has been the impact of the phenomenal Yugoslavian Rok Petrovic who notched up five spectacular slalom victories in the 20th World Cup series. Petrovic, from Slovenia in the north of the country, is emerging as one of the finest champions since 1974.

Bojan Krizaj, Boris Strel and Jure Franko all scored memorable successes in the World Cup and in the pursuit of medals. Franko became a national hero in Yugoslavia when he raced superbly in the Sarajevo giant slalom to become his country's first skier to gain an Olympic silver.

But Petrovic is something else. The 20-year-old son of a Ljubljana University professor, he is remarkably sensitive and intelligent in addition to being a highly gifted skier. At 15, he was already racing in the World Cup: World junior champion at Sestrière in 1983, he gained his first World Cup victory two years later.

Fascinated by the social sciences, Rok is particularly devoted to philosophy, poetry and foreign languages.

He and his father Kresimir are a well-matched pair: the elder Petrovic is a leading light of the Yugoslav sporting world and a

Rok Petrovic is the newest star in the World Cup. The Yugoslavian, who turned 20 in 1986, is also the most brilliant of the new generation, winning five slaloms so far. He is not only a great skier but also a fascinating character who enjoys writing and studying poetry and philosophy.

Veteran Bojan Krizaj was the first Yugoslavian skier to win a World Cup race – in Wengen in 1980. Since 1979, he has always finished among the top ten in the overall World Cup.

recognized expert in physical training and sports sociology. An excellent ski theorist, he has edited several books with the help of his son, the last being *The Way to Success.*

Petrovic has not been the only revelation of recent years: competitors like Austria's Gunther Mader, the Italians Oswald Totsch, Robert Erlacher and Richard Pramotton and the Swiss Karl Alpiger and Thomas Burgler have all brought a new dynamism to their respective teams.

Two champions born far from the Alps created sensations in 1984 and 1986 – the American Bill Johnson and the Scot Martin Bell. Johnson achieved something that would have been unimaginable ten years ago. He beat the top European specialists in the Sarajevo Olympic downhill and three World Cup races at Wengen, Aspen and Whistler Mountain.

What is more, it was a case of fact aping fiction. His 1984 Olympics win had been predicted some 20 years earlier when Robert Redford had starred in a movie about an American downhill racer who became an Olympic champion. The film had received a cool reception in Europe, especially in Austria. After a showing in Kitzbühel in the early 1970s the great Karl Schranz concluded scornfully that "everything is improbable in that film and especially the ending, because an American skier will never beat the Europeans in this great competition".

Add to this the fact that Billy Johnson was not only a superb skier, particularly at home on soft snow, but also a great actor who has played his part to perfection: he knew precisely how to use his wits and gift for conversation in interviews. And certain aspects of his colourful past – he almost went to prison for "borrowing" a car with some friends when he was 17 – made him an intriguing character.

Oswald Totsch has never won a race, unlike his team-mates Robert Erlacher and Richard Pramotton, but his trainers believe he can become one of the World Cup's strongest slalom specialists. He is very talented, but still rather nervous.

*Top:* Martin Bell has the talent to be the first Briton to win a World Cup race, a dream that Konrad Bartelski almost realized in 1981. A spectacular crash at Megêve first brought this courageous skier to the world's attention.

Johnson became a big star of the American and international circuits overnight, but did not repeat his brilliant success in the 1983-84 season in 1985 or 1986 – he never managed to finish in the top three in any downhill. His rivals were quick to gloat and treat him as a "phony champion", while still wondering how he could have been as good as he was on that day in 1984. Their reaction was unfair because Johnson had certainly achieved an exceptional performance in dominating both the Olympic and World Cup races, especially as he had put extra pressure on himself by announcing well in advance that he could not see how he could be beaten on the Bjelasnica Olympic course.

Martin Bell, as a Briton, is carrying on a long tradition. Since its origins, Alpine ski racing has always exercised a strong fascination for the British public. The primary role of the British in the development of the sport in the 1920s is well known. Today, British television sports programmes give wide coverage to skiing, especially downhills. And they are watched faithfully by between three and four million people every weekend in the season. England's Bill Bracken won the combined event, at that time the most important honour, in the first Lauberhorn at Wengen, one of the oldest "classics" of Alpine skiing – but since then no British skier has celebrated a victory at World Cup level.

Britons Divina Galica and Gina Hathorn came very close in the 1960s, while the amazing Konrad Bartelski (born in Holland of a Polish father who later moved to Austria) was placed second at Val Gardena in 1981.

Bartelski, an imaginative man capable – like Italy's Erwin Stricker – of having a bright new idea every 30 minutes, made a major contribution to improving the running of the British team which now enjoys solid logistical and financial support. But it was a spectacular crash at Megêve in 1975 that brought this courageous skier to the skiing world's attention. He fell again quite a few times after that, but fortunately never hurt himself too badly.

Bill Johnson became America's great ski hero in 1984 by winning a gold medal in Sarajevo. The same winter, the Californian also won three World Cup events, including the Lauberhorn at Wengen. His next goal is more gold in 1987 in Crans-Montana and 1988 in Calgary.

When he retired in 1983, he left a vacuum which was soon filled by his compatriot Martin Bell who had made rapid progress by studying at the famous Austrian ski school at Stams. Ranked only 80th in the world downhill standings at the start of the 1985-86 season, he shot up into the leading 20 by finishing in the top ten in several races – most notably at Åre in Sweden where he was fifth.

Let's hope he will not stop there – ski racing, traditionally dominated by the Alpine countries, has always been enriched by the emergence of stars from other parts of the world. The list of racers who helped spread Alpine competition internationally is a long one. Beyond them there are countless others who never finished a race among the first 30 or 40 but who were remarkable characters in their own right – like Lamine Gueye of Senegal.

The grandson of a leading politician, he discovered skiing during a stay in Switzerland and went on to indulge his passion for Alpine competition by racing on the international circuit.

# COACHES AND TRAINERS

There have been coaches of a sort ever since the first organized races. But when skiing became a highly competitive sport with its inclusion in the Winter Olympics and the creation of the World Championships, its new team managers enlisted the help of professional assistants to take charge of training.

More often than not these assistants were ex-racers or player coaches, stars still in competition but coming to the end of their careers. Toni Seelos, for example, raced in the 1936 Garmisch Winter Games and coached the German team which won two gold medals. A year later, he coached Emile Allais and the French squad for the 1938 World Championships.

While a slalom coach's job is mainly to help the skier perfect a turning technique and to indicate the correct line through a series of gates, a downhill coach has to be a psychologist, athlete, coach and nutritionist rolled into one.

In the days of group downhill training, which lasted until 1966, the coaches often led by example, schussing ahead of their racers during training runs and only stopping to occasionally point out the finer points of a particularly difficult section. One name symbolizes the epitome of coaching at that time: Fred Roessner. He took charge of the Austrian team in 1951, and became the most innovative and original coach of the 1950s.

He had been a world class cross-country skier and led a military patrol to victory in the 1941 Cortina World Championships, an event struck from the records books at the end of the war.

A downhill race – even among the top seeds – is won on the easiest sections of the course: building up a racer's physical strength and stamina is the primary objective of coaching. This was the essence of Roessner's method. And he was the man behind Toni Sailer's three Olympic gold medals.

Roessner was also the man of his time in the early 1950s in another sense. Doubly wounded by the Second World War, Austria found an ace in its hand: the Marshall Plan. With massive US aid, Austria was suddenly able to rebuild and expand its hotel accommodation. And the Allied occupation troops were all potential skiers. Roessner's *"Wunderteam"* provided the spark which fired both Austrian tourism and the equipment sales of its ski manufacturers. Snow rapidly became Austria's white gold, the most vital of its national resources.

The high standard of the Austrian team under Roessner's guidance was a gauntlet thrown down in front of its rivals. Roessner had retired four years earlier, but his team was still benefiting from the results of his coaching, when the French rose to the challenge in 1960. Honoré Bonnet took over French skiing and he did as well if not better than Roessner.

Hailing from Haute-Provence, Bonnet's colourful language masked his impressive intelligence and affection for those in his charge.

His basic weapon for results was psychology. It was an inner strength he imbued in so many of his champions – Guy Perillat, Leo Lacroix, Pierre Stamos, Jean Vuarnet, Adrien Duvillard, Albert Gacon, Michel Arpin, Marielle and Christine Goitschel, Annie Famose and Isabelle Mir – that helped them realize their full potential. Among them – at an utterly different level – was Jean-Claude Killy.

Bob Beattie's exemplary career also belongs to this time. Born on the East Coast of the United

Honoré Bonnet

Fred Roessner

States with a background in American football, Beattie landed in Europe in 1961 and, despite his youth, quickly gained respect as a coach. His dream was to forge an American team whose stars would rival Bonnet's and a squad whose group strength would match Austria's. His team came close to that goal, and that it did not quite reach it was not Beattie's fault. It was due to the fact that Americans prefer their children to get a college education, rather than spend all their time on the ski slopes. Yet Buddy Werner, Chuck Ferries, Billy Kidd, Cathy Nagel, Jean Saubert, Kiki Cutter, Spider Sabich, Jimmy Heuga, the Cochrans and many others were thrown into the breach against formidable European opponents and acquitted themselves with honour, some spectacularly so.

While Beattie's technical background was rather slim, he was a master of all the nuances of coaching American-style. This proved to be a powerful psychological weapon. Beattie also deserves credit for introducing ski racing to America's major networks as early as 1965.

The 1960 Olympic downhill champion Jean Vuarnet was one of Bonnet's boys – in 1957 Bonnet proposed him as coach of France's military ski team. In his early career, Vuarnet had been a jack-of-all trades. He was the brains and the promotional muscle behind the development of the Avoriaz resort above Morzine, the inventor of a type of sunglasses that made him rich, a sailor and a publisher. It was he who, as early as 1959, had invented the "egg position" – an early version of the "tuck" – which won him the Olympic gold medal a year later. And in collaboration with Georges Joubert, he had published numerous technical books on skiing, outlining teaching and racing methods.

In 1968, the Italians were seeking to replace Ermano Nogler. A master of technique, and a man ahead of his time in many ways, who went on to become Ingemar Stenmark's mentor, Nogler had fallen victim to the age-old conflict between German-speaking Alto-Adige and the rest of Italy. Once part of the Tyrol, the Alto-Adige, was one of the great centres of Italian skiing. In Nogler's days, German was the predominant language of the Italian squad. And some Italians found it easy to believe that a racer like Carlo Senoner, who was bred like Nogler in Val Gardena, found more favour with his coach than a talented Italian-speaking skier. So when Nogler was edged out, the Italians put their money on Vuarnet.

Jean Vuarnet paid scant attention to such nuances. He began by straightening out equipment matters with the manufacturers who supplied the team – thus raising important financial backing – and by reorganizing the various Italian regional ski districts. But when it came to evaluating the various team members inherited from Nogler, Vuarnet discovered that the most talented and best-prepared did, in fact, come from the German-speaking Alto-Adige.

Among the racers already in training were Helmut Schmalzl, Erwin Stricker and a young prodigy from Stelvio coached by his father who

Bob Beattie

Toni Sailer with Christian Pravda

was a ski instructor, Gustavo Thoeni. Winning his first World Cup race as early as December 1969 in Val d'Isère, Thoeni was to win the first of his overall World Cup titles a year later.

After the 1972 Sapporo Olympics, Vuarnet coached the French team. But there was not much he could do, given the parlous state of French skiing when he took over. His assignment was to last only two years.

Mario Cotelli was Vuarnet's successor with Italy's *"Azzurri"* team. There was much singing of the Montanara, an abundance of Valtelina wine, Pizzocheri and hams at his table, where Cotelli welcomed his friends. Though Cotelli only offered vague solutions to technical problems, his fine tactical sense, his persuasiveness, his sociability and his alert intelligence were a boon to an Italian team then becoming the world's best in the slalom and the giant slalom.

In Cotelli's shadow came Oreste Peccedi who had helped this magnificent ascent to success. He helped bolster the Italian squad with the inclusion of Piero Gros, the boy from Piedmont who became Olympic slalom champion in 1976.

Having failed with his own countrymen, Italy's Ermano Nogler went to Sweden where he built their slalom and giant slalom team. He also discovered the World Cup's greatest champion to date, Ingemar Stenmark, then aged only 12, and Stig Strand. He was also able to communicate with the young Stenmark who, most people found, was virtually inaccessible. And he recognized that Stenmark's greatest asset was his unique style. Instead of trying to alter it, he helped the young Swede refine it, and even refind it whenever Stenmark veered away from his instinctive technique which was to be in Nogler's custody for 13 years.

The Swiss skiers' return to form between 1963 and 1968 was due to Georges Schneider and Peter Baumgartner. In a single winter, Schneider spurred the men's team to victories led by Jos Minsch and Adolf Mathys, the Chaux-de-Fonds "cowboy" who was a brilliant slalomer cursed by a cruel fate. In 1963 Mathys came back to winning form. A year later, Minsch – until then the unknown son of a Klosters stationmaster – became an overnight star by winning Innsbruck's pre-Olympic downhill. And in Willy Favre and Stefan Kaelin, Schneider found two giant slalom specialists, the like of which Swiss skiing had not seen since Roger Staub,the 1960 Olympic champion.

Schneider met an untimely death in a hunting accident while visiting Mathys and Swiss skiing took two years to find another father figure – Peter Baumgartner, who raised the spirits of his squad demoralized by failure. This paid off at the 1968 Grenoble Winter Olympics in the form of a bronze medal in the downhill for Jean-Daniel Daetwyler and giant slalom medals for Willy Favre and Fernande Bochatay.

After a meteoric rise through the federation's ranks, it was the young Adolf Ogi who, starting in September 1969, was finally to turn Switzerland into one of the major World Cup contenders and – since 1984 – a leader in the Nations Cup. Ogi, who recently began a political career, had the foresight to modernize the Swiss Ski Federation. When he took over the job in the autumn of 1969, the federation had two employees, himself and a general secretary. When he left, ten years later, it had nearly 70 employees and coaches and a budget of several million Swiss francs. By then he'd also created the most powerful ski team in the world, replete with medals in the Olympic Games and the overall World Cup title which Peter Luescher won for the Swiss for the first time in 1979.

Professor Franz Hoppichler led the Austrian men and women's teams from 1966 to 1972. A man of great culture and intelligence and son-in-law and successor of Stefan Kruckenhauser, the grand master of Austrian ski teaching, Hoppichler greatly strengthened his federation's influence and extended its scouting programme beyond the Tyrol for the first time.

In the mid-1960s other skiing nations – the United States, Canada, Norway and Sweden – were vastly improving their performance and the days when a single nation could dominate the sport were numbered. Austria needed time to realize and accept it. Despite this, Hoppichler's leadership produced some memorable successes. Karl Schranz and Gertrud Gabl were overall World Cup winners in 1969. Schranz was overall winner again in 1970 and, at the World Championships the same year, he won the gold while Werner Bleiner won the silver in the giant slalom and Karl Cordin the silver in the downhill.

On Hoppichler's retirement, after the 1972 Sapporo Olympics where Austria's morale received a heavy blow by the barring of Schranz, Toni Sailer was elected head coach.

After a triumphal swan song at the Badgastein World Championships, Sailer had gone into show business. Acting in numerous films with skiing sequences, he had also recorded songs and dabbled in the theatre. Lucid, pragmatic, Sailer knew the ropes and the details which affect the outcome of a race. Boots, Sailer believed, were as crucial as the skis themselves. The new head coach immediately thrust forward unknown racers like Franz Klammer who, at the age of 19, beat Roland Collombin and Bernhard Russi – Switzerland's top downhillers – on Schladming's precipitous course.

When Toni Sailer retired, his successer, Karl Kahr, was already in the hierarchy. And just as Cotelli had made the Italian team into a squad of slalom and giant slalom specialists – neglecting fine downhillers like Marcello Varallo, Besson, Ansi and Herbert Plank – Kahr transformed Austria into a nation of downhill racers.

German coach Klaus Maier was the craftsman behind Rosi Mittermaier's 1976 Innsbruck triumphs and later built up a new men's team led by Markus Wasmaier, the 1985 World Champion in the giant slalom. He, along with Sepp Messner of Italy, Dieter Bartsch of Austria, Theo Nadig and Jean-Pierre Chatelard of the United States, Kurt Hoch of Norway, Andy Rauch who coaches the Austrian women's team, Jean-Pierre Fournier of the Swiss women's team, Toni Vogrinec of Yugoslavia and Roland Francey of France are – with their doyen Ermano Nogler – among the best qualified of today's head coaches. Karl Frehsner of Switzerland and Helmut Girardelli have been willing to take the risk of training brilliant all-round champions too. They are the men behind Pirmin Zurbriggen's and Marc Girardelli's domination of the World Cup since 1984.

Roland Francey (left)
and Karl Frehsner

KSC
TZBÜHE

# CLASSIC COURSES – DESIGN AND PREPARATION

The original World Cup locations were picked from the classic events that already held a particular significance among international competitions. But since then the World Cup has been held in 127 more or less well-known ski resorts.

In 1966 at Bob Beattie's suggestion three American resorts were added to the schedule: Franconia in New Hampshire which attracts thousands of Bostonian and New York spectators; Vail in Colorado, home to the 1965 Nations Cup; and Jackson Hole in Wyoming. It was built by rich rancher Paul McCollister at the base of the sheer rock face of the Grand Teton. By 1966, the US already had two classics – the Roch Cup at Aspen, Colorado, and the Harriman Cup at Sun Valley, Idaho. Heavenly Valley in California and Waterville Valley in New Hampshire are also regular World Cup venues.

Seven other resorts have been on the World Cup regular schedule since 1967. They are Adelboden, Berchtesgaden, Kitzbühel, Madonna di Campiglio, Megêve, Sestrière and Wengen, all in the Alps. With Grindelwald, Oberstaufen, Schruns and St. Gervais they are the historical nucleus of the World Cup. Val d'Isère joined the circuit in 1968.

Val d'Isère is one of the world's largest and most beautiful ski areas. Thanks to its early November snowfalls it is also one of the most reliable. Yet, since weather conditions have tended to retard winter towards the end of December, Val d'Isère has made a considerable investment in snow-making equipment for its La Daille runs. And it is in Val d'Isère – whose races are aptly named *le Criterium de la Première Neige* (the Criterion of the First Snows) – that many young racers like Henri Duvillard, Gustavo Thoeni,

*Opposite:* The downhill course at Kitzbühel, the famous "Streif", is known all round the skiing world. Over 20 World Cup races have been held there since 1967, attracting hundreds of thousands of spectators.

Piero Gros, Erik Haaker and Ken Read were first discovered.

But it is the giant slalom at Adelboden that has the unique distinction of never having once been cancelled. Adelboden is on the slopes of the Kuonisbergli with its ferocious final headwall and has a second smaller area above Schwanfeldspitze. The town itself has just one main street. The director of the tourist office is former champion Dr. Fred Rubi.

On 5 January 1967, the Jenner's rather bare slopes played host to the World Cup's European debut. Despite the Jenner's modest skiing area and its antique chairlift that carries only 300 skiers an hour, the resort town of Berchtesgaden has a charm all of its own. Tourists are attracted by the beauty of the Koenigsee Lake, the Watzmann mountains and one of the world's most famous bobsled runs. It was also the retreat of Adolf Hitler and is still a major resort for American service men.

Since 1973, Japan has hosted World Cup races, first at Naeba near Tokyo, then in Furano on Hokkaido Island. The competitions were always well organized and attracted large crowds.

Garmisch-Partenkirchen and Morzine are two resorts with great World Cup traditions. And the Kandahar at Garmisch and the Jean Vuarnet at Morzine figure prominently on the list of the world's finest downhills. That list also includes the "Streif" at Kitzbühel, the Kappal at St. Anton, the Mondiale at Bormio, the Lauberhorn at Wengen, the Patscherkofel at Innsbruck and the courses at Laax, Whistler Mountain and Lake Louise.

On the occasion of the 1936 Winter Olympics, Garmisch and Partenkirchen were joined together. With a combined population of just 10,000 inhabitants the resort is only an hour's drive from Munich and tens of thousands of spectators turn out to watch the finest skiers in the world perform there.

Morzine has in a few years joined the ranks of the most important resorts thanks to its most modern approach. Apart from its spectacular downhill, the side shows are a great carnival in themselves, taking place as they do under a huge tent.

There is a fair-sized skiing terrain at Morzine and at Avoriaz which is accessible on skis from Switzerland, by way of Champéry and the Portes du Soleil that offers almost 500 km of pistes to skiers of all standards. The proximity of large towns like Geneva, Evian and Thonon means that race organizers can count on a large number of spectators attending each event.

Kitzbühel, with its medieval architecture nestling in the shadow of the Horn and the Hahnenkamm, is the most beautiful city on the circuit. Its cosmopolitan atmosphere attracts rich tourists who come to the races to be seen, as much as to see.

Wengen in the Bernese Oberland has quite a different style.

Dominated by the Eiger's north face, the Monch and the Jungfrau, it lives in a world of ice and granite. Its success as a resort depends on the small Scheidegg cog railway, installed to carry climbers.

The World Cup first went to Val Gardena in 1969. Before the World Championships, Karl Schranz scandalized the natives by calling their downhill an "autostrada" or motorway. But skiing is not the valley's only source of income. For generations, the locals have thrived on sales of multi-coloured wooden sculptures.

On the far side of the Selva Pass from Val Gardena in a grand Dolomite valley is La Villa, the World Cup's latest addition.

The fine slalom hill of the "3-Tre" races at Madonna di Campiglio, at the foot of the impressive Brenta range in the Trentino Alps, draws thousands of spectators each year. The *tifosi* – or fans – come from Brescia, Trente, Bolzano and even Milan. It is there, switching from the Austrian "knödel" to spaghetti, that the World Cup gets into the Barbera and espresso mood.

Kranjska Gora in Yugoslavia's Julian Alps is at the cross roads

Crans Montana, home of the 1987 World Championships, has a great tradition of Alpine ski racing. One of the first international downhills was held there in 1911. It was organized by Arnold Lunn.

between Austria and Italy. There the Slovenes cheer on their heroes Bojan Krizaj and Rok Petrovic. Skiing is a sport of growing importance in Yugoslavia. Ingemar Stenmark even has his skis made there, near to the Kranjska Gora course.

It was in Oberstaufen, in southern Bavaria's Allgau, that the women skiers first took part in the World Cup in January 1967. Since then they have often returned to this rather special resort, whose specialty is not so much the skiing as the "Schrotkur", a fasting cure during which food is replaced by white wine.

Since 1977, the Cup's traditional Japanese port of call is Furano at the heart of Hokkaido Island. The resort is first class and everything and everybody involved in the "white circus" lives in the Prince Hotel which belongs to head organizer Joshihaki Tsutsumi.

The World Cup's most original stopover was Anchorage, where it paused en route to Tokyo in 1973. The Cup takes on a wild west flavour at its Canadian dates in Lake Louise, Whistler Mountain and Panorama. While the ultra modern Las Leñas resort, in Argentina, whose fine architecture is designed to blend into the Andes is another new addition to the circuit.

But it is Aspen – in the Rocky Mountains whose night-time cold works wonders in rejuvenating the snow – which is the jewel in the Cup's crown. Nestling in the Roaring Fork Valley it is a town where skiers now replace the hundreds of thousands of 19th century miners and adventurers drawn west by gold and silver. With its right-angled streets, its old red-brick houses, Aspen is a resort for the young and the rich, a resort of late nights. Added to that its downhill course, with its Aztec Wall, is one of the world's greatest classics.

The development of Alpine ski racing had a permanent effect on the nature of competition ski runs, particularly their design and preparation.

Since the beginning the European term for a ski run has been "piste", which is French for "trail". Essentially it was just the track left by other skiers, often delineated by wooden landmarks jutting out above the drifts.

At first there were no organized practice runs on these pistes. In the days when races were mostly regional this proved a definite advantage for the home-town skiers. James Couttet liked to recount the trials and tribulations that the French team suffered when they went to train for the Lauberhorn downhill.

"They played the same trick on us each year," said the champion from Chamonix. "We'd come ahead of time, hoping to repeat Jean

The Lauberhorn at Wengen is the oldest ski classic held every year in the same place. It was created in 1930 and has the same finish area for the downhill and slalom.

## RACERS INSPECT THE COURSE

The racers have one hour to inspect the slalom course before the race. They climb the slope from finish to start and try to memorize each detail. In other Alpine disciplines, they ski the course several times as practice.

The snow is iced – or hardened by chemicals – for the slalom and giant slalom. But it still degrades after 10 or 20 skiers. It is an advantage to be among the first 5. The best racers, like Rok Petrovic pictured here, are seeded in a group of 15 whose starting order is decided by a draw.

Blanc's coup – he was the only Frenchman to win the great classic (in 1946). Looking back though, I think we'd have been better off staying at home until the last moment. Early on in race week, the run was very icy and looked like a badly ploughed field. It stayed open to all recreational skiers, each of whom made his own ruts which grew into impressive bumps. But that did not bother us. In fact we rather liked it, coming from Mont Blanc country where the runs are anything but easy. In fact we felt very much at home on such terrain. Henri Oreiller [who won the downhill gold medal in the 1948 St. Moritz Olympics] used to say: 'For men like us, goat jumps on the course are exactly what we need.'

"Wengen locals like Karl Molitor would not practise. Only on the day of the race would he make his presence felt – by winning. He knew the piste like the back of his hand. And on the eve of the race, the run would be meticulously packed down and most of the bumps eliminated."

Given the increase in the number of starters, racers more often than not skied on snow rutted and hardened by the tracks of others. This practically became the norm when, during the 1930s, most of the downhills became accessible by cog-railway or téléphérique. This made for longer and more varied runs for tourists, but also allowed the organizers to force racers down more selective courses, with wickedly difficult sections such as Kitzbühel's Mausefalle, Steilhang and Hausberg ridge; the Hundsschopf in Wengen; the Bronze Wall in Megêve and the Bottleneck on Chamonix's famous Piste Verte.

In the 1930s, course preparation was minimal and the skiers mostly raced on soft or powder snow. The skis and the boots could also be very slack and the bindings did not need to be very sophisticated as the speed was low. Downhillers did not wear protective helmets until 1950.

The Americans were the first to use machines intensely to prepare slopes for tourists or racers. These mechanical methods were only introduced to Europe after the 1960 Winter Olympics at Squaw Valley, California. The use of machinery, like these Snowcats, has influenced the development of technique and equipment. Downhills became faster and easier, creating a gap between that and the other disciplines. Fortunately this tendency has stopped and courses are becoming harder again.

As lifts made more practice runs possible, races became more exact and exacting. For decades, only the start and the finish of downhills were marked. Racers could pick their own – often widely differing – routes.

Some runs, like the Kreuzeck in Garmisch, the Lauberhorn in Wengen and the Graukogel in Badgastein, allowed shortcuts. In 1957 a handful of Austrians were spotted on the Kreuzeck with a power saw. Twenty metres off the regular run they cut down a tree to allow Karl Schranz and his team-mates to take a faster line. But on the eve of the 1958 Badgastein World Championships the FIS finally had to step in. The locals had packed a line downhill which was to be hidden by a dozen friendly spectators until the Austrian stars appeared. From then on, this kind of practice was forbidden.

Finally, downhill courses were staked out by control gates, forcing all participants to ski the same route. This was done for reasons of safety, as well as for fairness and control. Gates at the top of a blind headwall, for example, are essential reference points rather than restraints.

The material, methods and machines used to prepare race courses have progressed in the last 20 years. These days extreme action can be taken in the event of a shortage of snow. In Kitzbühel, for example, where normal piste preparation would not ensure adequate coverage of some slopes, the run is mown and all the bumps are cut some ten days before the Hahnenkamm. What snow there is, is drenched with water, protecting the base with an

Many ski resorts now use expensive and sophisticated snow-making machinery. Artificial snow is easier to prepare for racing than natural snow, and it stands up better to heavy use. But it also requires a different skiing technique.

icy armour. This is then mechanically raked before the race, to allow the racers' edges to bite. In the case of an unexpected snowfall, certain sections of the course in need of hardening are foot-packed and, if necessary, watered.

The organizers of the 1974 World Championships in St. Moritz had an original idea that has since become a generally accepted method of piste preparation. The snow, particularly on the more exposed turns, is first melted by acetelyne torch. It then freezes again, rock hard.

This technique is used to maintain the snow only on the sunniest sections of a downhill course. But similar preparation is essential on the whole length of a slalom, particularly early in the season when there is little or no day-time thaw to make up for the night-time freeze.

Many of these advances were made by Willy Schaeffler, the American in charge of Alpine events at the 1960 Squaw Valley Winter Olympics. Twenty years ago, when this was all still considered devilish alchemy he was able to transform unpackable dry powder snow into a hard, weatherproof slalom surface or change warm slush into ice.

One of Schaeffler's successors, Hans Kung of Switzerland explains the secret: "Above all one must get cold air down into the snow's deepest layers. On a downhill's delicate section, where the snow is badly rutted after training runs, we leave it untouched, like a ploughed field and exposed to the night cold.

Early in the morning, we knead and plane it smooth. The kneading action hardens the snow and compacts it quickly.

One prepares a slalom hill way ahead of time, side-stepping it from start to finish. Once that is done, the run is packed and smoothed regularly until race day."

But new snow-packing machines have recently made these methods obsolete, though they have also made some runs almost too easy. Agricultural chemicals – mainly fertilizers – are also used to make raceable runs even in summer temperatures. And compacted machine-made snow is ideally tough and resistant.

Grooming machines were the first mechanical devices to revolutionize the business. These are a kind of rolling drill attached to the front of the machine which bite deeply into the snow along the whole of its length. This kneads fresh snow into the old icy surface, converting the whole thing into a hard, compact base.

After a thaw, or even rain, salt or the cereal fertilizer ammonium sulphate is sprinkled on the surface. This turns the melted snow back to ice within a few minutes. Salt is only good for three or four hours, but ammonium sulphate can be effective winter long, especially if it is poured into deep snow holes. However due to adverse environmental effects these products are banned in quite a number of countries.

The Americans at Squaw Valley in 1960 were also the first to use tracked vehicles. These Snow-cats were descended from Second World War-vintage Weasels. Since then more than 10,000 multi-tracked vehicles made by Ratrac, Rolba and Prinoth have come into operation.

Machine-made snow is produced by mixing compressed air and water. This turns into snow on contact with the atmosphere. The cost is between one and three Swiss francs per cubic metre, depending on the system used. The snow crystals produced are shaped like grains of rice. But, when compacted, it makes a great surface for skiing on. However, racers dread the dangerous transition from natural to machine-made snow.

Snow-making equipment has allowed the season to start as early as 15 November again, which is roughly when winter began before the climatic changes of the last few years. It can be produced as soon as the temperature drops below four degrees Celsius, so snow can be produced on mountains where no natural snow flake has ever fallen.

Since 1959, the FIS has taken steps to minimize stationary dangers on courses after Canadian John Semmelink was killed by falling to the bottom of a hidden gorge that February and a few weeks later Austrian Toni Mark was killed by crashing into a rock.

Dangerous trees, rocks and téléphérique towers have been removed or padded with foam and a network of safety nets have been erected across potential falls.

Organizers of early World Cup races often faced the tough problem of lack of snow. But in December 1983, Kranjska Gora in Yugoslavia was able to hold the season's opening events on a piste entirely covered with artificial snow. It was the only slope open in that part of the Alps.

# THE FUTURE OF THE ALPINE WORLD CUP

It would be wishful thinking to imagine that sport can single-handedly bring peace to the world. However, international sporting events such as the Olympic Games and the Alpine World Cup can have an effect on global politics. Before the Second World War, for example, it was said that no French government ever fell during the Tour de France. Jacques Goddet explained: "If a crisis had ever occurred, no-one would have noticed."

These days, with the television air time accorded around the world to events like the World Cup, it is often hard for the dedicated sports fan to notice anything else going on. And that air time is constantly increasing – as are the number of ski resorts which are asking to host World Cup events. So the Cup is in a healthy state and looks certain to survive until the year 2000 at least.

There are problems that have to be solved. Faced with pressure from the Winter Olympics and the World Championships, the World Cup must once and for all limit the number of races it includes. It must also take advantage of the spectators' and TV viewers' early season enthusiasm and progressively move its opening race back to November 15. With modern snow-making equipment, it is perfectly feasible to stage events reliably in Scandinavia, North America and the Alps that early in the season.

The World Cup must also add excitement to the fringes of the races. There can be a certain monotony watching one competitor after another crossing the finishing line. The Cup should be able to do it easily. It is not bound by the same decorum as the Olympics or the World Championships.

However, to achieve this, the Cup's organization must become professional. With the money that is now at stake, it can no longer continue to be run, essentially, by unpaid volunteers in their spare time. And the racers – the stars of the show – must also be considered professionals and be rewarded at the end of the season according to their performance.

The World Cup could also help skiing in general by drastically revamping its schedule and format. For example, the Nations Cup could become a bilateral country-versus-country match with competitions staged, once or twice a winter, by the countries in the first and second, third and fourth, and fifth and sixth places.

The World Cup's formula needs to be changed too. There is a pressing need for a simpler system whose rankings could also serve to determine the starting orders in each subsequent downhill, slalom, giant slalom and Super-G.

In the past, the World Cup occasionally suffered from the absence of one or more exceptional champions – while, on the other hand, only a handful of racers were ever in real contention. When neither the French, the Italians, the Germans, Canadians nor Americans can produce a man or woman with a real chance of winning the overall Cup, or one of its four components – or even a few individual races – public interest in that country dwindles. And with it dwindles audience participation.

If the World Cup was instrumental in making skiing a universal sport, it must achieve the same goal within the borders of its participating nations. It will only be profitable for the Cup to stage races in other countries in South America, New Zealand, Australia, Japan, China or India when those countries are able to produce racers of a championship calibre.

In years to come, despite the new technology – the electronic scoreboards, the computer graphics and the TV special effects – it will still be the skiers themselves, their achievements and the diversity of the countries they represent that will make or break the World Cup.

# ALPINE WORLD CUP RESULTS

## TOP 50 PLACINGS 1967/1986

### MEN 1966/67

| | | | |
|---|---|---|---|
| 1. | Killy J.-C. | FRA | 225 |
| 2. | Messner H. | AUT | 114 |
| 3. | Périllat G. | FRA | 108 |
| 4. | Lacroix L. | FRA | 93 |
| 5. | Mauduit G. | FRA | 82 |
| 6. | Heuga J. | USA | 70 |
| 7. | Schranz K. | AUT | 62 |
| 8. | Huber H. | AUT | 58 |
| 9. | Bleiner W. | AUT | 48 |
| 10. | Giovanoli D. | SUI | 46 |
| | Melquiond J. | FRA | 46 |
| | Jauffret L. | FRA | 46 |
| 13. | Nenning G. | AUT | 44 |
| 14. | Vogler F. | BRD | 36 |
| 15. | Henderson S. | CAN | 32 |
| 16. | Rohr H. | SUI | 31 |
| 17. | Orcel B. | FRA | 30 |
| 18. | Zimmermann E. | AUT | 23 |
| | Malknecht I. | ITA | 23 |
| 20. | Daetwyler J.-D. | SUI | 22 |
| 21. | Grahn B. E. | SWE | 20 |
| | Favre W. | SUI | 20 |
| 23. | Senoner C. | ITA | 16 |
| 24. | Barrows J. | USA | 15 |
| 25. | Minsch J. | SUI | 12 |
| 26. | Kaelin S. | SUI | 11 |
| 27. | Hebron R. | CAN | 10 |
| | Rohr P. | SUI | 10 |
| 29. | Rossat-M. R. | FRA | 8 |
| | Penz A. | FRA | 8 |
| | Rollen O. | SWE | 8 |
| | Swann B. | CAN | 8 |
| | Tischhauser J. | SUI | 8 |
| 34. | Sabich W. | USA | 6 |
| 35. | Sailer R. | AUT | 4 |
| 36. | Lindström R. | SWE | 3 |
| | Mussner G. | ITA | 3 |
| | Sodat S. | AUT | 3 |
| | Clough J. | CAN | 3 |
| | Sprecher A. | SUI | 3 |
| 41. | Bruggmann E. | SUI | 2 |
| | McCoy D. | USA | 2 |
| | Lesch W. | BRD | 2 |
| 44. | Duvillard H. | FRA | 1 |
| | Chaffee R. | USA | 1 |
| | Piazzalunga B. | ITA | 1 |
| | Olsson L. | SWE | 1 |

### WOMEN 1966/67

| | | | |
|---|---|---|---|
| 1. | Greene N. | CAN | 176 |
| 2. | Goitschel M. | FRA | 172 |
| 3. | Famose A. | FRA | 158 |
| 4. | Mir I. | FRA | 115 |
| 5. | Steurer F. | FRA | 114 |
| 6. | Schinegger E. | AUT | 110 |
| 7. | Hecher T. | AUT | 65 |
| | Färbinger B. | BRD | 65 |
| 9. | Demetz G. | ITA | 63 |
| 10. | Beranger C. | FRA | 48 |
| 11. | Bochatay F. | SUI | 39 |
| 12. | Jochum I. | AUT | 30 |
| 13. | McCoy P. | USA | 25 |
| 14. | Hathorn G. | GBR | 23 |
| 15. | Zryd A. | SUI | 22 |
| 16. | Chaffee S. | USA | 21 |
| 17. | Zimmermann H. | AUT | 20 |
| 18. | Gabl G. | AUT | 19 |
| 19. | Wuilloud M. | SUI | 16 |
| 20. | Hiltbrand E. | SUI | 15 |
| 21. | Pall O. | AUT | 14 |
| | Cipolla G. | ITA | 14 |
| 23. | Haas C. | AUT | 11 |
| | Fortna R. | USA | 11 |
| 25. | Adolf R. | SUI | 8 |
| 25. | Matheson C. | CAN | 8 |
| 27. | Mittermaier R. | BRD | 6 |
| | Cutter Ch. | USA | 6 |
| | Hafen M. | BRD | 6 |
| 30. | Pall L. | AUT | 5 |
| 31. | Jeangeorges M. | FRA | 3 |
| | Jones V. | USA | 3 |

### MEN 1967/68

| | | | |
|---|---|---|---|
| 1. | Killy J.-C. | FRA | 200 |
| 2. | Giovanoli D. | SUI | 119 |
| 3. | Huber H. | AUT | 112 |
| 4. | Nenning G. | AUT | 102 |
| 5. | Périllat G. | FRA | 83 |
| 6. | Bruggmann E. | SUI | 80 |
| 7. | Kidd W. | USA | 73 |
| 8. | Schranz K. | AUT | 69 |
| 9. | Russel P. | FRA | 67 |
| 10. | Messner H. | AUT | 63 |
| 11. | Mauduit G. | FRA | 57 |
| 12. | Mjoen H. | NOR | 52 |
| 13. | Matt A. | AUT | 51 |
| 14. | Chaffee R. | USA | 46 |
| 15. | Augert J.-P. | FRA | 44 |
| 16. | Tritscher R. | AUT | 43 |
| 17. | Sabich W. | USA | 41 |
| 18. | Orcel B. | FRA | 40 |
| 19. | Daetwyler J.-D. | SUI | 37 |
| | Kaelin S. | SUI | 37 |
| 21. | Bleiner W. | AUT | 31 |
| 22. | Favre W. | SUI | 28 |
| 23. | Huggler K. | SUI | 26 |
| 24. | Digruber F. | AUT | 20 |
| 25. | Sprecher A. | SUI | 15 |
| 26. | Bachleda A. | POL | 14 |
| 27. | Frei P. | SUI | 13 |
| 27. | Heuga J. | USA | 13 |
| 29. | Lindström R. | SWE | 11 |
| | Wendner N. | AUT | 11 |
| | Pazout M. | CSF | 11 |
| 32. | Minsch J. | SUI | 10 |
| | Sailer R. | AUT | 10 |
| | Vogler F. | BRD | 10 |
| 35. | Heckelmiller S. | BRD | 8 |
| | Sodat S. | AUT | 8 |
| | Phelps K. | USA | 8 |
| | Tischhauser J. | SUI | 8 |
| 39. | Lakota P. | YUG | 6 |
| | Loidl J. | AUT | 6 |
| | Pechtl J. | AUT | 6 |
| 42. | Mussner G. | ITA | 5 |
| | Penz A. | FRA | 5 |
| 44. | Hinterholzer H. | AUT | 4 |
| | Leitner L. | BRD | 4 |
| | McCoy D. | USA | 4 |
| | Prinzing G. | BRD | 4 |
| | Schlaber R. | BRD | 4 |
| | Strand B. | NOR | 4 |
| 50. | Duncan P. | CAN | 3 |

### WOMEN 1967/68

| | | | |
|---|---|---|---|
| 1. | Greene N. | CAN | 191 |
| 2. | Mir I. | FRA | 159 |
| 3. | Steurer F. | FRA | 153 |
| 4. | Goitschel M. | FRA | 128 |
| 5. | Bochatay F. | SUI | 126 |
| 6. | Famose A. | FRA | 123 |
| 7. | Gabl G. | AUT | 121 |
| 8. | Pall O. | AUT | 89 |
| 9. | Cutter C. | USA | 78 |
| 10. | Haas C. | AUT | 55 |
| 11. | Nagel J. | USA | 53 |
| 12. | Seiwald B. | AUT | 47 |
| 13. | Galica D. | GBR | 45 |
| 14. | Mittermaier R. | BRD | 44 |
| 15. | Allen W. | USA | 41 |
| 16. | Färbinger B. | BRD | 36 |
| 17. | Hathorn G. | GBR | 25 |
| 18. | Macchi F. | FRA | 22 |
| 19. | Lafforgue B. | FRA | 21 |
| 20. | Fortna R. | USA | 19 |
| | Beranger C. | FRA | 19 |
| | Zryd A. | SUI | 19 |
| 23. | Rauter B. | AUT | 14 |
| 24. | Skinger E. | USA | 13 |
| 25. | Budge K. | USA | 12 |
| 26. | Nagel C. | USA | 11 |
| | Rouvier J. | FRA | 11 |
| | Untermoser E. | AUT | 11 |
| 29. | Jeangeorges M. | FRA | 9 |
| 30. | Christiansen M. | NOR | 8 |
| | Inäbnit V. | SUI | 8 |
| | Joux R. | ITA | 8 |
| | Leinweber J. | CAN | 8 |
| | Wurmer D. | BRD | 8 |
| 35. | Blann S. | USA | 7 |
| | Chaffee S. | USA | 7 |
| | Jacot M. | FRA | 7 |
| 38. | Cochran B. | USA | 6 |
| | Drexel W. | AUT | 6 |
| | Field F. | GBR | 6 |
| | Rey A. | FRA | 6 |
| | Strauss P. | ITA | 6 |
| | Vogl M. | BRD | 6 |
| | Clifford B. | CAN | 6 |
| 45. | Cipolla G. | ITA | 5 |
| | Cochran M. | USA | 5 |
| 47. | Hubert V. | BRD | 4 |
| | Newall B. | GBR | 4 |
| 49. | Brusletto A. | NOR | 3 |
| | McCoy P. | USA | 3 |
| | Mercier M. C. | FRA | 3 |

### MEN 1968/69

| | | | |
|---|---|---|---|
| 1. | Schranz K. | AUT | 182 |
| 2. | Augert J.-N. | FRA | 123 |
| 3. | Tritscher R. | AUT | 108 |
| 4. | Matt A. | AUT | 104 |
| 5. | Penz A. | FRA | 98 |
| 6. | Duvillard H. | FRA | 91 |
| 7. | Messner H. | AUT | 89 |
| 8. | Russel P. | FRA | 80 |
| 9. | Giovanoli D. | SUI | 79 |
| 10. | Huber H. | AUT | 62 |
| 11. | Sabich W. | USA | 58 |
| 12. | Daetwyler J.-D. | SUI | 56 |
| 13. | Kidd W. | USA | 55 |
| | Tischhauser J. | SUI | 55 |
| 15. | Augert J.-P. | FRA | 49 |
| 16. | Bruggmann E. | SUI | 47 |
| 17. | Minsch J. | SUI | 44 |
| 18. | Cordin K. | AUT | 41 |
| 19. | Sailer R. | AUT | 34 |
| 20. | Orcel B. | FRA | 32 |
| | Sprecher A. | SUI | 32 |
| 22. | Chaffee F. | USA | 30 |
| 23. | Frei P. | SUI | 26 |
| 24. | De Tassis C. | ITA | 20 |
| 25. | Digruber F. | AUT | 19 |
| 26. | Rohr H. | SUI | 17 |
| 27. | Lindström R. | SWE | 16 |
| 28. | Clataud P. L. | ITA | 15 |
| 28. | Vogler F. | BRD | 15 |
| 30. | Bachleda A. | POL | 12 |
| | Périllat G. | FRA | 12 |
| 32. | Nenning G. | AUT | 9 |
| 33. | Hebron R. | CAN | 8 |
| | Heckelmiller S. | BRD | 8 |
| | Mjoen H. | NOR | 8 |
| | Schnider K. | SUI | 8 |
| 37. | Rossat-M. R. | FRA | 7 |
| 38. | Fernandez-O. F. | SPA | 6 |
| | Huggler K. | SUI | 6 |
| | Mauduit G. | FRA | 6 |
| 41. | Rollen O. | SWE | 5 |
| | Shepherd K. | CAN | 5 |
| | Zingre H. | SUI | 5 |
| 44. | Hamre L. | NOR | 4 |
| | Mussner G. | ITA | 4 |
| | Zwilling D. | AUT | 4 |
| 47. | McCoy D. | USA | 3 |
| | Kashiwa H. | USA | 3 |
| | Schmalzl E. | ITA | 3 |
| 50. | Ambroise J.-L. | FRA | 2 |

### WOMEN 1968/69

| | | | |
|---|---|---|---|
| 1. | Gabl G. | AUT | 131 |
| 2. | Steurer F. | FRA | 112 |
| 3. | Drexel W. | AUT | 111 |
| 4. | Cutter C. | USA | 107 |
| 5. | Lafforgue I. | FRA | 103 |
| 6. | Famose A. | FRA | 101 |
| 7. | Mittermaier R. | BRD | 98 |
| 8. | Jacot M. | FRA | 92 |
| 9. | Nagel J. | USA | 85 |
| | Mir I. | FRA | 85 |
| 11. | Rauter B. | AUT | 82 |
| 12. | Cochran M. | USA | 76 |
| 13. | Pall O. | AUT | 61 |
| 14. | Budge K. | USA | 40 |
| 15. | Macchi F. | FRA | 38 |
| 16. | Nagel C. | USA | 37 |
| 17. | Proell A. | AUT | 31 |
| | Bochatay-Schm. | SUI | 31 |
| 19. | Cochran B. | USA | 28 |
| 20. | Hathorn G. | GBR | 23 |
| 21. | Zimmermann H. | AUT | 22 |
| 22. | Clifford B. | CAN | 19 |
| 23. | Zryd A. | SUI | 18 |
| 24. | Demetz G. | ITA | 14 |
| | Kaserer M. | AUT | 14 |
| 26. | Lafforgue B. | FRA | 11 |
| | Skinger E. | USA | 11 |
| 28. | Cipolla G. | ITA | 10 |
| 29. | Knobloch J. | AUT | 9 |
| 30. | Galica D. | GBR | 7 |
| 31. | Crawford J. | CAN | 6 |
| | Färbinger B. | BRD | 6 |
| | Jochum I. | AUT | 6 |
| 34. | Fasolis C. | ITA | 4 |
| | Wolcott J. | USA | 4 |
| 36. | Fortna R. | USA | 3 |
| 37. | Rouvier J. | FRA | 2 |
| 38. | Schranz M. R. | ITA | 1 |
| | Treichl T. | BRD | 1 |

### MEN 1969/70

| | | | |
|---|---|---|---|
| 1. | Schranz K. | AUT | 148 |
| 2. | Russel P. | FRA | 145 |
| 3. | Thoeni G. | ITA | 140 |
| 4. | Augert J.-N. | FRA | 120 |
| 5. | Penz A. | FRA | 119 |
| 6. | Giovanoli D. | SUI | 116 |
| 7. | Bleiner W. | AUT | 83 |
| 8. | Duvillard H. | FRA | 81 |
| | Messner H. | AUT | 81 |
| 10. | Cordin K. | AUT | 65 |
| 11. | Bréchu H. | FRA | 62 |
| 12. | Orcel B. | FRA | 52 |
| 13. | Bachleda A. | POL | 50 |
| 14. | Russi B. | SUI | 49 |
| 15. | Milne M. | AUS | 48 |
| 16. | Kidd W. | USA | 45 |
| | Rieger M. | BRD | 45 |
| 18. | Loidl J. | AUT | 44 |
| 19. | Bruggmann E. | SUI | 40 |
| 20. | Tischhauser J. | SUI | 39 |
| 21. | Huggler K. | SUI | 37 |
| | Rofner H. | AUT | 37 |
| | Vogler F. | BRD | 37 |
| 24. | Schnider K. | SUI | 35 |
| 25. | Mauduit G. | FRA | 30 |
| 26. | Heckelmiller J. | BRD | 29 |
| 27. | Daetwyler J.-D. | SUI | 28 |
| 28. | Tresch W. | SUI | 27 |
| 29. | Chaffee F. | USA | 25 |
| 30. | Neureuther Ch. | BRD | 24 |
| | Sailer R. | AUT | 24 |
| | Zwilling D | AUT | 24 |
| 33. | Grosfilley B. | FRA | 23 |
| 34. | Huber H. | AUT | 22 |
| 35. | Hemmi H. | SUI | 21 |
| 36. | Pinel J.-L. | FRA | 20 |
| | Sprecher A. | SUI | 20 |
| 38. | Sabich W. | USA | 19 |
| 39. | Bonnevie M. | FRA | 17 |
| 40. | Cochran R. | USA | 15 |
| 41. | Frei P. | SUI | 14 |
| 42. | Mitterer P. | AUT | 13 |
| | Riml G. | AUT | 13 |
| 44. | Duncan P. | CAN | 11 |
| | Kashiwa H. | USA | 11 |
| | Poulsen E. | USA | 11 |
| 47. | Bozon M. | FRA | 10 |
| | Steufer H. | AUT | 10 |
| 49. | Berthold K. | AUT | 8 |
| | Bonnevie G. | FRA | 8 |

### WOMEN 1969/70

| | | | |
|---|---|---|---|
| 1. | Jacot M. | FRA | 180 |
| 2. | Macchi F. | FRA | 145 |
| 3. | Steurer F. | FRA | 133 |
| 4. | Lafforgue I. | FRA | 132 |
| 5. | Cochran B. | USA | 120 |
| 6. | Nagel J. | USA | 118 |
| 7. | Proell A. | AUT | 110 |
| 8. | Clifford B. | CAN | 101 |
| 9. | Mir I. | FRA | 100 |
| 10. | Lafforgue B. | FRA | 87 |
| 11. | Famose A. | FRA | 81 |
| 12. | Mittermaier R. | BRD | 76 |
| 13. | Rauter B. | AUT | 67 |
| 14. | Cochran M. | USA | 62 |
| 15. | Budge K. | USA | 58 |
| 16. | Drexel W. | AUT | 51 |
| 17. | Gabl G. | AUT | 45 |
| 18. | Mathieux D. | FRA | 42 |
| 19. | Cutter Ch. | USA | 40 |
| 20. | Zryd A. | SUI | 31 |
| 21. | Jeangeorges M. | FRA | 22 |
| 22. | Crawford J. | CAN | 15 |
| 23. | Gfölner I. | AUT | 14 |
| 24. | Christiansen K. | NOR | 13 |
| | Fortna R. | USA | 13 |
| 26. | Hafen M. | BRD | 10 |
| | Hathorn G. | GBR | 10 |
| | Wolcott J. | USA | 10 |
| 29. | Galica D. | GBR | 9 |
| 30. | Pall O. | AUT | 8 |
| 31. | Boydstun P. | USA | 6 |
| | Corrock S. | USA | 6 |
| 33. | Culver D. | CAN | 5 |
| 34. | Demetz G. | ITA | 4 |
| | Foerland I. | NOR | 4 |
| 36. | Rolland Ch. | FRA | 2 |
| | Sprecher E. | SUI | 2 |
| | Treichl T. | BRD | 2 |
| 39. | Field F. | GBR | 1 |
| | Hintermaier C. | AUT | 1 |
| | Ray C. | FRA | 1 |
| | Rouvier J. | FRA | 1 |
| | Ruud K. | NOR | 1 |
| | Spettel J. | AUT | 1 |

### MEN 1970/71

| | | | |
|---|---|---|---|
| 1. | Thoeni G. | ITA | 155 |
| 2. | Duvillard H. | FRA | 135 |
| 3. | Russel P. | FRA | 125 |
| 4. | Augert J.-N. | FRA | 107 |
| 5. | Russi B. | SUI | 95 |
| 6. | Bruggmann E. | SUI | 94 |
| 7. | Zwilling D. | AUT | 86 |
| 8. | Neureuther C. | BRD | 66 |
| 9. | Orcel B. | FRA | 63 |
| 10. | Palmer T. | USA | 60 |
| 11. | Schranz K. | AUT | 57 |
| 12. | Cordin K. | AUT | 56 |
| 13. | Tresch W. | SUI | 52 |
| 14. | Penz A. | FRA | 51 |
| 15. | Rofner H. | AUT | 50 |
| 16. | Heckelmiller S. | BRD | 46 |
| 17. | Daetwyler J.-D. | SUI | 44 |
| 18. | Bachleda A. | POL | 41 |
| 19. | Anzi S. | ITA | 40 |

| | | | |
|---|---|---|---|
| 20. | Loidl S. | AUT | 34 |
| 21. | Chaffee R. | USA | 31 |
| | Rieger M. | BRD | 31 |
| 23. | Messner H. | AUT | 30 |
| 24. | Rosti A. | SUI | 28 |
| 25. | Bleiner W. | AUT | 25 |
| | Sprecher A. | SUI | 25 |
| | Vogler F. | BRD | 25 |
| 28. | Stefani M. | ITA | 23 |
| 29. | Daetwyler M. | SUI | 22 |
| 30. | Poulsen E. | USA | 17 |
| 31. | Matt A. | AUT | 14 |
| 32. | Frei P. | SUI | 10 |
| 33. | Tritscher R. | AUT | 9 |
| 34. | Garcia A. | SPA | 8 |
| | Jakober M. | SUI | 8 |
| | Kashiwa H. | USA | 8 |
| | Rossat-M. R. | FRA | 8 |
| | Shanholzer G. | USA | 8 |
| 39. | Bréchu H. | FRA | 7 |
| | Fernandez-O. F. | SPA | 7 |
| | Milner M. | AUS | 7 |
| 42. | Grosfilley B. | FRA | 6 |
| 43. | Thoeni R. | ITA | 4 |
| | Tschudi O. | NOR | 4 |
| 45. | Berthod R. | SUI | 3 |
| | Charvin B. | FRA | 3 |
| | Hemmi H. | SUI | 3 |
| | Huggler K. | SUI | 3 |
| | Lesch W. | BRD | 3 |
| 50. | Cochran B. | USA | 2 |

## WOMEN 1970/71

| | | | |
|---|---|---|---|
| 1. | Proell A. | AUT | 210 |
| 2. | Jacot M. | FRA | 177 |
| 3. | Mir I. | FRA | 133 |
| 4. | Drexel W. | AUT | 124 |
| 5. | Macchi M. | FRA | 122 |
| 6. | Lafforgue B. | FRA | 112 |
| 7. | Rouvier J. | FRA | 101 |
| 8. | Cochran B. | USA | 90 |
| 9. | Gabl G. | AUT | 87 |
| 10. | Clifford B. | CAN | 76 |
| 11. | Cochran M. | USA | 74 |
| 12. | Rauter B. | AUT | 63 |
| 13. | Steurer F. | FRA | 61 |
| 14. | Mittermaier R. | BRD | 59 |
| 15. | Famose A. | FRA | 45 |
| 16. | Périllat J. | FRA | 38 |
| 17. | Budge K. | USA | 34 |
| 18. | Debernard D. | FRA | 33 |
| 19. | Kaserer M. | AUT | 30 |
| 20. | Puig C. | SPA | 27 |
| 21. | Crawford J. | CAN | 21 |
| 22. | Poulsen S. | USA | 17 |
| 23. | Galica D. | GBR | 15 |
| 24. | Corrock S. | USA | 14 |
| | Gfölner I. | AUT | 14 |
| 26. | Boydstun P. | USA | 12 |
| 27. | Hafen M. | BRD | 9 |
| 28. | Hathorn G. | GBR | 7 |
| 29. | Good R. | SUI | 5 |
| 30. | Fortna R. | USA | 4 |
| | Rolland C. | FRA | 4 |
| 32. | Inäbnit V. | SUI | 3 |
| | Schranz M. R. | ITA | 3 |
| | Spettel J. | AUT | 3 |
| 35. | Chalvin O. | FRA | 2 |
| | Treichl T. | BRD | 2 |

## MEN 1971/72

| | | | |
|---|---|---|---|
| 1. | Thoeni G. | ITA | 154 |
| 2. | Duvillard H. | FRA | 142 |
| 3. | Bruggmann E. | SUI | 140 |
| 4. | Augert J.-N. | FRA | 125 |
| 5. | Russi B. | SUI | 114 |
| 6. | Bachleda A. | POL | 112 |
| 7. | Thoeni R. | ITA | 93 |
| 8. | Schranz K. | AUT | 83 |
| 9. | Lafferty M. | USA | 63 |
| 10. | Messner H. | AUT | 61 |
| 11. | Rossat-M. R. | FRA | 55 |
| 12. | Haker E. | NOR | 50 |
| 13. | Tresch W. | SUI | 49 |
| 14. | Vogler F. | BRD | 47 |
| 15. | Zwilling D. | AUT | 46 |
| 16. | Penz A. | FRA | 41 |
| 17. | Rösti A. | SUI | 40 |
| 18. | Sprecher A. | SUI | 39 |
| | Daetwyler J.-D. | SUI | 39 |
| 20. | Schmalzl E. | ITA | 38 |
| 21. | Daetwyler M. | SUI | 37 |
| 22. | Hagn A. | BRD | 36 |
| 23. | Berthod R. | SUI | 32 |
| 24. | Heckelmiller S. | BRD | 28 |
| 25. | Tritscher R. | AUT | 27 |
| 26. | Mattle A. | SUI | 26 |
| 27. | Palmer T. | USA | 25 |
| 28. | Cordin K. | AUT | 24 |
| 29. | Cochran B. | USA | 22 |
| 30. | Loidl S. | AUT | 21 |
| 31. | Rieger M. | BRD | 20 |
| 32. | Neureuther C. | BRD | 18 |
| 33. | Fernandez-O. P. | SPA | 17 |
| 34. | Rofner H. | AUT | 15 |
| | Schmalzl H. | ITA | 15 |
| 36. | Poulsen E. | USA | 12 |
| 37. | Hinterseer H. | AUT | 10 |
| 38. | Milne M. | AUS | 9 |
| 39. | Collombine R. | SUI | 8 |
| | Bleiner W. | AUT | 8 |
| 41. | Russel P. | FRA | 6 |
| | Garcia A. | SPA | 6 |
| 43. | Besson G. | ITA | 5 |
| 44. | Sonnenberger G. | BRD | 4 |
| | Pargätzi E. | SUI | 4 |
| 46. | Hemmi H. | SUI | 3 |
| 47. | Hunter J. | CAN | 2 |
| | Palmer T. | USA | 2 |
| | Tschudi O. | NOR | 2 |
| | Matt A. | AUT | 2 |
| | Zingre H. | SUI | 2 |

## WOMEN 1971/72

| | | | |
|---|---|---|---|
| 1. | Proell A. | AUT | 269 |
| 2. | Macchi F. | FRA | 187 |
| 3. | Lafforgue B. | FRA | 128 |
| 4. | Kaserer M. | AUT | 120 |
| 5. | Nadig M.-T. | SUI | 111 |
| 6. | Mittermaier R. | BRD | 110 |
| 7. | Drexel W. | AUT | 106 |
| 8. | Steurer F. | FRA | 96 |
| 9. | Debernard D. | FRA | 90 |
| 10. | Mir I. | FRA | 89 |
| 11. | Jacot M. | FRA | 70 |
| 12. | Cochran B. | USA | 67 |
| | Cochran M. | USA | 67 |
| 14. | Rouvier J. | FRA | 60 |
| 15. | Behr P. | BRD | 29 |
| 16. | Poulsen S. | USA | 26 |
| | Rolland C. | FRA | 26 |
| 18. | Clifford B. | CAN | 24 |
| 19. | Corrock S. | USA | 23 |
| | Gabl G. | AUT | 23 |
| 21. | Treichl T. | BRD | 21 |
| 22. | Kreiner L. | CAN | 17 |
| 23. | Speiser | BRD | 15 |
| 24. | Zurbriggen B. | SUI | 14 |
| | Boydstun P. | USA | 14 |
| | Puig C. | SPA | 14 |
| 27. | Totschnig B. | AUT | 13 |
| 28. | Crawford J. | CAN | 11 |
| 29. | Périllat J. | FRA | 10 |
| 30. | Rauter B. | AUT | 9 |
| 31. | Mayr E. | BRD | 8 |
| | Famose A. | FRA | 8 |
| | Kreiner K. | CAN | 8 |
| 34. | Chalvin O. | FRA | 7 |
| | Budge K. | USA | 7 |
| 36. | Christiansen K. | NOR | 6 |
| | Hathorn G. | GBR | 6 |
| 38. | Oughton C. | CAN | 4 |
| 39. | Coughlin C. | USA | 2 |
| 40. | Schranz M. R. | ITA | 1 |
| | Good R. | SUI | 1 |
| | Ranner M. | AUT | 1 |
| | Bechmot P. | USA | 1 |
| | Teague C. | USA | 1 |
| | Wenzel H. | LIE | 1 |

## MEN 1972/73

| | | | |
|---|---|---|---|
| 1. | Thoeni G. | ITA | 168 |
| 2. | Zwilling D. | AUT | 151 |
| 3. | Collombin R. | SUI | 131 |
| 4. | Neureuther C. | BRD | 120 |
| | Hinterseer H. | AUT | 120 |
| 6. | Russi B. | SUI | 106 |
| 7. | Augert J.-N. | FRA | 104 |
| 8. | Klammer F. | AUT | 93 |
| | Cochran B. | USA | 93 |
| 10. | Gros P. | ITA | 91 |
| 11. | Duvillard H. | FRA | 90 |
| 12. | Rösti A. | SUI | 74 |
| 13. | Haker E. | MOR | 72 |
| 14. | Tresch W. | SUI | 65 |
| 15. | Varallo M. | ITA | 64 |
| 16. | Schmalzl H. | ITA | 59 |
| 17. | Tritscher R. | AUT | 58 |
| 18. | Cordin K. | AUT | 53 |
| 19. | Roux Ph. | SUI | 45 |
| 20. | Rieger M. | BRD | 39 |
| | Pegorari J. | ITA | 39 |
| 22. | Bachleda A. | POL | 38 |
| 23. | Perrot C. | FRA | 31 |
| 24. | Stricker E. | ITA | 30 |
| 25. | Grissmann W. | AUT | 29 |
| | Pietrogiovana T. | ITA | 29 |
| 27. | Pechtl J. | AUT | 21 |
| 28. | Walcher S. | AUT | 20 |
| | Matt A. | AUT | 20 |
| 30. | Hauser T. | AUT | 17 |
| 31. | Bachleda J. | POL | 16 |
| 32. | Kniewasser J. | AUT | 15 |
| 33. | Besson G. | ITA | 14 |
| 34. | Sprecher A. | SUI | 13 |
| | Fernandez-O. F. | SPA | 13 |
| | Engstler K. | AUT | 13 |
| 37. | Pargätzi E. | SUI | 12 |
| | Schlager H.-J. | BRD | 12 |
| 39. | Hunter J. | CAN | 11 |
| 40. | Feyersinger P. | AUT | 10 |
| 41. | Lafferty M. | USA | 9 |
| | Bieler F. | ITA | 9 |
| 43. | Thœni R. | ITA | 7 |
| | Junginger W. | BRD | 7 |
| 45. | Berchtold H. | AUT | 6 |
| 46. | Zingre H. | SUI | 5 |
| | Rossat-M. R. | FRA | 5 |
| | Heckelmiller S. | BRD | 5 |
| 49. | Schmalzl E. | ITA | 4 |
| | Loidl S. | AUT | 4 |

## WOMEN 1972/73

| | | | |
|---|---|---|---|
| 1. | Proell A. | AUT | 297 |
| 2. | Kaserer M. | AUT | 223 |
| 3. | Emonet P. | FRA | 163 |
| 4. | Mittermaier R. | BRD | 131 |
| 5. | Wenzel H. | LIE | 112 |
| 6. | Drexel W. | AUT | 106 |
| 7. | Rouvier J. | FRA | 103 |
| 8. | Cochran M. | USA | 84 |
| 9. | Gfölner I. | AUT | 83 |
| 10. | Lukasser I. | AUT | 65 |
| 11. | Zurbriggen B. | SUI | 64 |
| | Behr P. | BRD | 64 |
| 13. | Debernard D. | FRA | 61 |
| 14. | Treichl T. | BRD | 57 |
| | Rolland Ch. | FRA | 57 |
| 16. | Crawford J. | CAN | 51 |
| 17. | Nadig M.-T. | SUI | 48 |
| 18. | Totschnig B. | AUT | 46 |
| 19. | Schroll B. | AUT | 45 |
| 20. | Serrat F. | FRA | 44 |
| 21. | Cochran B. | USA | 39 |
| 22. | Giordani C. | ITA | 34 |
| 23. | Kreiner L. | CAN | 28 |
| 24. | Zechmeister Ch. | BRD | 27 |
| 25. | Förland T. | NOR | 25 |
| | Kreiner K. | CAN | 25 |
| 27. | Chalvin O. | FRA | 24 |
| 28. | Puig C. | SPA | 19 |
| | Poulsen S. | USA | 19 |
| | Lafforgue B. | FRA | 19 |
| 31. | Mir I. | FRA | 15 |
| 32. | Ranner M. | AUT | 13 |
| 33. | Morerod L.-M. | SUI | 10 |
| 34. | Eberle S. | AUT | 6 |
| 35. | Corrock S. | USA | 5 |
| | Hefti M. | SUI | 5 |
| | Schnider R. | SUI | 5 |
| | Matous E. | SMA | 5 |
| 39. | Stumpf S. | SUI | 4 |
| | Rauter B. | AUT | 4 |
| 41. | Epple M. | BRD | 3 |
| | Tisot C. | ITA | 3 |
| 43. | Hauser B. | AUT | 2 |
| | Hofer P. | ITA | 2 |
| 45. | Graswander | AUT | 1 |
| | Olikka R. | FIN | 1 |

## MEN 1973/74

| | | | |
|---|---|---|---|
| 1. | Gros P. | ITA | 181 |
| 2. | Thoeni G. | ITA | 165 |
| 3. | Hinterseer H. | AUT | 162 |
| 4. | Collombin R. | SUI | 140 |
| 5. | Klammer F. | AUT | 125 |
| 6. | Stricker E. | ITA | 98 |
| 7. | Zwilling D. | AUT | 95 |
| 8. | Kniewasser J. | AUT | 67 |
| 9. | Neureuther C. | BRD | 66 |
| | Plank H. | ITA | 66 |
| 11. | Schmalzl H. | ITA | 65 |
| 12. | Stenmark I. | SWE | 62 |
| 13. | Tritscher R. | AUT | 59 |
| 14. | Radici F. | ITA | 49 |
| 15. | Fernandez-O. F. | SPA | 46 |
| 16. | Grissmann W. | AUT | 42 |
| 17. | Russi B. | SUI | 40 |
| 18. | Cordin K. | AUT | 37 |
| 19. | Besson G. | ITA | 30 |
| 20. | Tresch W. | SUI | 29 |
| 21. | Berchtold H. | AUT | 25 |
| | Anzi S. | ITA | 25 |
| | Hunter J. | CAN | 25 |
| 24. | Hauser T. | AUT | 24 |
| 25. | Pargätzi E. | SUI | 23 |
| 26. | Rieger M. | BRD | 20 |
| | Cochran B. | USA | 20 |
| 28. | Schlager H.-J. | BRD | 19 |
| 29. | Walcher J. | AUT | 17 |
| | Grabler M. | AUS | 17 |
| | Roux P. | SUI | 17 |
| | Haker E. | NOR | 17 |
| | Bachleda A. | POL | 17 |
| 34. | Feyersinger P. | AUT | 16 |
| 35. | Pechtl J. | AUT | 13 |
| 36. | Bruggmann E. | SUI | 12 |
| 37. | Derezinski R. | POL | 11 |
| | Pietrogiovana T. | ITA | 11 |
| 39. | Jakober M. | SUI | 8 |
| 40. | Junginger W. | BRD | 7 |
| 41. | Demetz C. | ITA | 6 |
| | Vesti W. | SUI | 6 |
| | Morgenstern A. | AUT | 6 |
| | Varallo M. | ITA | 6 |
| | Bachleda J. | POL | 6 |
| 46. | Perrot C. | FRA | 5 |
| 47. | Beeli R. | SUI | 4 |
| | Berger O. | BRD | 4 |
| 49. | Frommelt W. | LIE | 3 |
| | Rowles D. | USA | 3 |

## WOMEN 1973/74

| | | | |
|---|---|---|---|
| 1. | Moser-Proell A. | AUT | 268 |
| 2. | Kaserer M. | AUT | 153 |
| 3. | Wenzel H. | LIE | 144 |
| 4. | Zechmeister Ch. | BRD | 129 |
| 5. | Serrat F. | FRA | 127 |
| 6. | Nadig M.-T. | SUI | 123 |
| 7. | Mittermaier R. | BRD | 116 |
| 8. | Morerod L.-M. | SUI | 77 |
| 9. | Drexel W. | AUT | 72 |
| 10. | Kreiner K. | CAN | 70 |
| 11. | Lukasser I. | AUT | 63 |
| 12. | Treichl T. | BRD | 56 |
| 13. | Giordani C. | ITA | 55 |
| 14. | Cochran B. | USA | 46 |
| 15. | Nelson C. | USA | 43 |
| 16. | Gfölner I. | AUT | 42 |
| 17. | Rouvier J. | FRA | 41 |
| 18. | Clifford B. | CAN | 32 |
| 19. | Debernard D. | FRA | 24 |
| 20. | Cochran L. | USA | 23 |
| 21. | Emonet P. | FRA | 19 |
| | Jäger M. | SUI | 19 |
| 23. | Cochran M. | USA | 17 |
| 24. | Totschnig B. | AUT | 9 |
| | Poulsen S. | USA | 9 |
| 26. | Jacot M. | FRA | 7 |
| 27. | Crawford J. | CAN | 6 |
| | Tisot C. | ITA | 6 |
| 29. | Schroll B. | AUT | 5 |
| 30. | Ducroz M. | FRA | 4 |
| | Patterson S. | USA | 4 |
| 32. | Rolland C. | FRA | 3 |
| | Sackl R. | AUT | 3 |
| 34. | Chalvin O. | FRA | 2 |
| | Förland T. | NOR | 2 |
| | Epple I. | BRD | 2 |
| | Eberle I. | AUT | 2 |
| | Ranner M. | AUT | 2 |
| | Zurbriggen B. | SUI | 2 |
| 40. | Kreiner L. | CAN | 1 |

## MEN 1974/75

| | | | |
|---|---|---|---|
| 1. | Thoeni G. | ITA | 250 |
| 2. | Stenmark I. | SWE | 245 |
| 3. | Klammer F. | AUT | 240 |
| 4. | Gros P. | ITA | 196 |
| 5. | Haker E. | NOR | 147 |
| 6. | Hinterseer H. | AUT | 117 |
| 7. | Plank H. | ITA | 92 |
| 8. | Grissmann W. | AUT | 87 |
| 9. | F.-Ochoa F. | SPA | 79 |
| 10. | De Chiesa P. | ITA | 74 |
| 11. | Russi B. | SUI | 58 |
| 12. | Berthod R. | SUI | 57 |
| 13. | Veith M. | BRD | 55 |
| 14. | Tresch W. | SUI | 50 |
| 15. | Radici F. | ITA | 49 |
| 16. | Hauser T. | AUT | 47 |
| 17. | Hemmi H. | SUI | 45 |
| 18. | Roux P. | SUI | 42 |
| 19. | Jones G. | USA | 41 |
| 20. | Vesti W. | SUI | 39 |
| 21. | Neureuther C. | BRD | 36 |
| 22. | Cordin K. | AUT | 31 |
| 23. | Walcher J. | AUT | 30 |
| 24. | Pietrogiovana T. | ITA | 27 |
| | Bachleda J. | POL | 27 |
| 26. | Zwilling D. | AUT | 22 |
| | Schlager H. | BRD | 22 |
| 28. | Bruce G. | USA | 19 |
| 29. | Frommelt W. | LIE | 18 |
| | Schmalzl H. | ITA | 18 |
| 31. | Pargätzi E. | SUI | 17 |
| 32. | Grabler M. | AUS | 16 |
| 33. | Mattle W. | SUI | 15 |
| | Hunter J. | CAN | 15 |
| 35. | Junginger W. | BRD | 13 |
| | Thoeni R. | ITA | 12 |
| 37. | Mill A. | USA | 11 |
| 38. | Tritscher R. | AUT | 10 |
| | Kniewasser J. | AUT | 10 |
| 40. | Berger A. | BRD | 9 |
| 41. | Ferstl S. | BRD | 8 |
| | Winkler E. | AUT | 8 |
| | Margreiter W. | AUT | 8 |
| | Anderson K. | USA | 8 |
| 45. | Roche R. | FRA | 6 |
| | Irwin D. | CAN | 6 |
| | Murray D. | CAN | 6 |
| | Berchtold H. | AUT | 6 |
| 49. | Besson G. | ITA | 5 |
| | Jakober M. | SUI | 5 |
| | Read K. | CAN | 5 |

## WOMEN 1974/75

| | | | |
|---|---|---|---|
| 1. | Moser-Proell A. | AUT | 305 |
| 2. | Wenzel H. | LIE | 199 |
| 3. | Mittermaier R. | BRD | 166 |
| 4. | Nadig M.-T. | SUI | 154 |
| 5. | Serrat F. | FRA | 153 |
| | Zurbriggen B. | SUI | 153 |
| 7. | Morerod L.-M. | SUI | 141 |
| 8. | Nelson C. | USA | 138 |
| 9. | Kaserer M. | AUT | 136 |
| 10. | Zechmeister C. | BRD | 127 |
| 11. | Drexel W. | AUT | 82 |
| 12. | Kreiner C. | CAN | 62 |
| 13. | Epple I. | BRD | 60 |
| 14. | Debernard D. | FRA | 57 |
| 15. | Schroll B. | AUT | 42 |
| | Clifford B. | CAN | 42 |
| 17. | Schmid-Gfolner I. | AUT | 35 |
| 18. | Giordani C. | ITA | 31 |
| 19. | Rouvier J. | FRA | 23 |
| 20. | Lukasser I. | AUT | 19 |
| | Jacot M. | FRA | 19 |
| 22. | Fjelstad T. | NOR | 17 |
| 23. | Treichl T. | BRD | 16 |
| 24. | Tisot C. | ITA | 15 |
| 25. | Ducroz M. | FRA | 13 |
| | Berwen M. | BRD | 13 |
| 27. | Matous H. | SMA | 11 |
| | Chalvin O. | FRA | 11 |
| 29. | Deufl E. | AUT | 10 |
| | Sackl R. | AUT | 10 |
| | Behr P. | BRD | 10 |
| 32. | Totschnig B. | AUT | 8 |
| | Fischer A. | USA | 8 |
| | Fleckenstein W. | USA | 8 |
| 35. | Emonet P. | FRA | 6 |
| | Spiess N. | USA | 6 |
| | Mittermaier E. | BRD | 6 |
| 38. | Pröll E. | AUT | 5 |
| 39. | Moesenlechner R. | BRD | 4 |
| | Cochran C. | USA | 4 |
| 41. | Dorsey B. | USA | 2 |
| | Smith L. | USA | 2 |
| 43. | Blackburn G. | USA | 1 |
| | Mumford K. | USA | 1 |

## MEN 1975/76

| | | | |
|---|---|---|---|
| 1. | Stenmark I. | SWE | 249 |
| 2. | Gros P. | ITA | 205 |
| 3. | Thoeni G. | ITA | 190 |
| 4. | Klammer F. | AUT | 181 |
| 5. | Hinterseer H. | AUT | 98 |
| | Tresch W. | SUI | 98 |
| 7. | Plank H. | ITA | 77 |
| 8. | Russi B. | SUI | 72 |
| 9. | Roux Ph. | SUI | 71 |
| 10. | Pargätzi E. | SUI | 67 |
| 11. | Bieler F. | ITA | 63 |
| 12. | Good E. | SUI | 59 |
| 13. | Hunter J. | CAN | 58 |
| 14. | Mahre P. | USA | 57 |
| 15. | Radici F. | ITA | 55 |
| 16. | Steiner A. | AUT | 50 |
| 17. | Irwin D. | CAN | 47 |
| 18. | Jones G. | USA | 44 |
| 19. | Eberhard K. | AUT | 41 |
| | Hauser Th. | AUT | 41 |
| | Hemmi H. | SUI | 41 |
| 22. | Grissmann W. | AUT | 39 |
| 23. | Haker E. | NOR | 35 |
| 24. | Read K. | CAN | 34 |
| 25. | Luescher P. | SUI | 31 |
| 26. | Neureuther C. | BRD | 30 |
| 27. | Mahre S. | USA | 26 |
| 28. | Winkler E. | AUT | 24 |
| 29. | Berthod R. | SUI | 22 |
| 30. | Walcher J. | AUT | 20 |
| | Veith M. | BRD | 20 |
| 32. | Murray D. | USA | 16 |
| 33. | Stricker E. | ITA | 15 |
| 34. | Adgate G. | USA | 14 |
| 35. | Morgenstern A. | AUT | 13 |
| 35. | Nöckler B. | ITA | 13 |
| | Junginger W. | BRD | 13 |
| 38. | Amplatz D. | ITA | 12 |
| | Ferstl S. | BRD | 12 |
| | Burger A. | BRD | 12 |
| 41. | Sörli O. | NOR | 11 |
| | De Chiesa P. | ITA | 11 |
| 43. | Podborsky S. | CAN | 10 |
| 44. | Zeman B. | CSF | 8 |
| | Patterson P. | USA | 8 |
| 46. | Cordin K. | AUT | 7 |
| | Pellat-Finet P. | FRA | 7 |
| 48. | Senoner A. | ITA | 6 |
| 49. | Frommelt W. | LIE | 5 |
| 50. | Fischer P. | BRD | 4 |
| | Ichimura M. | JAP | 4 |
| | Heidegger K. | AUT | 4 |

## WOMEN 1975/76

| | | | |
|---|---|---|---|
| 1. | Mittermaier R. | BRD | 281 |
| 2. | Morerod L.-M. | SUI | 214 |
| 3. | Kaserer M. | AUT | 171 |
| 4. | Zurbriggen B. | SUI | 170 |
| 5. | Debernard D. | FRA | 164 |
| 6. | Totschnig B. | AUT | 155 |
| 7. | Serrat F. | FRA | 125 |
| 8. | Nelson C. | USA | 122 |
| 9. | Wenzel H. | LIE | 83 |
| 10. | Epple I. | BRD | 73 |
| 11. | Giordani C. | ITA | 67 |
| 12. | Lukasser I. | AUT | 62 |
| | Spiess N. | AUT | 62 |
| 14. | Nadig M.-T. | SUI | 58 |
| | Emonet P. | FRA | 58 |
| 16. | Behr P. | BRD | 51 |
| 17. | Zechmeister C. | BRD | 50 |
| 18. | Deufl E. | AUT | 46 |
| | Mittermaier E. | BRD | 46 |
| 20. | Drexel W. | AUT | 31 |
| | Cochran L. | USA | 31 |
| 22. | Clifford E. | CAN | 30 |
| 23. | Kreiner K. | CAN | 28 |
| 24. | De Agostini D. | SUI | 25 |
| | Berwein M. | BRD | 25 |
| 26. | Oberholzer M. | SUI | 24 |
| 27. | Matous E. | IRA | 21 |
| | Fisher A. | USA | 21 |
| 29. | Sackl R. | AUT | 19 |
| 30. | Rouvier J. | FRA | 17 |
| 31. | Eilmer M. | AUT | 13 |
| 32. | Gatta W. | ITA | 11 |
| | Bieler W. | ITA | 11 |
| | Sölkner L. | AUT | 11 |
| 35. | Seaton M. | USA | 10 |
| 35. | Fleckenstein W. | USA | 10 |
| 37. | Patterson S. | USA | 9 |
| 38. | Epple M. | BRD | 7 |
| | Schmidt-Gfölner | AUT | 7 |
| 40. | Soltysova J. | CSR | 6 |
| 41. | Mathis M. | AUT | 5 |
| 42. | Blackburn G. | USA | 3 |
| 43. | Kusmanova D. | CSR | 2 |
| | Eberle I. | AUT | 2 |
| | Tisot-Arrigoni C. | ITA | 2 |
| | Kurlander J. | USA | 2 |
| 47. | Schroll B. | AUT | 1 |
| | Michelet G. | SUI | 1 |
| | Couttet M. | FRA | 1 |

## MEN 1976/77

| | | | |
|---|---|---|---|
| 1. | Stenmark I. | SWE | 339 |
| 2. | Heidegger K. | AUT | 250 |
| 3. | Klammer F. | AUT | 203 |
| 4. | Gros P. | ITA | 165 |
| 5. | Russi B. | SUI | 148 |
| 6. | Thoeni G. | ITA | 145 |
| 7. | Hemmi H. | SUI | 133 |
| 8. | Walcher S. | AUT | 115 |
| 9. | Mahre P. | USA | 100 |
| 10. | Frommelt P. | LIE | 99 |
| 11. | Ferstl S. | BRD | 97 |
| 12. | Bieler F. | ITA | 92 |
| 13. | Tresch W. | SUI | 89 |
| 14. | Hinterseer H. | AUT | 82 |
| 15. | Hemmi C. | SUI | 69 |
| 16. | Winkler E. | AUT | 66 |
| 17. | Radici F. | ITA | 60 |
| 18. | Plank H. | ITA | 58 |
| 19. | Frommelt W. | LIE | 52 |
| 20. | Grissmann W. | AUT | 48 |
| 21. | Wenzel A. | LIE | 42 |
| 22. | Nöckler B. | ITA | 40 |
| 23. | Fischer P. | BRD | 39 |
| 24. | Müller P. | SUI | 37 |
| | Wirnsberger P. | AUT | 37 |
| 26. | Berthod R. | SUI | 35 |
| 27. | Steiner A. | AUT | 33 |
| 28. | Brunner M. | AUT | 32 |
| | Neureuther Ch. | BRD | 32 |
| | Veith M. | BRD | 32 |
| 31. | Stock L. | AUT | 31 |
| 32. | Gensbichler B. | AUT | 29 |
| 33. | Morgenstern A. | AUT | 27 |
| | Josi E. | SUI | 27 |
| 35. | Enn H. | AUT | 26 |
| 36. | Luescher P. | SUI | 24 |
| 37. | Spiess U. | AUT | 22 |
| 38. | Sochor M. | CSR | 21 |
| 39. | Haker E. | NOR | 19 |
| | Adgate G. | USA | 19 |
| | Jakobson T. | SWE | 19 |
| 42. | Good E. | SUI | 18 |
| 43. | Mahre S. | USA | 15 |
| | Pargätzi E. | SUI | 15 |
| | Krizay B. | YUG | 15 |
| 46. | Strand S. | SWE | 6 |
| | Berthod M. | SUI | 6 |
| | Anderson K. | USA | 6 |
| 49. | De Chiesa P. | ITA | 5 |
| 50. | Kaiwa T. | JAP | 4 |

## WOMEN 1976/77

| | | | |
|---|---|---|---|
| 1. | Morerod L.-M. | SUI | 319 |
| 2. | Moser-Proell A. | AUT | 246 |
| 3. | Kaserer M. | AUT | 196 |
| 4. | Habersatter B. | AUT | 186 |
| 5. | Wenzel H. | LIE | 150 |
| 6. | Nadig M.-T. | SUI | 133 |
| 7. | Pelen P. | FRA | 132 |
| 8. | Giordani C. | ITA | 121 |
| 9. | Serrat F. | FRA | 85 |
| 10. | Zurbriggen B. | SUI | 78 |
| 11. | Mittermaier E. | BRD | 77 |
| 12. | Sackl R. | AUT | 74 |
| 13. | Kreiner K. | CAN | 65 |
| 14. | Spiess N. | AUT | 61 |
| 15. | Sölkner L. | AUT | 59 |
| 16. | Emonet P. | FRA | 53 |
| 17. | Fischer A. | USA | 51 |
| 18. | Epple I. | BRD | 49 |
| 19. | Behr P. | BRD | 41 |
| | Nelson C. | USA | 41 |
| 21. | Zechmeister C. | BRD | 40 |
| 22. | Matous E. | IRA | 39 |
| 23. | Debernard D. | FRA | 37 |
| 24. | Eberle B. | AUT | 35 |
| 25. | Dorsey B. | USA | 31 |
| 26. | Kerscher B. | AUT | 28 |
| 27. | Fleckenstein W. | USA | 16 |
| 28. | De Agostini D. | SUI | 15 |
| | Konzett U. | LIE | 15 |
| 30. | Ellmer M. | AUT | 11 |
| 31. | Berwein M. | BRD | 7 |
| 32. | Deufl E. | AUT | 6 |
| 33. | Epple M. | BRD | 5 |
| | Patterson S. | USA | 5 |
| 35. | Cooper C. | USA | 4 |
| | Kurlander J. | USA | 4 |
| | Oberholzer M. | SUI | 4 |
| | Seaton M. | USA | 4 |
| 39. | Schlechter M. | AUT | 2 |
| 40. | Mandrillon M. | FRA | 1 |
| | Kinshofer C. | BRD | 1 |

## MEN 1977/78

| | | | |
|---|---|---|---|
| 1. | Stenmark I. | SWE | 150 |
| 2. | Mahre P. | USA | 116 |
| 3. | Wenzel A. | LIE | 100 |
| 4. | Heidegger K. | AUT | 95 |
| 5. | Klammer F. | AUT | 70 |
| | Plank H. | ITA | 70 |
| 7. | Walcher S. | AUT | 65 |
| 8. | Hemmi H. | SUI | 60 |
| | Gros P. | ITA | 60 |
| 10. | Bernardi M. | ITA | 54 |
| 11. | Read K. | CAN | 47 |
| 12. | Spiess U. | AUT | 43 |
| | Popangelov P. | BUL | 43 |
| 14. | Ferstl S. | BRD | 41 |
| | Veith M. | BRD | 41 |
| 16. | Luescher P. | SUI | 40 |
| 17. | Wirnsberger P. | AUT | 39 |
| 18. | Haker E. | NOR | 37 |
| 19. | Fournier J.-L. | SUI | 32 |
| 20. | Krizay B. | YUG | 31 |
| 21. | Stock L. | AUT | 29 |
| 22. | Grissmann W. | AUT | 27 |
| 23. | Mahre S. | USA | 25 |
| | De Chiesa P. | ITA | 25 |
| 25. | Vesti W. | SUI | 24 |
| 26. | Thoeni G. | ITA | 22 |
| 27. | Radici F. | ITA | 21 |
| 28. | Murray D. | CAN | 20 |
| | Russi B. | SUI | 20 |
| 30. | Eberhard K. | AUT | 19 |
| 31. | Podborski | CAN | 18 |
| 32. | Antonioli R. | ITA | 16 |
| 33. | Frommelt P. | LIE | 15 |
| 34. | Neureuther C. | BRD | 14 |
| | Gensbichler B. | AUT | 14 |
| 36. | Müller P. | SUI | 13 |
| | Adgate C. | USA | 13 |
| 38. | Enn H. | AUT | 12 |
| 39. | Brunner M. | AUT | 11 |
| | Roux P. | SUI | 11 |
| | Steiner A. | AUT | 11 |
| 42. | Nöckler B. | ITA | 10 |
| 43. | Josi E. | SUI | 9 |
| | Aellig P. | SUI | 9 |
| | Kaiwa T. | JAP | 9 |
| 46. | Morgenstern A. | AUT | 8 |
| | Hemmi C. | SUI | 8 |
| | Pellat-Finet P. | FRA | 8 |
| | Ortner W. | AUT | 8 |
| | Mally P. | ITA | 8 |

## WOMEN 1977/78

| | | | |
|---|---|---|---|
| 1. | Wenzel H. | LIE | 154 |
| 2. | Moser-Proell A. | AUT | 147 |
| 3. | Morerod L.-M. | SUI | 135 |
| 4. | Serrat F. | FRA | 105 |
| 5. | Nelson C. | USA | 97 |
| 6. | Pelen P. | FRA | 96 |
| 7. | Epple M. | BRD | 94 |
| 8. | Kaserer M. | AUT | 76 |
| 9. | Sölkner L. | AUT | 70 |
| 10. | Nadig M.-T. | SUI | 63 |
| 11. | Epple I. | BRD | 62 |
| 12. | Mittermaier E. | BRD | 60 |
| 13. | Becky D. | USA | 45 |
| 14. | De Agostini D. | SUI | 37 |
| | Fisher A. | USA | 37 |
| 16. | Lukasser I. | AUT | 27 |
| 17. | Eberle I. | AUT | 26 |
| 18. | Cooper C. | USA | 24 |
| 19. | Zurbriggen B. | SUI | 23 |
| 20. | Fleckenstein W. | USA | 20 |
| 21. | Habersatter B. | AUT | 19 |
| 22. | Konzett U. | LIE | 17 |
| 23. | Bader M. | BRD | 16 |
| 24. | Zechmeister C. | BRD | 14 |
| 25. | Kreiner K. | CAN | 12 |
| 26. | Sackl R. | AUT | 10 |
| | Matous E. | IRA | 10 |
| 28. | Hess E. | SUI | 7 |
| | Moesenlechner R. | BRD | 7 |
| 30. | Bieler W. | ITA | 6 |
| | Totschnig S. | AUT | 6 |
| 32. | Ellmer M. | AUT | 5 |
| 33. | Behr P. | BRD | 4 |
| | Dirren E. | SUI | 4 |
| | Emonet P. | FRA | 4 |
| 36. | Oberholzer M. | SUI | 3 |
| 37. | Giordani C. | ITA | 2 |
| | Gravina Ch. | ITA | 2 |
| | Kerscher B. | AUT | 2 |
| | Wiesler H. | BRD | 2 |
| 41. | Spiess N. | AUT | 1 |
| | Liouche M. | FRA | 1 |
| | Patterson S. | USA | 1 |

## MEN 1978/79

| | | | |
|---|---|---|---|
| 1. | Luescher P. | SUI | 186 |
| 2. | Stock L. | AUT | 163 |
| 3. | Mahre P. | USA | 155 |
| 4. | Gros P. | ITA | 152 |
| 5. | Stenmark I. | SWE | 150 |
| 6. | Wenzel A. | LIE | 148 |
| 7. | Steiner A. | AUT | 107 |
| 8. | Krizaj B. | JUG | 106 |
| 9. | Thoeni G. | ITA | 92 |
| 10. | Mahre St. | USA | 86 |
| 11. | David L. | ITA | 85 |
| 12. | Enn H. | AUT | 81 |
| 13. | Lüthy J. | SUI | 79 |
| 14. | Neureuther C. | BRD | 74 |
| 15. | Müller P. | SUI | 72 |
| | Wirnsberger P. | AUT | 72 |
| 17. | Frommelt P. | LIE | 68 |
| | Zeman B. | TCH | 68 |
| 19. | Pogangelov P. | BUL | 67 |
| | Bürgler T. | SUI | 67 |
| 21. | Jakobsson T. | SWE | 62 |
| 22. | Read K. | CAN | 61 |
| 23. | Hemmi H. | SUI | 60 |
| | Plank H. | ITA | 60 |
| 25. | Strel B. | JUG | 58 |
| | Orlainsky C. | AUT | 58 |
| 27. | Spiess U. | AUT | 56 |
| | Ferstl S. | BRD | 56 |
| | Donnet M. | SUI | 56 |
| 30. | Fournier J.-L. | SUI | 52 |
| | Heidegger K. | AUT | 52 |
| | Gruber F. | AUT | 52 |
| 33. | Grissmann W. | AUT | 51 |
| | Kuralt J. | JUG | 51 |
| 35. | Ortner W. | AUT | 49 |
| 36. | Podborski S. | CAN | 47 |
| | Murray D. | CAN | 47 |
| 38. | Haker E. | NOR | 41 |
| 39. | Walcher S. | AUT | 40 |
| 40. | Giorgi A. | ITA | 37 |
| 41. | Makejew W. | SOV | 35 |
| 42. | Patterson P. | USA | 32 |
| 43. | Trojer K. | ITA | 31 |
| 44. | Rhyner W. | SUI | 30 |
| 45. | Mally P. | ITA | 29 |
| 46. | Gstrein H. | AUT | 27 |
| | Räber U. | SUI | 27 |
| | Spiss H. | AUT | 27 |
| 49. | Roux Ph. | SUI | 26 |
| 50. | Vesti W. | SUI | 25 |

## WOMEN 1978/79

| | | | |
|---|---|---|---|
| 1. | Moser-Proell A. | AUT | 243 |
| 2. | Wenzel H. | LIE | 240 |
| 3. | Epple I. | BRD | 189 |
| 4. | Nelson C. | USA | 168 |
| 5. | Nadig M.-T. | SUI | 156 |
| 6. | Serrat F. | FRA | 151 |
| 7. | Sackl R. | AUT | 112 |
| 8. | Kinshofer C. | BRD | 110 |
| 9. | Pelen P. | FRA | 100 |
| 10. | Giordani C. | ITA | 98 |
| 11. | Sölkner L. | AUT | 95 |
| 12. | Mösenlechner R. | BRD | 85 |
| 13. | Quaria M. R. | ITA | 84 |
| 14. | Zini D. | ITA | 82 |
| 15. | Hess E. | SUI | 76 |
| 16. | Glur B. | SUI | 74 |
| 17. | Charvatova O. | CSR | 70 |
| 18. | Preuss H. | USA | 69 |
| 19. | Fleckenstein F. | USA | 62 |
| 20. | Kaserer M. | AUT | 61 |
| 21. | Zurbriggen B. | SUI | 60 |
| 22. | Mittermaier E. | BRD | 60 |
| 23. | Cooper Ch. | USA | 60 |
| 23. | Wiesler H. | BRD | 60 |
| 25. | McKinney T. | USA | 59 |
| 26. | Peter E. | AUT | 57 |
| 27. | Fisher A. | USA | 51 |
| 28. | Attia C. | FRA | 50 |
| 29. | Flanders H. | USA | 50 |
| 30. | Bischofberger A. | SUI | 49 |
| 31. | Zechmeister C. | BRD | 48 |
| 32. | Vickova L. | TCH | 47 |
| 33. | Behr P. | BRD | 46 |
| | Soltysova J. | CSR | 46 |
| 35. | Gatta W. | ITA | 43 |
| 36. | Habersatter B. | AUT | 41 |
| | Pröll C. | AUT | 41 |
| 38. | Kurz-Schlechter | AUT | 38 |
| 39. | Dorsey B. | USA | 37 |
| 40. | Konzett U. | LIE | 35 |
| 41. | Dirren E. | SUI | 34 |
| 42. | De Agostini D. | SUI | 33 |
| 43. | Bader M. | BRD | 32 |
| | Gros-Gaudenier | FRA | 32 |
| | Kurlander J. | USA | 32 |
| 46. | Lukasser I. | AUT | 29 |
| 47. | Ellmer M. | AUT | 27 |
| 48. | Wenzel P. | LIE | 27 |
| 49. | Haas Z. | SUI | 26 |
| 50. | Liouche M. | FRA | 24 |

## MEN 1979/80

| | | | |
|---|---|---|---|
| 1. | Wenzel A. | LIE | 204 |
| 2. | Stenmark I. | SWE | 200 |
| 3. | Mahre P. | USA | 132 |
| 4. | Krizaj B. | YUG | 131 |
| 5. | Steiner A. | AUT | 130 |
| 6. | Lüthy J. | SUI | 116 |
| 7. | Enn H. | AUT | 100 |
| 8. | Plank H. | ITA | 91 |
| 9. | Müller P. | SUI | 87 |
| | Luescher P. | SUI | 87 |
| 11. | Read K. | CAN | 79 |
| 12. | Mahre S. | USA | 72 |
| 13. | Popangelov P. | BUL | 70 |
| 14. | Zhirov A. | SOV | 68 |
| 15. | Weirather H. | AUT | 64 |
| 16. | Neureuther C. | BRD | 62 |
| 17. | Orlainsky C. | AUT | 61 |
| | Gaspoz J. | SUI | 61 |
| 19. | Wirnsberger P. | AUT | 58 |
| 20. | Haker E. | NOR | 57 |
| 21. | Grissmann W. | AUT | 53 |
| 22. | Zeman B. | TCH | 51 |
| | Walcher J. | AUT | 51 |
| 24. | Halsnes J. | NOR | 44 |
| 25. | Frommelt P. | LIE | 43 |
| | Strel B. | YUG | 43 |
| 27. | Nöckler B. | ITA | 42 |
| 28. | Tsyganov V. | SOV | 41 |
| 29. | Gros P. | ITA | 40 |
| 30. | Podborski S. | CAN | 35 |
| 31. | Jäger G. | AUT | 31 |
| 32. | Heidegger K. | AUT | 28 |
| 33. | F.-Ochoa F. | SPA | 27 |
| | Klammer F. | AUT | 27 |
| | Spiss H. | AUT | 27 |
| 36. | Spiss U. | AUT | 25 |
| 37. | Vion M. | FRA | 24 |
| | Veith M. | BRD | 24 |
| | Ferstl S. | BRD | 24 |
| 40. | Kuralt J. | JUG | 23 |
| | Sörli O. | NOR | 23 |
| | Wörndl F. | BRD | 23 |
| 43. | Mill A. | USA | 22 |
| | Bernardi M. | ITA | 22 |
| 45. | Gruber F. | AUT | 21 |
| | Josi E. | SUI | 21 |
| | Stock L. | AUT | 21 |
| | De Chiesa P. | ITA | 21 |
| 49. | Bürgler T. | SUI | 20 |
| 50. | Jakobsson T. | SWE | 19 |

## WOMEN 1979/80

| | | | |
|---|---|---|---|
| 1. | Wenzel H. | LIE | 311 |
| 2. | Moser-Proell A. | AUT | 259 |
| 3. | Nadig M.-T. | SUI | 221 |
| 4. | Pelen P. | FRA | 192 |
| 5. | Epple I. | BRD | 141 |
| 6. | Serrat F. | FRA | 124 |
| 7. | Hess E. | SUI | 109 |

| | | |
|---|---|---|
| 8. Giordani C. | ITA | 107 |
| 9. Zini D. | ITA | 99 |
| 10. Nelson C. | USA | 98 |
| 11. Kinshofer C. | BRD | 79 |
| 12. Preuss H. | USA | 78 |
| 13. Soltysova J. | CSR | 72 |
| 14. McKinney T. | USA | 65 |
| 15. Moesenlechner R. | BRD | 60 |
| 16. Eberle I. | AUT | 56 |
| 17. Sölkner L. | AUT | 45 |
| 18. Cooper C. | USA | 44 |
| Sackl R. | AUT | 44 |
| 20. Patrakeeva N. | SOV | 43 |
| 21. De Agostini D. | SUI | 42 |
| 22. Fisher A. | USA | 41 |
| Flanders H. | USA | 41 |
| Graham L. | CAN | 41 |
| 25. Konzett U. | LIE | 40 |
| 26. Bieler W. | ITA | 38 |
| 27. Pröll C. | AUT | 37 |
| 28. Fjeldstad T. | NOR | 36 |
| Mittermaier E. | BRD | 36 |
| Epple M. | BRD | 36 |
| 31. Quario M.-R. | ITA | 35 |
| Kreiner C. | CAN | 35 |
| 33. Bischofsberger | SUI | 32 |
| 34. Charvatova O. | CSR | 28 |
| 35. Wiesler H. | BRD | 24 |
| 36. Bader M. | BRD | 23 |
| 37. Gatta W. | ITA | 22 |
| 38. Attia C. | FRA | 19 |
| Haaser A. | AUT | 19 |
| Macchi P. | ITA | 19 |
| 41. Fleckenstein V. | USA | 16 |
| 42. Melander A. | SWE | 15 |
| 43. Glur B. | SUI | 14 |
| Dirren E. | SUI | 14 |
| 45. Zechmeister M. | BRD | 13 |
| 46. Kraml E. | AUT | 12 |
| 47. Wenzel P. | LIE | 11 |
| Valt C. | ITA | 11 |
| 49. Vickova L. | CSR | 9 |
| Waldmeier M.-L. | FRA | 9 |

## MEN 1980/81

| | | |
|---|---|---|
| 1. Mahre P. | USA | 266 |
| 2. Stenmark I. | SWE | 260 |
| 3. Zhirov A. | SOV | 185 |
| 4. Mahre S. | USA | 155 |
| 5. Müller P. | SUI | 140 |
| 6. Krizaj B. | JUG | 137 |
| 7. Wenzel A. | LIE | 130 |
| 8. Weirather H. | AUT | 115 |
| 9. Podborski S. | CAN | 110 |
| 10. Orlainski C. | AUT | 105 |
| 11. Gaspoz J. | SUI | 102 |
| 12. Stock L. | AUT | 97 |
| 13. Halsnes J. | NOR | 96 |
| 14. Enn H. | AUT | 93 |
| 15. Lüthy J. | SUI | 84 |
| 16. Nockler B. | ITA | 79 |
| 17. Frommelt P. | LIE | 77 |
| 18. Wirnsberger P. | AUT | 73 |
| Tsyganov V. | SOV | 73 |
| 20. Andreev V. | SOV | 72 |
| 21. Fournier J. L. | SUI | 62 |
| Strel B. | JUG | 62 |
| 23. Spiess U. | AUT | 56 |
| 24. Bürgler T. | SUI | 55 |
| 25. Gruber F. | AUT | 53 |
| 26. Girardelli M. | LUX | 51 |
| 27. Plank H. | ITA | 49 |
| 28. Gros P. | ITA | 48 |
| Pfaffenbichler | AUT | 48 |
| 30. Hoeflehner | AUT | 47 |
| 31. Zurbriggen P. | SUI | 46 |
| Strand S. | SWE | 46 |
| 33. Fjällberg B. | SWE | 45 |
| Spiss H. | AUT | 45 |
| 35. Jaeger G. | AUT | 44 |
| 36. De Chiesa P. | ITA | 43 |
| Heinzer F. | SUI | 43 |
| 38. Read K. | CAN | 42 |
| 39. Ortner W. | AUT | 41 |
| 40. Klammer F. | AUT | 37 |
| 41. Walcher J. | AUT | 33 |
| 42. Resch | AUT | 32 |
| Kuralt J. | JUG | 32 |
| 44. Kerschbaumer S. | ITA | 31 |
| 45. Skajem P. A. | NOR | 28 |
| 46. Soerli O. | NOR | 27 |
| Grissmann W. | AUT | 27 |
| 48. Makeev V. | SOV | 26 |
| 49. Veith M. | BRD | 25 |
| 50. Cathomen C. | SUI | 24 |
| Popangelov P. | BUL | 24 |

## WOMEN 1980/81

| | | |
|---|---|---|
| 1. Nadig M.-T. | SUI | 289 |
| 2. Hess E. | SUI | 251 |
| 3. Wenzel H. | LIE | 241 |
| 4. Cooper C. | USA | 198 |
| 5. Epple I. | BRD | 181 |
| 6. McKinney T. | USA | 176 |
| Pelen P. | FRA | 176 |
| 8. Nelson C. | USA | 168 |
| 9. Kinshofer C. | BRD | 165 |
| 10. Serrat F. | FRA | 149 |
| 11. Zini D. | ITA | 137 |
| 12. Walliser M. | SUI | 112 |
| 13. De Agostini D. | SUI | 110 |
| 14. Epple M. | BRD | 102 |
| 15. Charvatova O. | TCH | 84 |
| 16. Proell C. | AUT | 78 |
| 17. Bieler W. | ITA | 75 |
| 18. Quario M. R. | ITA | 64 |
| 19. Flanders H. | USA | 63 |
| 20. Fjeldstad T. | NOR | 62 |
| 21. Moesenlechner R. | BRD | 61 |
| Giordani C. | ITA | 61 |
| Soltysova J. | TCH | 61 |
| 24. Haas Z. | SUI | 58 |
| 25. Haecher T. | BRD | 55 |
| 26. Macchi P. | ITA | 52 |
| 27. Kreiner C. | CAN | 49 |
| Patrakeeva N. | SOV | 49 |
| 29. Fisher A. | USA | 47 |
| 30. Preuss H. | USA | 46 |
| 31. Sorensen G. | CAN | 45 |
| Soelkner L. | AUT | 45 |
| 33. Kirchler E. | AUT | 42 |
| 34. Glur B. | SUI | 37 |
| 35. Peter E. | AUT | 35 |
| 36. Waldmeier Ml. | FRA | 33 |
| 37. Gros-Gauden. M. | FRA | 32 |
| 38. Konsett U. | LIE | 30 |
| 39. Oak C. | USA | 25 |
| 40. Wiessler H. | BRD | 22 |
| 41. Eberle I. | AUT | 21 |
| Dornig B. | JUG | 21 |
| Chaud E. | FRA | 21 |
| 44. Attia C. | FRA | 20 |
| 45. Rey A. F. | FRA | 18 |
| 46. Wenzel P. | LIE | 17 |
| Gerg M. | BRD | 17 |
| 48. Bischofsberger | SUI | 14 |
| 49. Zavadlav A. | JUG | 13 |
| Steiner R. | AUT | 13 |

## MEN 1981/82

| | | |
|---|---|---|
| 1. Mahre P. | USA | 309 |
| 2. Stenmark I. | SWE | 211 |
| 3. Mahre S. | USA | 183 |
| 4. Müller P. | SUI | 132 |
| 5. Wenzel A. | LIE | 129 |
| 6. Girardelli M. | LUX | 121 |
| 7. Gaspoz J. | SUI | 119 |
| 8. Podborski S. | CAN | 115 |
| 9. Krizaj B. | JUG | 108 |
| 10. Weirather H. | AUT | 97 |
| 11. Zurbriggen P. | SUI | 96 |
| 12. Resch E. | AUT | 76 |
| 13. Enn H. | AUT | 75 |
| 14. Klammer F. | AUT | 71 |
| 15. Gruber F. | AUT | 69 |
| 16. De Chiesa P. | ITA | 68 |
| 17. Read K. | CAN | 65 |
| 18. Stock L. | AUT | 64 |
| 19. Lüthy J. | SUI | 63 |
| 20. Strolz H. | AUT | 59 |
| 21. Meli S. | SUI | 56 |
| 22. Bürgler T. | SUI | 54 |
| 23. Wirnsberger P. | AUT | 53 |
| 24. Ortner W. | AUT | 51 |
| Höflehner H. | AUT | 51 |
| 26. Heinzer F. | SUI | 50 |
| 27. Orlainski C. | AUT | 48 |
| 28. Luescher P. | SUI | 46 |
| Cathomen C. | SUI | 46 |
| 30. Oerli G. | SUI | 45 |
| 31. Frommelt P. | LIE | 44 |
| 32. Brooker T. | CAN | 43 |
| Fournier J.-L. | SUI | 43 |
| 34. Strand S. | SWE | 39 |
| 35. Vion M. | FRA | 38 |
| Zhirov A. | SOV | 38 |
| 37. Nöckler B. | ITA | 37 |
| Hole E. | NOR | 37 |
| 39. Tsyganov V. | SOV | 36 |
| 40. Steiner A. | AUT | 34 |
| 41. Halsnes J. | NOR | 31 |
| 42. Mair M. | ITA | 29 |
| Strel B. | JUG | 29 |
| Von Hohenlohe H. | MEX | 29 |
| 45. Gatterman K. | BRD | 28 |
| Julen M. | SUI | 28 |
| 47. Pfaffenbichler G. | AUT | 27 |
| Irwin D. | CAN | 27 |
| Giorgi A. | ITA | 27 |
| 50. Gros P. | ITA | 26 |
| Walcher J. | AUT | 26 |

## WOMEN 1981/82

| | | |
|---|---|---|
| 1. Hess E. | SUI | 297 |
| 2. Epple I. | BRD | 282 |
| 3. Cooper C. | USA | 198 |
| 4. Epple M. | BRD | 166 |
| 5. Nelson C. | USA | 158 |
| 6. Sölkner L. | AUT | 137 |
| Konsett U. | LIE | 137 |
| 8. Pelen P. | FRA | 125 |
| 9. McKinney T. | USA | 116 |
| 10. Quario M. | ITA | 109 |
| 11. Chaud E. | FRA | 98 |
| 12. Sorensen G. | CAN | 90 |
| Flanders H. | USA | 90 |
| 14. Zini D. | ITA | 88 |
| 15. G.-Gaudenier M. | FRA | 87 |
| 16. De Agostini D. | SUI | 84 |
| 17. Walliser M. | SUI | 75 |
| 18. Serrat F. | FRA | 73 |
| 19. Wenzel H. | LIC | 72 |
| 20. Eberle I. | AUT | 68 |
| 21. Eder S. | AUT | 66 |
| 22. Kronbichler A. | AUT | 60 |
| 23. Steiner R. | AUT | 58 |
| 24. Kinshofer C. | BRD | 56 |
| 25. Wenzel P. | LIE | 55 |
| 26. Charvatova O. | CSR | 49 |
| 27. Kirchler E. | AUT | 45 |
| Melander A. | SWE | 45 |
| 29. Graham L. | CAN | 44 |
| 30. Tlalka M. | POL | 43 |
| 31. Leskovsek A. | JUG | 42 |
| Hächer T. | BRD | 42 |
| Zavadlav A. | JUG | 42 |
| 34. Haas Z. | SUI | 41 |
| 35. Macchi P. | ITA | 38 |
| 36. Tlalka D. | POL | 37 |
| 37. Fisher A. | USA | 35 |
| 38. Hess M. | SUI | 30 |
| 39. Waldmeier M.-L. | FRA | 26 |
| Wolf S. | AUT | 26 |
| 41. Lehodey D. | CAN | 22 |
| Fjeldstad T. | NOR | 22 |
| 43. Lancaster K. | USA | 21 |
| 44. Rey A.-F. | FRA | 20 |
| 45. Jerman M. | JUG | 18 |
| 46. Pröll C. | AUT | 16 |
| Frigo L. | ITA | 16 |
| Haight D. | CAN | 16 |
| Riedl C. | AUT | 16 |
| 50. Preuss H. | USA | 15 |
| Henkel M. | BRD | 15 |
| Winkler S. | AUT | 15 |

## MEN 1982/83

| | | |
|---|---|---|
| 1. Mahre P. | USA | 285 |
| 2. Stenmark I. | SWE | 218 |
| 3. Wenzel A. | LIE | 177 |
| 4. Girardelli M. | LUX | 168 |
| 5. Luescher P. | SUI | 164 |
| 6. Zurbriggen P. | SUI | 161 |
| 7. Müller P. | SUI | 125 |
| 8. Julen M. | SUI | 116 |
| 9. Gruber F. | AUT | 112 |
| Krizaj B. | JUG | 112 |
| 11. Strand S. | SWE | 110 |
| 12. Mahre S. | USA | 108 |
| 13. Weirather H. | AUT | 102 |
| 14. Cathomen C. | SUI | 100 |
| 15. Orlainsky C. | AUT | 99 |
| Räber U. | SUI | 99 |
| 17. Lüthy J. | SUI | 96 |
| 18. Klammer F. | AUT | 95 |
| 19. Meli S. | SUI | 85 |
| 20. Enn H. | AUT | 84 |
| 21. Mair M. | ITA | 78 |
| 22. Kernen B. | SUI | 77 |
| 23. Read K. | CAN | 76 |
| 24. Höflehner H. | AUT | 74 |
| 25. Resch E. | AUT | 73 |
| Heinzer F. | SUI | 73 |
| 27. Brooker T. | CAN | 67 |
| De Chiesa P. | ITA | 67 |
| 29. Erlacher R. | ITA | 65 |
| 30. Podborski S. | CAN | 63 |
| 31. Canac M. | FRA | 59 |
| 32. Franko J. | JUG | 56 |
| 33. Stock L. | AUT | 55 |
| 34. Fjaellberg B. | SWE | 49 |
| 35. Giorgi A. | ITA | 47 |
| 36. Strel B. | JUG | 43 |
| 37. Pfaffenbichler G. | AUT | 40 |
| 38. Edalini I. | ITA | 39 |
| 39. Strolz H. | AUT | 38 |
| 40. Bürgler T. | SUI | 36 |
| 41. Frommelt P. | LIE | 34 |
| 42. Popangelov P. | BUL | 33 |
| 43. Wirnsberger P. | AUT | 32 |
| 44. Halvarsson L. G. | SWE | 27 |
| 45. Wörndl F. | BRD | 26 |
| 46. Heidegger K. | AUT | 23 |
| Makeev V. | SOV | 23 |
| 48. Lee S. | AUS | 22 |
| Sbardellotto D. | ITA | 22 |
| Kuralt J. | JUG | 22 |

## WOMEN 1982/83

| | | |
|---|---|---|
| 1. McKinney | USA | 225 |
| 2. Wenzel H. | LIE | 193 |
| 3. Hess E. | SUI | 192 |
| 4. Kirchler E. | AUT | 163 |
| 5. Walliser M. | SUI | 135 |
| 6. Epple I. | BRD | 117 |
| 7. Nelson C. | USA | 115 |
| 8. Charvatova O. | CSR | 111 |
| 9. Epple M. | BRD | 109 |
| 10. De Agostini D. | SUI | 96 |
| 11. Kronbichler A. | AUT | 93 |
| 12. Cooper C. | USA | 87 |
| 13. Serrat F. | FRA | 86 |
| 14. Quario M. R. | ITA | 82 |
| 15. Gerg M. | BRD | 70 |
| 16. Pelen P. | FRA | 69 |
| 17. Chaud E. | FRA | 67 |
| 18. Graham L. | CAN | 66 |
| 19. Wenzel P. | LIE | 65 |
| 20. Rey A.-F. | FRA | 63 |
| 21. Attia C. | FRA | 62 |
| 22. Tlalka M. | POL | 61 |
| 23. Steiner R. | AUT | 60 |
| 24. Eder S. | AUT | 55 |
| 25. Haas Z. | SUI | 53 |
| 26. Figini M. | SUI | 52 |
| 27. Zini D. | ITA | 51 |
| 28. Tlalka D. | POL | 50 |
| 29. Ganterova J. | TCH | 48 |
| 30. Emonet P. | FRA | 44 |
| Konzett U. | LIE | 44 |
| 32. Sölkner L. | AUT | 42 |
| 33. Armstrong D. | USA | 41 |
| Wiesler H. | BRD | 41 |
| 35. Hess M. | SUI | 38 |
| Oertli B. | SUI | 38 |
| 37. Ehrat A. | SUI | 37 |
| 38. Merle C. | FRA | 35 |
| 39. Vitzthum V. | AUT | 34 |
| Waldmeier M.-L. | FRA | 34 |
| Sörensen G. | CAN | 34 |
| Magoni P. | ITA | 34 |
| 43. Ouittet C. | FRA | 33 |
| 44. Barbier H. | FRA | 28 |
| 45. Winkler S. | AUT | 27 |
| 46. Frigo L. | ITA | 23 |
| 47. Gutensohn K. | AUT | 21 |
| 48. Maricich M. | USA | 20 |
| 49. Zavadlav A. | JUG | 16 |
| Wolf S. | AUT | 16 |

## MEN 1983/84

| | | |
|---|---|---|
| 1. Zurbriggen P. | SUI | 256 |
| 2. Stenmark I. | SWE | 230 |
| 3. Girardelli M. | LUX | 222 |
| 4. Wenzel A. | LIE | 191 |
| 5. Steiner A. | AUT | 148 |
| 6. Heinzer F. | SUI | 129 |
| 7. Räber U. | SUI | 118 |
| 8. Gruber F. | AUT | 113 |
| 9. Giorgi A. | ITA | 107 |
| 10. Krizaj B. | JUG | 106 |
| 11. Enn H. | AUT | 105 |
| 12. Resch E. | AUT | 91 |
| Julen M. | SUI | 91 |
| 14. Johnson B. | USA | 87 |
| 15. Mahre P. | USA | 85 |
| Höflehner H. | AUT | 85 |
| 17. Bürgler T. | SUI | 84 |
| 18. Popangelov P. | BUL | 82 |
| 19. Jure F. | JUG | 81 |
| 20. Klammer F. | AUT | 79 |
| 21. Podborski S. | CAN | 76 |
| Strolz H. | AUT | 76 |
| 23. Hinterseer G. | AUT | 71 |
| 24. Müller P. | SUI | 66 |
| 25. Brooker T. | CAN | 64 |
| Hangl M. | SUI | 64 |
| 27. Weirather H. | AUT | 58 |
| 28. Kernen B. | SUI | 57 |
| De Chiesa P. | ITA | 57 |
| Gaspoz J. | SUI | 57 |
| 31. Zoller R. | AUT | 55 |
| 32. Meli S. | SUI | 54 |
| 33. Mader G. | AUT | 51 |
| 34. Erlacher R. | ITA | 50 |
| 35. Wirnsberger P. | AUT | 45 |
| 36. Halvarsson L. | SWE | 44 |
| 37. Cathomen C. | SUI | 43 |
| 38. Strel B. | JUG | 40 |
| 39. Strand S. | SWE | 39 |
| 40. Frommelt P. | LIE | 37 |
| 41. Heidegger K. | AUT | 36 |
| 42. Mair M. | ITA | 34 |
| 43. Stock L. | AUT | 33 |
| Nilsson J. | SWE | 33 |
| 45. Kuralt J. | JUG | 32 |
| Niederseer S. | AUt | 32 |
| 47. Mahre S. | USA | 30 |
| 48. Lee S. | AUS | 29 |
| 49. Bouvet D. | FRA | 27 |
| 50. Lüthy J. | SUI | 25 |
| Fjaellberg B. | SWE | 25 |
| Pfaffenbichler G. | AUT | 25 |

## WOMEN 1983/84

| | | |
|---|---|---|
| 1. Hess E. | SUI | 247 |
| 2. Wenzel H. | LIE | 238 |
| 3. McKinney T. | USA | 195 |
| 4. Epple I. | BRD | 178 |
| 5. Figini M. | SUI | 166 |
| 6. Cooper C. | USA | 161 |
| 7. Charvatova O. | CSR | 153 |
| 8. Walliser M. | SUI | 131 |
| 9. Kiehl M. | BRD | 126 |
| 10. Kirchler E. | AUT | 122 |
| Pelen P. | FRA | 122 |
| 12. Sorensen G. | CAN | 100 |
| 13. Sölkner L. | AUT | 95 |
| 14. Epple M. | BRD | 92 |
| 15. Steiner R. | AUT | 91 |
| 16. Oertli B. | SUI | 89 |
| 17. Quario M. R. | ITA | 69 |
| 18. Eder S. | AUT | 67 |
| 19. Graham L. | CAN | 65 |
| 20. Flanders H. | USA | 60 |
| 21. Tlalka D. | POL | 59 |
| 22. Ehrat A. | SUI | 57 |
| 23. Tlalka M. | POL | 56 |
| 24. Armstrong D. | USA | 55 |
| Zini D. | ITA | 55 |
| Hess M. | SUI | 55 |
| 27. Kronbichler A. | AUT | 52 |
| 28. Merle C. | FRA | 45 |
| 29. Gadient B. | SUI | 44 |
| 30. Gantnerova J. | TCH | 43 |
| 31. Savijarvi L. | CAN | 41 |
| 32. Barbier H. | FRA | 39 |
| 33. Gerg M. | BRD | 36 |
| 34. Vitzthum V. | AUT | 35 |
| 35. Moesenlechner R. | BRD | 34 |
| 36. Fernandez B. | SPA | 33 |
| 37. Waldmeier M.-L. | FRA | 32 |
| 38. Magoni P. | ITA | 31 |
| 39. Zavadlav A. | JUG | 29 |
| 40. Tome N. | JUG | 27 |
| 41. Guignard C. | FRA | 26 |
| Nelson C. | USA | 26 |
| 43. Valesova I. | CSR | 24 |
| Quittet C. | FRA | 24 |
| 45. Von Grünigen C. | SUI | 23 |
| 46. Chaud E. | FRA | 22 |
| Stemmle K. | CAN | 21 |
| Konzett U. | LIE | 21 |
| Haas Z. | SUI | 21 |
| Rey A.-F. | FRA | 21 |

## MEN 1984/85

| | | | |
|---|---|---|---|
| 1. | Girardelli M. | LUX | 262 |
| 2. | Zurbriggen P. | SUI | 244 |
| 3. | Wenzel A. | LIE | 172 |
| 4. | Müller P. | SUI | 156 |
| 5. | Heinzer F. | SUI | 137 |
| 6. | Stenmark I. | SWE | 135 |
| 7. | Bürgler T. | SUI | 131 |
| 8. | Höflehner H. | AUT | 116 |
| 9. | Wirnsberger P. | AUT | 111 |
| 10. | Wasmaier M. | BRD | 101 |
| | Krizaj B. | JUG | 101 |
| | Mahrer D. | SUI | 101 |
| 13. | Alpiger K. | SUI | 100 |
| 14. | Julen M. | SUI | 97 |
| 15. | Hangl M. | SUI | 93 |
| 16. | Tötsch O. | ITA | 92 |
| | Luescher P. | SUI | 92 |
| 18. | Erlacher R. | ITA | 91 |
| 19. | Enn H. | AUT | 80 |
| | Frommelt P. | LIE | 80 |
| 21. | Pramotton R. | ITA | 74 |
| 22. | Giorgi A. | ITA | 72 |
| 23. | De Chiesa P. | ITA | 70 |
| | Kernen B. | SUI | 70 |
| 25. | Nilsson J. | SWE | 69 |
| 26. | Mair M. | ITA | 65 |
| 27. | Steiner A. | AUT | 63 |
| 28. | Wildgruber S. | BRD | 62 |
| 29. | Brooker T. | CAN | 60 |
| 30. | Petrovic R. | JUG | 58 |
| 31. | Roth P. | BRD | 57 |
| | Popangelov P. | BUL | 57 |
| 33. | Edalini I. | ITA | 53 |
| 34. | Heidegger K. | AUT | 51 |
| 35. | Cathomen C. | SUI | 50 |
| 36. | Strolz H. | AUT | 49 |
| | Stangassinger T. | AUT | 49 |
| 38. | Franko J. | JUG | 46 |
| 39. | Vion M. | FRA | 45 |
| 40. | Gaspoz J. | SUI | 44 |
| | Zoller R. | AUT | 44 |
| 42. | Lee S. | AUS | 41 |
| 43. | Beck F. | BRD | 37 |
| 44. | Niederseer S. | AUT | 33 |
| 45. | Riedlsperger E. | AUT | 31 |
| | Piccard F. | FRA | 31 |
| 47. | Bouvet D. | FRA | 30 |
| 48. | Gruber F. | AUT | 28 |
| 49. | Rambaud G. | FRA | 27 |
| 50. | Eder M. | BRD | 26 |

## WOMEN 1984/85

| | | | |
|---|---|---|---|
| 1. | Figini M. | SUI | 259 |
| 2. | Oertli B. | SUI | 218 |
| 3. | Walliser M. | SUI | 197 |
| 4. | Hess E. | SUI | 168 |
| | Kiehl M. | BRD | 168 |
| 6. | Charvatova O. | CSR | 167 |
| 7. | Kirchler E. | AUT | 156 |
| 8. | McKinney T. | USA | 139 |
| 9. | Schneider V. | SUI | 112 |
| 10. | Fernandez B. | SPA | 108 |
| 11. | Haas Z. | SUI | 107 |
| 12. | Pelen P. | FRA | 106 |
| | Epple M. | BRD | 106 |
| 14. | Guignard C. | FRA | 97 |
| 15. | Hächer T. | BRD | 89 |
| 16. | Twardokens E. | USA | 83 |
| 17. | Graham L. | CAN | 73 |
| 18. | Gerg M. | BRD | 70 |
| 19. | Quario M. R. | ITA | 65 |
| 20. | Armstrong D. | USA | 62 |
| 21. | Quittet C. | FRA | 61 |
| 22. | Gadient B. | SUI | 59 |
| | Gutensohn K. | AUT | 59 |
| 24. | Magoni P. | ITA | 58 |
| 25. | Roffe D. | USA | 57 |
| 26. | Eder S. | AUT | 50 |
| 27. | Ehrat A. | SUI | 46 |
| 28. | Tlalka M. | POL | 45 |
| 29. | Zini D. | ITA | 41 |
| 30. | Svet M. | JUG | 40 |
| | Moesenlechner R. | BRD | 40 |
| | Tlalka D. | POL | 40 |
| 33. | Schmidhauser C. | SUI | 36 |
| | Savijarvi L. | CAN | 36 |
| 35. | Epple I. | BRD | 35 |
| 36. | Kronbichler A. | AUT | 34 |
| 37. | Steiner R. | AUT | 31 |
| 38. | Flanders H. | USA | 30 |
| | Aiejae M. | SWE | 30 |
| | Stemmle K. | CAN | 30 |
| 41. | Vitzthum V. | AUT | 29 |
| | Barbier H. | FRA | 29 |
| 43. | Winkler S. | AUT | 28 |
| 44. | Emonet C. | FRA | 27 |
| 45. | Rey A.-F. | FRA | 26 |
| 46. | Dedler K. | BRD | 24 |
| 47. | Wolf S. | AUT | 22 |
| 48. | Nelson C. | USA | 21 |
| 49. | Zavadlav A. | JUG | 19 |
| | Haight D. | CAN | 19 |

## MEN 1985/86

| | | | |
|---|---|---|---|
| 1. | Girardelli M. | LUX | 294 |
| 2. | Zurbriggen P. | SUI | 284 |
| 3. | Wasmaier M. | BRD | 214 |
| 4. | Mueller P. | SUI | 204 |
| 5. | Stenmark I. | SWE | 196 |
| 6. | Stock L. | AUT | 174 |
| 7. | Petrovic, R. | JUG | 170 |
| 8. | Wirnsberger P. | AUT | 148 |
| 9. | Strolz H. | AUT | 147 |
| 10. | Mader G. | AUT | 143 |
| 11. | Mair M. | ITA | 129 |
| 12. | Erlacher R. | ITA | 125 |
| 13. | Heinzer F. | SUI | 124 |
| 14. | Wenzel A. | LIE | 119 |
| 15. | Krizaj B. | JUG | 115 |
| 16. | Pramotton R. | ITA | 111 |
| 17. | Alpiger K. | SUI | 110 |
| 18. | Steiner A. | AUT | 109 |
| 19. | Gaspoz, J. | SUI | 101 |
| 20. | Frommelt P. | LIC | 100 |
| 21. | Oehrli G. | SUI | 87 |
| | Nilsson J. | SWE | 87 |
| 23. | Hangl, M. | SUI | 82 |
| 24. | Gaidet Ch. | FRA | 76 |
| 25. | Tonazzi M. | ITA | 72 |
| | Bouvet D. | FRA | 72 |
| | Resch E. | AUT | 72 |
| 28. | Hoeflehner H. | AUT | 71 |
| 29. | Mahrer D. | SUI | 68 |
| 30. | Piccard F. | FRA | 62 |
| 31. | Edalini I. | ITA | 55 |
| | Niederseer S. | AUT | 55 |
| 33. | Koehlbichler D. | AUT | 53 |
| 34. | Pfaffenbichler G. | AUT | 51 |
| 35. | Eder M. | BRD | 49 |
| 36. | Wallner J. | SWE | 47 |
| | Enn H. | AUT | 47 |
| 38. | Buergler, T. | SUI | 45 |
| 39. | Lewis, D. | USA | 43 |
| | Bell M. | GBR | 43 |
| 41. | Johnson B. | USA | 40 |
| | Giorgi A. | ITA | 40 |
| | Stuffer H. | BRD | 40 |
| 44. | Sbardellotto D. | ITA | 39 |
| 45. | Roth P. | BRD | 38 |
| 46. | Shaw T. | USA | 37 |
| | Henning N. | SWE | 37 |
| 48. | Kernen B. | SUI | 36 |
| 49. | Schick J. | BRD | 35 |
| | Heidegger K. | AUT | 35 |

## WOMEN 1985/86

| | | | |
|---|---|---|---|
| 1. | Walliser M. | SUI | 287 |
| 2. | Hess E. | SUI | 242 |
| 3. | Schneider V. | SUI | 216 |
| 4. | Charvatova O. | CSR | 199 |
| 5. | Oertli B. | SUI | 181 |
| 6. | Figini M. | SUI | 178 |
| 7. | Svet M. | JUG | 159 |
| 8. | Kiehl M. | BRD | 157 |
| 9. | Haecher T. | BRD | 153 |
| 10. | Gerg M. | BRD | 151 |
| 11. | Gutensohn K. | AUT | 145 |
| 12. | Savijarvi L. | CAN | 136 |
| 13. | Pelen P. | FRA | 117 |
| 14. | Graham L. | CAN | 116 |
| 15. | Steiner R. | AUT | 110 |
| 16. | Wolf S. | AUT | 93 |
| 17. | Wachter A. | AUT | 91 |
| 18. | Eder S. | AUT | 90 |
| 19. | Zeller H. | SUI | 81 |
| 20. | Moesenlechner R. | BRD | 80 |
| 21. | Schmidhauser C. | SUI | 69 |
| 22. | Magore M. | FRA | 67 |
| 23. | Fletcher P. | USA | 66 |
| 24. | Twardokens E. | USA | 63 |
| | McKinney T. | USA | 63 |
| 26. | Haas Z. | SUI | 57 |
| | Winkler S. | AUT | 57 |
| 28. | Marzola M. | ITA | 55 |
| 29. | Hess M. | SUI | 52 |
| | Ladstaetter I. | AUT | 52 |
| 31. | Fernandez-Ochoa B. | SPA | 51 |
| | Kirchler E | AUT | 51 |
| 33. | Wiesler H. | BRD | 50 |
| 34. | Rey A.-F. | FRA | 49 |
| 35. | Armstrong D. | USA | 47 |
| 36. | Gadient B. | SUI | 44 |
| | Kronbichler A. | AUT | 44 |
| 38. | Quittet C. | FRA | 42 |
| | Strobl C. | AUT | 42 |
| 40. | Bonfini N. | ITA | 41 |
| | Merle C. | FRA | 41 |
| 42. | Epple Beck M. | BRD | 39 |
| 43. | Percy K. | CAN | 32 |
| 44. | Kinshofer C. | NED | 31 |
| 45. | Delago K. | ITA | 30 |
| 46. | Flanders H. | USA | 26 |
| | Zajc K. | JUG | 26 |
| | Wallinger V. | AUT | 26 |
| 49. | Lacasse J. | CAN | 25 |
| | Beer, C. | AUT | 25 |

# ALPINE WORLD CUP RACE RESULTS
## 1967/1986

## MEN 1966/67

### DOWNHILL

**Wengen**

| | | |
|---|---|---|
| 1. Killy J.-C. | FRA | 3.06.76 |
| 2. Lacroix L. | FRA | 3.07.05 |
| 3. Dätwyler J.-D. | SUI | 3.07.61 |

**Kitzbühel**

| | | |
|---|---|---|
| 1. Killy J.-C. | FRA | 2.11.82 |
| 2. Vogler F. | BRD | 2.13.29 |
| 3. Messner H. | AUT | 2.14.69 |

**Megêve**

| | | |
|---|---|---|
| 1. Killy J.-C. | FRA | 2.13.73 |
| 2. Rohr H. | SUI | 2.15.77 |
| 3. Vogler F. | BRD | 2.15.80 |

**Sestrière (AK)**

| | | |
|---|---|---|
| 1. Killy J.-C. | FRA | 1.46.86 |
| 2. Orcel B. | FRA | 1.48.59 |
| 3. Périllat G. | FRA | 1.49.36 |

**Franconia**

| | | |
|---|---|---|
| 1. Killy J.-C. | FRA | 1.29.08 |
| 2. Périllat G. | FRA | 1.29.91 |
| 3. Barrows J. | USA | 1.30.03 |

### GIANT SLALOM

**Berchtesgaden**

| | | |
|---|---|---|
| 1. Mauduit G. | FRA | 1.46.91 |
| 2. Lacroix L. | FRA | 1.47.30 |
| 3. Killy J.-C. | FRA | 1.48.05 |

**Adelboden**

| | | |
|---|---|---|
| 1. Killy J.-C. | FRA | 3.30.71 |
| 2. Favre W. | SUI | 3.32.53 |
| 3. Mauduit G. | FRA | 3.32.58 |

**Franconia**

| | | |
|---|---|---|
| 1. Killy J.-C. | FRA | 1.35.63 |
| 2. Mauduit G. | FRA | 1.35.65 |
| 3. Giovanoli D. | SUI | 1.38.75 |

**Vail**

| | | |
|---|---|---|
| 1. Killy J.-C. | FRA | 1.42.83 |
| 2. Heuga J. | USA | 1.44.65 |
| 3. Messner H. | AUT | 1.46.06 |

**Jackson Hole**

| | | |
|---|---|---|
| 1. Killy J.-C. | FRA | 3.53.34 |
| 2. Heuga J. | USA | 3.55.01 |
| 3. Bleiner W. | AUT | 3.55.56 |

### SLALOM

**Berchtesgaden**

| | | |
|---|---|---|
| 1. Messner H. | AUT | 1.37.26 |
| 2. Melquiond J. | FRA | 1.27.31 |
| 3. Giovanoli D. | SUI | 1.37.39 |

**Wengen**

| | | |
|---|---|---|
| 1. Killy J.-C. | FRA | 1.52.90 |
| 2. Messner H. | AUT | 1.54.01 |
| 3. Melquiond J. | FRA | 1.54.92 |

**Kitzbühel**

| | | |
|---|---|---|
| 1. Killy J.-C. | FRA | 1.52.09 |
| 2. Grahn B.-E. | SWE | 1.54.30 |
| 3. Jauffret L. | FRA | 1.54.43 |

**Megêve**

| | | |
|---|---|---|
| 1. Périllat G. | FRA | 2.01.32 |
| 2. Killy J.-C. | FRA | 2.01.79 |
| 3. Schranz K. | AUT | 2.02.84 |

**Madonna di Campiglio**

| | | |
|---|---|---|
| 1. Périllat G. | FRA | 1.27.14 |
| 2. Jauffret L. | FRA | 1.27.60 |
| 3. Lacroix L. | FRA | 1.27.62 |

**Franconia**

| | | |
|---|---|---|
| 1. Killy J.-C. | FRA | 1.28.05 |
| 2. Heuga J. | USA | 1.28.12 |
| 3. Huber H. | AUT | 1.28.85 |

**Jackson Hole**

| | | |
|---|---|---|
| 1. Huber H. | AUT | 2.05.03 |
| 2. Mauduit G. | FRA | 2.05.64 |
| 3. Bleiner W. | AUT | 2.07.54 |

## WOMEN 1966/67

### DOWNHILL

**Grindelwald**

| | | |
|---|---|---|
| 1. Green N. | CAN | 2.05.32 |
| 2. Mir I. | FRA | 2.06.79 |
| 3. Steurer F. | FRA | 2.07.48 |

**Schruns**

| | | |
|---|---|---|
| 1. Goitschel M. | FRA | 2.12.23 |
| 2. Schinegger E. | AUT | 2.12.54 |
| 3. Famose A. | FRA | 2.12.60 |

**Sestrière (AK)**

| | | |
|---|---|---|
| 1. Goitschel M. | FRA | 2.01.75 |
| Demetz G. | ITA | 2.01.75 |
| 3. Steurer F. | FRA | 2.02.49 |

**Franconia**

| | | |
|---|---|---|
| 1. Mir I. | FRA | 1.28.74 |
| 2. Schinegger E. | AUT | 1.28.96 |
| 3. Famose A. | FRA | 1.30.58 |

### GIANT SLALOM

**Oberstaufen**

| | | |
|---|---|---|
| 1. Green N. | CAN | 1.18.58 |
| 2. Färbinger B. | BRD | 1.19.82 |
| 3. Bochatay F. | SUI | 1.20.28 |

**Saint-Gervais**

| | | |
|---|---|---|
| 1. Schinegger E. | AUT | 3.16.26 |
| 2. Goitschel M. | FRA | 3.17.13 |
| 3. Famose A. | FRA | 3.18.91 |

**Franconia**

| | | |
|---|---|---|
| 1. Béranger C. | FRA | 1.18.18 |
| 2. Steurer F. | FRA | 1.18.32 |
| 3. Green N. | CAN | 1.18.36 |

**Vail**

| | | |
|---|---|---|
| 1. Green N. | CAN | 1.16.14 |
| 2. Schinegger E. | AUT | 1.16.68 |
| 3. Famose A. | FRA | 1.17.99 |

**Jackson Hole**

| | | |
|---|---|---|
| 1. Green N. | CAN | 2.50.03 |
| 2. Schinegger E. | AUT | 2.51.75 |
| 3. Hecher T. | AUT | 2.52.95 |

**Grindelwald**

| | | |
|---|---|---|
| 1. Green N. | CAN | 1.36.06 |
| 2. Famose A. | FRA | 1.36.93 |
| 3. Goitschel M. | FRA | 1.37.47 |

### SLALOM

**Oberstaufen**

| | | |
|---|---|---|
| 1. Green N. | CAN | 1.19.33 |
| 2. Bochatay F. | SUI | 1.19.43 |
| 3. Famose A. | FRA | 1.20.69 |

**Grindelwald**

| | | |
|---|---|---|
| 1. Famose A. | FRA | 1.21.80 |
| 2. Hathorn G. | GBR | 1.22.12 |
| 3. Mir I. | FRA | 1.23.57 |

**Schruns**

| | | |
|---|---|---|
| 1. Goitschel M. | FRA | 1.43.38 |
| 2. Famose A. | FRA | 1.44.40 |
| 3. Green N. | CAN | 1.44.68 |

**Saint-Gervais**

| | | |
|---|---|---|
| 1. Famose A. | FRA | 1.31.50 |
| 2. Goitschel M. | FRA | 1.32.41 |
| 3. Steurer F. | FRA | 1.32.67 |

**Monte Bondone**

| | | |
|---|---|---|
| 1. Fäbinger B. | BRD | 1.12.98 |
| 2. Famose A. | FRA | 1.13.79 |
| 3. Hecher T. | AUT | 1.14.33 |

**Franconia**

| | | |
|---|---|---|
| 1. Goitschel M. | FRA | 1.26.22 |
| 2. Mir I. | FRA | 1.26.58 |
| 3. Famose A. | FRA | 1.27.04 |

**Jackson Hole**

| | | |
|---|---|---|
| 1. Green N. | CAN | 1.30.67 |
| 2. Goitschel M. | FRA | 1.30.74 |
| 3. Steurer F. | FRA | 1.33.02 |

## MEN 1967/68

### DOWNHILL

**Wengen**

| | | |
|---|---|---|
| 1. Nenning G. | AUT | 1.59.98 |
| 2. Schranz K. | AUT | 2.01.19 |
| 3. Bruggmann E. | SUI | 2.01.80 |

**Kitzbühel**

| | | |
|---|---|---|
| 1. Nenning G. | AUT | 2.14.49 |
| 2. Killy J.-C. | FRA | 2.14.95 |
| 3. Sprecher A. | SUI | 2.15.10 |

**Grenoble (JO)**

| | | |
|---|---|---|
| 1. Killy J.-C. | FRA | 1.59.85 |
| 2. Périllat G. | FRA | 1.59.93 |
| 3. Dätwyler J.-D. | SUI | 2.00.32 |

**Chamonix (AK)**

| | | |
|---|---|---|
| 1. Orcel B | FRA | 2.16.96 |
| 2. Huggler K. | SUI | 2.19.00 |
| 3. Périllat G. | FRA | 2.19.21 |

**Aspen**

| | | |
|---|---|---|
| 1. Nenning G. | AUT | 1.59.49 |
| 2. Messner H. | AUT | 2.01.82 |
| 3. Killy J.-C. | FRA | 2.02.15 |

### GIANT SLALOM

**Oslo**

| | | |
|---|---|---|
| 1. Bleiner W. | AUT | 2.32.61 |
| 2. Giovanoli D. | SUI | 2.32.93 |
| 3. Bruggmann E. | SUI | 2.33.36 |

**Méribel**

| | | |
|---|---|---|
| 1. Killy J.-C. | FRA | 2.46.01 |
| 2. Mauduit G. | FRA | 2.46.05 |
| 3. Périllat G. | FRA | 2.49.07 |

**Hindelang**

| | | |
|---|---|---|
| 1. Bruggmann E. | SUI | 3.49.56 |
| 2. Killy J.-C. | FRA | 3.51.39 |
| 3. Giovanoli D. | SUI | 3.51.87 |

**Adelboden**
1. Killy J.-C. FRA 3.02.61
2. Bruggmann E. SUI 3.04.16
3. Kälin S. SUI 3.05.48

**Grenoble (JO)**
1. Killy J.-C. FRA 3.29.28
2. Favre W. SUI 3.31.50
3. Messner H. AUT 3.31.83

**Rossland**
1. Huber H. AUT 3.07.61
2. Tritscher R. AUT 3.07.71
3. Périllat G. FRA 3.08.39

**Heavenly Valley**
1. Huber H. AUT 2.53.58
2. Mauduit G. FRA 2.54.49
3. Tritscher R. AUT 2.54.53

### SLALOM

**Oslo**
1. Russel P. FRA 1.47.35
2. Giovanoli D. SUI 1.47.50
3. Mjön H. NOR 1.47.89

**Kranjska Gora**
1. Russel P. FRA 1.47.41
2. Digruber F. AUT 1.48.32
3. Kälin S. SUI 1.49.87

**Wengen**
1. Giovanoli D. SUI 1.56.10
2. Mjön H. NOR 1.56.16
3. Matt A. AUT 1.56.95

**Kitzbühel**
1. Giovanoli D. SUI 2.03.22
2. Matt A. AUT 2.03.40
3. Killy J.-C. FRA 2.05.57

**Grenoble (JO)**
1. Killy J.-C. FRA 1.39.73
2. Huber H. AUT 1.39.82
3. Matt A. AUT 1.40.09

**Aspen**
1. Kidd B. USA 2.06.18
2. Huber H. AUT 2.06.28
3. Matt A. AUT 2.06.56

**Rossland**
1. Killy J.-C. FRA 1.42.85
2. Augert J.-P. FRA 1.43.12
3. Chaffee F. USA 1.43.38

**Heavenly Valley**
1. Sabich S. USA 1.45.93
2. Huber H. AUT 1.46.32
3. Chaffee F. USA 1.46.77

## WOMEN 1967/68

### DOWNHILL

**Badgastein**
1. Pall O. AUT 2.02.40
2. Haas C. AUT 2.02.66
3. Galica D. GBR 2.03.87

**Saint-Gervais**
1. Mir I. FRA 2.00.35
2. Famose A. FRA 2.01.50
3. Haas C. AUT 2.02.44

**Grenoble (JO)**
1. Pall O. AUT 1.40.87
2. Mir I. FRA 1.41.33
3. Haas C. AUT 1.41.41

**Chamonix (AK)**
1. Greene N. CAN 2.05.61
2. Haas C. AUT 2.05.70
3. Galica D. GBR 2.08.52

**Abetone**
1. Mir I. FRA 1.28.69
2. Famose A. FRA 1.30.71
3. Steurer F. FRA 1.31.38
   Macchi F. FRA 1.31.38

**Aspen**
1. Greene N. CAN 1.33.29
2. Pall O. AUT 1.34.17
3. Goitschel M. FRA 1.35.06

### GIANT SLALOM

**Oberstaufen**
1. Bochatay F. SUI 1.27.24
2. Steurer F. FRA 1.28.33
3. Greene N. CAN 1.28.76

**Grindelwald**
1. Greene N. CAN 1.23.29
2. Goitschel M. FRA 1.23.89
3. Bochatay F. SUI 1.24.13

**Grenoble (JO)**
1. Greene N. CAN 1.51.97
2. Famose A. FRA 1.54.61
3. Bochatay F. SUI 1.54.74

**Oslo**
1. Bochatay F. SUI 1.25.70
2. Mir I. FRA 1.25.73
3. Cutter K. USA 1.25.95

**Aspen**
1. Greene N. CAN 1.26.02
2. Goitschel M. FRA 1.27.69
3. Mittermaier R. BRD 1.29.07

**Rossland**
1. Greene N. CAN 1.26.85
2. Steurer F. FRA 1.28.41
3. Gabl G. AUT 1.29.41

**Heavenly Valley**
1. Gabl G. AUT 1.01.39
2. Steurer F. FRA 1.01.81
3. Mir I. FRA 1.02.72

### SLALOM

**Oberstaufen**
1. Goitschel M. FRA 1.19.62
2. Gabl G. AUT 1.19.84
3. Green N. CAN 1.20.28

**Grindelwald**
1. Gabl G. AUT 1.16.83
2. Mir I. FRA 1.17.79
3. Goitschel M. FRA 1.17.84

**Badgastein**
1. Steurer F. FRA 1.31.25
2. Goitschel M. FRA 1.32.34
3. Gabl G. AUT 1.32.45

**Saint-Gervais**
1. Bochatay F. FRA 1.18.93
2. Steurer F. FRA 1.19.00
3. Cutter K. USA 1.19.07

**Grenoble (JO)**
1. Goitschel M. FRA 1.25.86
2. Greene N. CAN 1.26.15
3. Famose A. FRA 1.27.89

**Oslo**
1. Cutter K. USA 1.33.41
2. Mir I. FRA 1.33.95
3. Allen W. USA 1.35.06

**Abetone**
1. Steurer F. FRA 1.23.86
2. Famose A. FRA 1.26.86
3. Lafforgue B. FRA 1.27.78

**Aspen**
1. Greene N. CAN 1.28.48
2. Gabl G. AUT 1.28.87
3. Cutter K. USA 1.28.92

**Rossland**
1. Goitschel M. FRA 1.30.91
2. Bochatay F. SUI 1.31.96
3. Cutter K. USA 1.32.95

**Heavenly Valley**
1. Gabl G. AUT 1.48.23
2. Greene N. CAN 1.48.84
3. Nagel J. USA 1.48.56

## MEN 1968/69

### DOWNHILL

**Wengen**
1. Schranz K. AUT 3.01.60
2. Messner H. AUT 3.01.99
3. Cordin K. AUT 3.03.03

**Megève**
1. Duvillard H. FRA 2.14.75
2. Messner H. AUT 2.16.44
3. Matt A. AUT 2.16.80

**Kitzbühel**
1. Schranz K. AUT 2.18.80
2. Dätwyler J.-D. SUI 2.19.41
3. Duvillard H. FRA 2.21.28
   Cordin K. AUT 2.21.28

**St. Anton (AK)**
1. Schranz K. AUT 2.27.48
2. Messner H. AUT 2.27.77
3. Vogler F. BRD 2.28.32

**Cortina**
1. Minsch J. SUI 2.17.53
2. Augert J.-P. FRA 2.17.67
3. Rohr H.-P. SUI 2.18.01

**Val Gardena**
1. Dätwyler J.-D. SUI 2.07.75
2. Duvillard H. FRA 2.08.54
3. Sailer R. AUT 2.08.68

### GIANT SLALOM

**Adelboden**
1. Augert J.-N. FRA 3.20.18
2. Augert J.-P. FRA 3.21.44
3. Schranz K. AUT 3.21.60

**Val d'Isère**
1. Schranz K. AUT 3.17.73
2. Orcel B. FRA 3.17.83
3. Duvillard H. FRA 3.18.00

**Åre**
1. Augert J.-N. FRA 3.35.89
2. Tischhauser J. SUI 3.38.30
3. Penz A. FRA 3.40.61

**Kranjska Gora**
1. Tritscher R. AUT 2.52.33
2. Matt A. AUT 2.52.43
3. Digruber F. AUT 2.53.30

**Squaw Valley**
1. Tritscher R. AUT 2.19.56
2. Tischhauser J. SUI 2.19.67
3. Messner H. AUT 2.19.74

**Mont-Sainte-Anne**
1. Schranz K. AUT 3.29.27
2. Giovanoli D. SUI 3.30.88
3. Tischhauser J. SUI 3.31.62

**Waterville Valley**
1. Giovanoli D. SUI 2.36.72
2. Schranz K. AUT 2.36.90
3. Tischhauser J. SUI 2.37.73

### SLALOM

**Berchtesgaden**
1. Matt A. AUT 1.48.31
2. Schranz K. AUT 1.50.34
3. Russel P. FRA 1.50.83

**Wengen**
1. Tritscher R. AUT 2.01.58
2. Sabich S. USA 2.02.01
3. Frei P. SUI 2.02.15

**Megêve**
1. Penz A. FRA 2.06.10
2. Huber H. AUT 2.08.20
3. Sabich S. USA 2.08.25

**Kitzbühel**
1. Russel P. FRA 2.00.37
2. Huber H. AUT 2.00.39
3. Giovanoli D. SUI 2.00.64

**Åre**
1. Russel P. FRA 1.54.50
2. Augert J.-N. FRA 1.55.41
3. Matt A. AUT 1.56.11

**Kranjska-Gora**
1. Bruggmann E. SUI 1.48.56
2. Penz A. FRA 1.50.18
3. Huber H. AUT 1.50.56

**Squaw Valley**
1. Kidd W. USA 1.36.55
2. Penz A. FRA 1.36.95
3. Russel P. FRA 1.37.17

**Mont-Sainte-Anne**
1. Matt A. AUT 1.33.50
2. Augert J.-N. FRA 1.34.49
3. Kidd W. USA 1.34.60

**Waterville Valley**
1. Augert J.-N. FRA 1.24.10
2. Huber H. AUT 1.24.11
3. Russel P. FRA 1.24.34

## WOMEN 1968/69

### DOWNHILL

**Grindelwald**
1. Drexel W. AUT 2.04.68
2. Mittermaier R. BRD 2.06.69
3. Mir I. FRA 2.07.14

**Schruns-Montafon**
1. Drexel W. AUT 2.16.76
2. Steurer F. AUT 2.18.01
3. Famose A. FRA 2.18.07

**Saint-Gervais**
1. Mir I. FRA 1.55.27
2. Famose A. FRA 1.55.48
   Pröll A.-M. AUT 1.55.48

**St. Anton (AK)**
1. Pall O. AUT 1.37.79
2. Mir I. FRA 1.38.23
3. Drexel W. AUT 1.38.30

### GIANT SLALOM

**Oberstaufen**
1. Cutter K. USA 1.33.19
2. Pall O. AUT 1.33.60
   Gabl G. AUT 1.33.60

**Val d'Isère**
1. Macchi F. FRA 1.35.17
2. Mittermaier R. BRD 1.36.74
3. Famose A. FRA 1.36.81

**Vipiteno**
1. Jacot M. FRA 1.15.27
2. Cochran M. USA 1.15.48
3. Lafforgue I. FRA 1.15.82

**Vysoke Tatry**
1. Gabl G. AUT 1.14.24
2. Cochran M. USA 1.14.99
3. Steurer F. FRA 1.15.47

**Squaw Valley**
1. Steurer F. FRA 1.12.43
2. Cochran M. USA 1.12.80
3. Rauter B. AUT 1.13.43

**Mont-Sainte-Anne**
1. Jacot M. FRA 1.20.23
2. Lafforgue I. FRA 1.20.59
3. Cochran M. USA 1.20.70

**Waterville Valley**
1. Rauter B. AUT 1.11.98
2. Budge K. USA 1.11.99
   Cochran M. USA 1.11.99

### SLALOM

**Oberstaufen**
1. Gabl G. AUT 1.15.72
2. Nagel J. USA 1.16.51
3. Cochran M. USA 1.16.80

**Grindelwald**
1. Gabl G. AUT 1.27.56
2. Famose A. FRA 1.29.15
3. Cutter K. USA 1.29.54

**Schruns-Montafon**
1. Mittermaier R. BRD 1.45.90
2. Gabl G. AUT 1.46.23
3. Cutter K. USA 1.46.53

**Saint-Gervais**
1. Lafforgue I. FRA 1.19.31
2. Famose A. FRA 1.19.58
3. Nagel J. USA 1.19.93

**Vipiteno**
1. Nagel J. USA 1.36.34
2. Nagel C. USA 1.38.57
3. Steurer F. FRA 1.39.27

**Vysoke Tatry**
1. Gabl G. AUT 1.29.27
2. Cutter K. USA 1.29.82
3. Lafforgue I. FRA 1.30.12

**Squaw Valley**
1. Rauter B. AUT 1.29.16
2. Lafforgue I. FRA 1.29.95
3. Nagel J. USA 1.30.03

**Mont-Sainte-Anne**
1. Cutter K. USA 1.09.80
2. Lafforgue I. FRA 1.09.81
3. Steurer F. FRA 1.09.94

**Waterville Valley**
1. Cutter K. USA 1.18.18
2. Mittermaier R. BRD 1.18.68
3. Nagel J. USA 1.18.69

## MEN 1969/70

### DOWNHILL

**Val d'Isère**
1. Milne M. AUS 2.13.79
2. Dätwyler J.-D. SUI 2.14.69
3. Schranz K. AUT 2.15.02

**Wengen**
1. Duvillard H. FRA 1.50.21
2. Cordin K. AUT 1.50.91
3. Messner H. AUT 1.51.13

**Megêve**
1. Schranz K. AUT 2.12.80
2. Messner H. AUT 2.13.83
3. Duvillard H. FRA 2.14.35

**Jackson Hole**
1. Cordin K. AUT 2.00.52
2. Orcel B. FRA 2.01.39
3. Duvillard J.-D. FRA 2.01.91

**Garmisch-Part. (AK)**
1. Schranz K. AUT 1.58.08
2. Cordin K. AUT 1.58.90
3. Vogler F. BRD 1.59.19

**Val Gardena**
1. Russi B. SUI 2.24.57
2. Cordin K. AUT 2.24.79
3. Milne M. AUS 2.25.09

### GIANT SLALOM

**Val d'Isère**
1. Thoeni G. ITA 3.01.10
2. Russel P. FRA 3.02.21
3. Augert J.-N. FRA 3.02.67

**Lienz**
1. Russel P. FRA 3.21.09
2. Thoeni G. ITA 3.21.53
3. Tischhauser J. SUI 3.23.41

**Adelboden**
1. Schranz K. AUT 3.22.76
2. Heckelmiller S. BRD 3.23.73
3. Giovanoli D. SUI 3.23.84

**Kitzbühel**
1. Giovanoli D. SUI 3.20.67
2. Bachleda A. POL 3.22.74
3. Schranz K. AUT 3.22.88

**Kranjska Gora**
1. Giovanoli D. SUI 3.16.64
2. Russel P. FRA 3.17.41
3. Mauduit G. FRA 3.18.60

**Vancouver**
1. Penz A. FRA 3.04.47
2. Bleiner W. AUT 3.04.49
3. Russel P. FRA 3.06.37

**Heavenly Valley**
1. Russel P. FRA 3.55.58
2. Bleiner W. AUT 3.56.30
3. Schranz K. AUT 3.56.73

**Voss**
1. Bleiner W. AUT 3.19.32
2. Augert J.-N. FRA 3.19.90
3. Schranz K. AUT 3.19.92

**Madonna di Campiglio**
1. Thoeni G. ITA 3.13.75
2. Bruggmann E. SUI 3.14.74
3. Augert J.-N. FRA 3.15.20

**Val Gardena (CDM)**
1. Schranz K. AUT 4.19.19
2. Bleiner W. AUT 4.19.58
3. Giovanoli D. SUI 4.21.15

**Madonna di Campiglio**
1. Thoeni G. ITA 3.28.83
2. Giovanoli D. SUI 3.30.15
3. Augert J.-N. FRA 3.31.11

### SLALOM

**Lienz**
1. Augert J.-N. FRA 1.41.76
2. Huber H. AUT 1.43.56
3. Sabich S. USA 1.45.16

**Hindelang**
1. Thoeni G. ITA 1.37.88
2. Russel P. FRA 1.38.74
3. Augert J.-N. FRA 1.39.19

**Wengen**
1. Russel P. FRA 1.49.55
2. Giovanoli D. SUI 1.50.56
3. Bréchu H. FRA 1.50.85

**Kitzbühel**
1. Russel P. FRA 1.50.77
2. Thoeni G. ITA 1.51.27
3. Augert J.-N. FRA 1.52.88

**Jackson Hole**
1. Penz A. FRA 1.44.88
2. Bréchu H. FRA 1.54.97
3. Thoeni G. ITA 1.46.64

**Vancouver**
1. Penz A. FRA 2.07.73
2. Thoeni G. ITA 2.07.78
3. Russel P. FRA 2.07.97

**Heavenly Valley**
1. Penz A. FRA 1.34.16
2. Chaffee F. USA 1.34.96
3. Messner H. AUT 1.35.44

**Voss**
1. Russel P. FRA 1.20.23
2. Augert J.-N. FRA 1.21.17
3. Bréchu H. FRA 1.21.80

**Megève**
1. Russel P. FRA 1.25.85
2. Penz A. FRA 1.26.93
3. Bréchu H. FRA 1.27.30

**Madonna di Campiglio**
1. Bréchu H. FRA 1.41.04
2. Thoeni G. ITA 1.41.52
3. Giovanoli D. SUI 1.42.20

**Val Gardena (CDM)**
1. Augert J.-N. FRA 1.39.47
2. Russel P. FRA 1.39.51
3. Kidd B. USA 1.39.53

## WOMEN 1969/70

### DOWNHILL

**Grindelwald**
1. Mir I. FRA 1.50.62
2. Famose A. FRA 1.51.11
3. Steurer F. FRA 1.51.25

**Badgastein**
1. Mir I. FRA 1.44.02
2. Steurer F. FRA 1.45.78
3. Jacot M. FRA 1.46.07

**Val Gardena (CDM)**
1. Zryd A. SUI 1.58.34
2. Mir I. FRA 1.58.84
3. Proell A. AUT 2.00.43

**Jackson Hole**
1. Mir I. FRA 1.57.86
2. Famose A. FRA 1.59.36
3. Jacot M. FRA 1.59.40

**Garmisch**
1. Macchi F. FRA 1.08.62
2. Drexel W. AUT 1.08.65
3. Jacot M. FRA 1.09.46

### GIANT SLALOM

**Val d'Isère**
1. Macchi F. FRA 1.49.81
2. Cochran B. USA 1.50.55
3. Jacot M. FRA 1.50.79

**Lienz**
1. Nagel J. USA 1.26.97
2. Jacot M. FRA 1.27.34
3. Cochran B. USA 1.28.39

**Oberstaufen**
1. Jacot M. FRA 1.38.86
2. Macchi F. FRA 1.39.05
3. Cochran B. USA 1.40.18

**Maribor**
1. Proell A. AUT 1.24.34
2. Steurer F. FRA 1.24.49
3. Cochran B. USA 1.24.77

**Saint-Gervais**
1. Macchi F. FRA 1.36.41
2. Proell A. AUT 1.38.12
3. Nagel J. USA 1.38.46

**Abetone**
1. Lafforgue B. FRA 1.46.05
2. Jeang M.-F. FRA 1.47.62
3. Nagel J. USA 1.47.92

**Val Gardena (CDM)**
1. Clifford B. CAN 1.20.46
2. Lafforgue I. FRA 1.20.53
3. Macchi F. FRA 1.20.60

**Vancouver**
1. Jacot M. FRA 1.38.84
2. Cochran B. USA 1.39.21
3. Nagel J. USA 1.39.98

**Voss**
1. Lafforgue I. FRA 1.19.43
2. Drexel W. AUT 1.19.56
3. Proell A. AUT 1.19.92

### SLALOM

**Val d'Isère**
1. Jacot M. FRA 1.12.80
2. Cochran M. USA 1.13.10
3. Steurer F. FRA 1.13.25

**Lienz**
1. Nagel J. USA 1.20.28
2. Lafforgue I. FRA 1.20.44
3. Rauter B. AUT 1.20.56

**Oberstaufen**
1. Rauter B. AUT 1.31.11
2. Mir I. FRA 1.41.53
3. Macchi F. FRA 1.33.78

**Grindelwald**
1. Jacot M. FRA 1.37.49
2. Clifford B. CAN 1.37.67
3. Cochran M. USA 1.37.75

**Badgastein**
1. Lafforgue I. FRA 1.27.81
2. Clifford B. CAN 1.29.22
3. Mathieux D. FRA 1.29.70

**Maribor**
1. Cochran B. USA 1.34.41
2. Lafforgue B. FRA 1.35.81
3. Rauter B. AUT 1.36.20

**Saint-Gervais**
1. Cutter K. USA 1.32.58
2. Lafforgue I. FRA 1.33.04
3. Steurer F. FRA 1.33.17

**Abetone**
1. Lafforgue I. FRA 1.18.15
2. Nagel J. USA 1.19.10
3. Mathieux D. FRA 1.19.17

**Val Gardena (CHM)**
1. Lafforgue I. FRA 1.40.44
2. Cochran B. USA 1.42.15
3. Jacot M. FRA 1.42.20

**Jackson Hole**
1. Lafforgue I. FRA 1.39.84
2. Cochran B. USA 1.41.41
3. Lafforgue B. FRA 1.41.99

**Vancouver**
1. Lafforgue I. FRA 1.53.78
2. Lafforgue B. FRA 1.54.25
3. Clifford B. CAN 1.53.31

**Voss**
1. Mittermaier R. BRD 1.07.97
2. Steurer F. FRA 1.08.12
3. Lafforgue B. FRA 1.08.59

## MEN 1970/71

### DOWNHILL

**Sestrière**
1. Duvillard H. FRA 1.48.30
2. Orcel B. FRA 1.49.58
3. Schranz K. AUT 1.49.72

**Val d'Isère**
1. Cordin K. AUT 2.09.08
2. Orcel B. FRA 2.09.62
3. Schranz K. AUT 2.09.83

**St. Moritz**
1. Tresch W. SUI 1.55.12
2. Russi B. SUI 1.55.20
3. Sprecher A. SUI 1.55.61

**Megève I**
1. Dätwyler J.-D. SUI 2.11.70
2. Orcel B. FRA 2.12.21
3. Tresch W. SUI 2.12.54

**Megève II**
1. Russi B. SUI 2.07.93
2. Vogler F. BRD 2.08.49
Dätwyler M. SUI 2.08.53

**Sugarloaf I**
1. Russi B. SUI 1.31.41
2. Duvillard H. FRA 1.31.95
3. Anzi S. ITA 1.31.98

**Sugarloaf II**
1. Anzi S. ITA 1.32.05
2. Cordin K. AUT 1.32.09
3. Thoeni G. ITA 1.32.13

### GIANT SLALOM

**Val d'Isere**
1. Russel P. FRA 2.34.65
2. Augert J.-N. FRA 2.35.29
3. Thoeni G. ITA 2.36.72

**Berchtesgaden**
1. Bruggmann E. SUI 2.40.91
2. Russel P. FRA 2.41.80
3. Zwilling D. AUT 2.42.40

**Madonna di Campiglio**
1. Duvillard H. FRA 3.35.27
2. Russel P. FRA 3.36.12
3. Thoeni G. ITA 3.36.72

**Adelboden**
1. Russel P. FRA 2.23.47
2. Thoeni G. ITA 2.24.95
3. Duvillard H. FRA 2.25.43

**Mont-Sainte-Anne**
1. Russi B. SUI 4.42.18
2. Bruggmann E. SUI 4.42.24
3. Bleiner W. AUT 4.42.35

**Sugarloaf**
1. Thoeni G. ITA 2.57.59
2. Bruggmann E. SUI 2.57.81
3. Duvillard H. FRA 3.00.00

**Heavenly Valley**
1. Thoeni G. ITA 1.36.71
2. Neureuther C. BRD 1.38.90
3. Duvillard H. FRA 1.39.80

**Åre**
1. Zwilling D. AUT 2.55.95
2. Heckelmiller S. BRD 2.57.27
3. Russel P. FRA 2.57.43

### SLALOM

**Berchtesgaden**
1. Augert J.-N. FRA 1.59.55
2. Messner H. AUT 2.02.01
3. Rieger M. BRD 2.02.78

**Madonna di Campiglio**
1. Thoeni G. ITA 1.35.15
2. Augert J.-N. FRA 1.36.26
3. Russel P. FRA 1.36.63

**St. Moritz**
1. Palmer T. USA 1.28.27
2. Rofner H. AUT 1.29.01
3. Thoeni G. ITA 1.29.27

**Kitzbühel**
1. Augert J.-N. FRA 1.48.17
2. Penz A. FRA 1.48.51
3. Rofner H. AUT 1.49.04

**Megève**
1. Augert J.-N. FRA 1.36.70
2. Thoeni G. ITA 1.37.95
3. Neureuther C. BRD 1.38.33

**Mürren (AK)**
1. Augert J.-N. FRA 1.40.30
2. Palmer T. USA 1.40.78
3. Russel P. FRA 1.42.61

**Mont-Saint-Anne**
1. Russel P. FRA 1.39.95
2. Thoeni G. ITA 1.40.05
3. Penz A. FRA 1.40.47

**Heavenly Valley**
1. Thoeni G. ITA 1.44.89
2. Neureuther C. BRD 1.46.56
3. Palmer T. USA 1.46.62

**Åre**
1. Augert J.-N. FRA 1.40.67
2. Thoeni G. ITA 1.41.33
3. Bruggmann E. SUI 1.42.19

## WOMEN 1970/71

### DOWNHILL

**Bardonecchia**
1. Macchi F. FRA 1.23.84
2. Proell A. AUT 1.25.58
3. Mir I. FRA 1.25.74

**Val d'Isére**
1. Mir I. FRA 1.29.44
2. Drexel W. AUT 1.29.92
3. Jacot M. FRA 1.30.08

**Schruns**
1. Jacot M. FRA 2.01.54
2. Macchi F. FRA 2.02.17
3. Drexel W. AUT 2.02.34

**Sugarloaf II**
1. Proell A. AUT 1.23.04
2. Rouvier J. FRA 1.23.24
3. Famose A. FRA 1.23.44

**Pra-Loup**
1. Drexel W. AUT 1.53.52
2. Proell A. AUT 1.53.89
3. Rouvier J. FRA 1.53.95

**Sugarloaf I**
1. Proell A. AUT 1.20.27
2. Rouvier J. FRA 1.20.49
3. Mir I. FRA 1.20.67

### GIANT SLALOM

**Maribor**
1. Macchi F. FRA 1.32.32
2. Gabl G. AUT 1.32.81
3. Proell A. AUT 1.33.14

**Oberstaufen**
1. Jacot M. FRA 1.29.83
2. Lafforgue B. FRA 1.30.73
3. Périllat J. FRA 1.31.34

**Sugarloaf**
1. Jacot M. FRA 1.37.26
2. Proell A. AUT 1.37.52
3. Mittermaier R. BRD 1.37.90

**Heavenly Valley**
1. Cochran B. USA 1.09.44
2. Budge K. USA 1.10.08
3. Mir I. FRA 1.11.44

**Abetone I**
1. Proell A. AUT 1.36.35
2. Jacot M. FRA 1.38.10
3. Macchi F. FRA 1.38.33

**Abetone II**
1. Proell A. AUT 1.32.37
2. Macchi F. FRA 1.35.33
3. Gabl G. AUT 1.36.39

**Åre**
1. Proell A. AUT 1.19.17
2. Cochran M. USA 1.21.13
3. Gabl G. AUT 1.21.49

**Mont-Sainte-Anne**
1. Mir I. FRA 1.44.17
2. Rouvier J. FRA 1.44.13
3. Macchi F. FRA 1.45.03

### SLALOM

**Val d'Isère**
1. Clifford B. CAN 1.11.63
2. Steurer F. FRA 1.12.22
3. Drexel W. AUT 1.12.43

**Maribor**
1. Proell A. AUT 1.39.95
2. Rauter B. AUT 1.41.01
3. Cochran USA 1.41.23

**Oberstaufen**
1. Jacot M. FRA 1.36.25
2. Gabl G. AUT 1.38.86
3. Périllat J. FRA 1.39.91

**Grindelwald**
1. Lafforgue B. FRA 1.27.52
2. Jacot M. FRA 1.28.27
3. Debernard D. FRA 1.28.66

**Heavenly Valley**
1. Cochran B. USA 1.36.37
2. Clifford B. CAN 1.37.28
3. Proell A. AUT 1.38.03

**Mürren (AK)**
1. Lafforgue B. FRA 1.39.09
2. Steurer F. FRA 1.39.27
3. Debernard D. FRA 1.40.17

**Schruns**
1. Clifford B. CAN 1.33.50
2. Lafforgue B. FRA 1.34.03
3. Drexel W. AUT 1.34.04

**Saint Gervais**
1. Proell A. AUT 1.31.90
2. Cochran B. USA 1.33.09
3. Mittermaier R. BRD 1.33.15

**Mont-Saint-Anne**
1. Cochran M. USA 1.22.20
2. Cochran B. USA 1.23.45
3. Drexel W. AUT 1.23.97

## MEN 1971/72

### DOWNHILL

**St. Moritz**
1. Russi B. SUI 1.53.93
2. Messner H. AUT 1.53.98
3. Tresch W. SUI 1.54.63

**Val d'Isère**
1. Schranz K. AUT 2.06.58
2. Messner H. AUT 2.06.87
3. Daetwyler M. SUI 2.06.90

**Kitzbühel I**
1. Schranz K. AUT 2.23.70
2. Duvillard H. FRA 2.23.95
3. Russi B. SUI 2.24.85

**Kitzbühel II**
1. Schranz K. AUT 2.24.36
2. Duvillard H. FRA 2.24.55
3. Messner H. AUT 2.24.86

**Crystal Mountain I**
1. Russi B. SUI 1.25.97
2. Lafferty M. USA 1.26.84
3. Dätwyler J.-D. SUI 1.26.92

**Crystal Mountain II**
1. Vogler F. BRD 1.26.36
2. Russi B. SUI 1.27.13
3. Dätwyler J.-D. SUI 1.27.21

**Val Gardena**
1. Russi B. SUI 2.06.06
2. Berthod R. SUI 2.07.23
3. Lafferty M. USA 2.07.57

### GIANT SLALOM

**Val d'Isère**
1. Haker E. NOR 2.59.55
2. Augert J.-N. FRA 2.59.90
3. Duvillard H. FRA 3.00.89

**Berchtesgaden**
1. Rossat-M. R. FRA 2.07.65
2. Thoeni G. ITA 2.07.93
3. Tresch W. SUI 2.08.49

**Adelboden**
1. Mattle W. SUI 3.00.91
2. Rösti A. SUI 3.00.96
3. Thoeni G. ITA 3.01.45

**Banff**
1. Haker E. NOR 2.40.95
2. Heckelmiller S. BRD 2.42.25
3. Schmalzl H. ITA 2.42.29

**Heavenly Valley**
1. Thoeni G. ITA 2.41.30
2. Duvillard H. FRA 2.41.94
3. Zwilling D. AUT 2.42.10

**Val Gardena**
1. Bruggmann E. SUI 3.41.61
2. Tritscher R. AUT 3.44.82
3. Thoeni R. ITA 3.45.06

**Pra-Loup**
1. Bruggmann E. SUI 2.27.13
2. Thoeni G. ITA 2.27.91
3. Rossat-M. R. FRA 2.28.23

### SLALOM

**Sestrière**
1. Palmer T. USA 1.55.30
2. Augert J.-N. FRA 1.55.84
3. Rofner H. AUT 1.56.15

**Berchtesgaden**
1. Duvillard H. FRA 1.39.36
2. Rieger M. BRD 1.39.79
3. Bachleda A. POL 1.39.89

**Kitzbühel**
1. Augert J.-N. FRA 1.50.98
2. Bruggmann E. SUI 1.52.33
3. Bachleda A. POL 1.53.17

**Wengen**
1. Augert J.-N. FRA 1.37.92
2. Thoeni G. ITA 1.38.04
3. Cochran B. USA 1.38.69

**Banff**
1. Bachleda A. POL 1.44.45
2. Augert J.-N. FRA 1.45.27
3. Thoeni G. ITA 1.45.58

**Madonna di Campiglio**
1. Thoeni R. ITA 1.44.07
2. Penz A. FRA 1.45.66
3. Bachleda A. POL 1.45.77

**Pra-Loup**
1. Thoeni R. ITA 1.28.44
2. Thoeni G. ITA 1.29.39
3. Bruggmann E. SUI 1.29.44

## WOMEN 1971/72

### DOWNHILL

**St. Moritz**
1. Proell A. AUT 1.46.60
2. Macchi F. FRA 1.47.69
3. Rouvier J. FRA 1.48.13

**Val d'Isère**
1. Rouvier J. FRA 1.26.89
2. Proell A. AUT 1.27.26
3. Macchi F. FRA 1.28.17

**Sestrières**
1. Proell A. AUT 1.44.58
2. Rouvier J. FRA 1.45.28
3. Macchi F. FRA 1.45.45

**Badgastein**
1. Proell A. AUT 1.30.59
2. Drexel W. AUT 1.32.65
3. Mir I. FRA 1.32.99

**Grindelwald**
1. Proell A. AUT 1.53.51
2. Nadig M.-T. SUI 1.54.07
3. Mir I. FRA 1.54.10

**Crystal Mountain I**
1. Proell A. AUT 1.32.82
2. Nadig M.-T. SUI 1.33.09
Drexel W. AUT 1.33.09

**Crystal Mountain II**
1. Drexel W. AUT 1.31.33
2. Proell A. AUT 1.31.48
3. Nadig M.-T. SUI 1.31.65

### GIANT SLALOM

**Oberstaufen**
1. Macchi F. FRA 1.38.27
2. Proell A. AUT 1.38.97
3. Cochran M. USA 1.40.55

**Maribor**
1. Macchi F. FRA 2.11.69
2. Jacot M. FRA 2.12.52
3. Proell A. AUT 2.13.57

**Saint-Gervais**
1. Proell A. AUT 3.12.03
2. Kaserer M. AUT 3.14.80
3. Nadig M.-T. SUI 3.16.13

**Banff**
1. Proell A. AUT 1.07.42
2. Drexel W. AUT 1.08.49
3. Kaserer M. AUT 1.08.69

**Heavenly Valley**
1. Proell A. AUT 1.18.96
2. Mittermaier R. BRD 1.19.26
3. Lafforgue G. FRA 1.19.31

**Pra-Loup I**
1. Debernard D. FRA 1.21.97
2. Kaserer M. AUT 1.22.10
3. Nadig M.-T. SUI 1.22.20

**Pra-Loup II**
1. Lafforgue B. FRA 1.23.16
2. Proell A. AUT 1.23.79
3. Kaserer M. AUT 1.24.04

### SLALOM

**Sestrière**
1. Macchi F. FRA 1.43.30
2. Mittermaier R. BRD 1.44.98
3. Kaserer M. AUT 1.45.34

**Grindelwald**
1. Lafforgue B. FRA 1.29.50
2. Kaserer M. AUT 1.30.89
3. Cochran B. USA 1.30.99

**Banff**
1. Lafforgue B. FRA 1.27.83
2. Cochran B. USA 1.28.09
3. Steurer F. FRA 1:28.17

**Oberstaufen**
1. Macchi F. FRA 1.18.47
2. Mittermaier R. BRD 1.18.91
3. Debernard D. FRA 1.19.13

**Badgastein**
1. Lafforgue B. FRA 1.13.96
2. Macchi F. FRA 1.14.11
3. Proell A. AUT 1.14.22

**Heavenly Valley**
1. Steurer F. FRA 1.30.07
2. Jacot M. FRA 1.13.15
3. Cochran M. USA 1.31.18

**Pra-Loup**
1. Debernard D. FRA 1.27.36
2. Behr P. BRD 1.27.54
3. Mittermaier R. BRD 1.27.62

## MEN 1972/73

### DOWNHILL

**Val d'Isère**
1. Tritscher R. AUT 2.11.89
2. Zwilling D. AUT 2.12.03
3. Varallo M. ITA 2.12.66

**Val Gardena**
1. Collombin R. SUI 2.05.67
2. Cordin K. AUT 2.06.13
3. Zwilling D. AUT 2.06.15

**Garmisch-Partenk. I**
1. Collombin R. SUI 1.47.38
2. Roux P. SUI 1.48.05
Varallo M. ITA 1.48.05

**Garmisch-Partenk. II**
1. Collombin R. SUI 1.46.30
2. Varallo M. ITA 1.46.53
3. Russi B. SUI 1.47.13

**Grindelwald**
1. Russi B. SUI 2.07.78
2. Collombin R. SUI 2.07.88
3. Tritscher R. AUT 2.08.33

**Kitzbühel**
1. Collombin R. SUI 2.13.32
2. Russi B. SUI 2.13.49
3. Cochran B. USA 2.14.38

**St. Anton**
1. Russi B. SUI 2.25.66
2. Klammer F. AUT 2.27.75
3. Roux P. SUI 2.27.95

**St. Moritz**
1. Grissmann W. AUT 2.06.06
2. Walcher J. AUT 2.07.68
3. Klammer F. AUT 2.08.18

### GIANT SLALOM

**Val d'Isère**
1. Gros P. ITA 3.27.89
2. Haaker E. NOR 3.28.07
3. Schmalzl E. ITA 3.29.73

**Madonna di Campiglio**
1. Zwilling D. AUT 3.41.99
2. Rösti A. SUI 3.42.52
3. Schmalzl E. ITA 3.44.31

**Adelboden**
1. Thoeni G. ITA 2.15.63
2. Hinterseer H. AUT 2.16.01
3. Haaker E. NOR 2.16.39

**Megêve**
1. Duvillard H. FRA 2.54.15
2. Hinterseer H. AUT 2.54.37
3. Thoeni G. ITA 2.55.70

**Québec**
1. Rieger M. BRD 3.13.52
2. Hinterseer H. AUT 3.13.63
3. Klammer F. AUT 3.14.51

**Anchorage**
1. Hinterseer H. AUT 3.45.37
2. Rösti A. SUI 3.47.75
3. Pechtl J. AUT 3.47.89

**Naeba**
1. Haaker E. NOR 3.33.10
2. Hinterseer H. AUT 3.33.35
3. Rösti A. SUI 3.35.57

**Heavenly Valley**
1. Cochran B. USA 3.08.27
2. Stricker E. ITA 3.08.37
3. Augert J.-N. FRA 3.08.81

### SLALOM

**Madonna di Campiglio**
1. Gros P. ITA 1.40.41
2. Thoeni G. ITA 1.40.48
3. Neureuther C. BRD 1.40.68

**Wengen**
1. Neureuther C. BRD 1.32.38
2. Tresch W. SUI 1.33.35
3. Perrot C. FRA 1.33.40

**Megêve**
1. Neureuther C. BRD 1.51.55
2. Thoeni G. ITA 1.52.56
3. Tresch W. SUI 1.52.70

**Kitzbühel**
1. Augert J.-N. FRA 1.46.22
2. Thoeni G. ITA 1.47.07
3. Bachleda A. POL 1.47.56

**St. Anton**
1. Thoeni G. ITA 1.46.94
2. Neureuther C. BRD 1.47.54
3. Duvillard H. FRA 1.47.92

**Québec**
1. Thoeni G. ITA 1.38.59
2. Pegorari I. ITA 1.38.76
3. Neureuther C. BRD 1.38.83

**Naeba**
1. Augert J.-N. FRA 1.50.34
2. Neureuther C. BRD 1.52.24
3. Pegorari I. ITA 1.53.22

**Heavenly Valley**
1. Augert J.-N. FRA 1.46.02
2. Cochran B. USA 1.56.38
3. Pietrogiov T. ITA 1.47.36

## WOMEN 1972/73

### DOWNHILL

**Val d'Isère**
1. Proell A. AUT 1.27.94
2. Rouvier J. FRA 1.28.29
3. Lukasser I. AUT 1.30.24

**Saalbach**
1. Proell A. AUT 1.29.58
2. Rouvier J. FRA 1.32.20
3. Totschnig B. AUT 1.32.56

**Pfronten I**
1. Proell A. AUT 1.17.32
2. Kaserer M. AUT 1.18.68
3. Lukasser I. AUT 1.18.89

**Pfronten II**
1. Proell A. AUT 1.16.79
2. Lukasser I. AUT 1.17.97
3. Gfölner I. AUT 1.18.51

**Grindelwald**
1. Proell A. AUT 2.27.92
2. Drexel W. AUT 2.28.50
3. Totschnig B. AUT 2.33.25

**Chamonix**
1. Proell A. AUT 2.06.61
2. Drexel W. AUT 2.09.57
3. Rouvier J. FRA 2.11.12

**Schruns**
1. Proell A. AUT 1.36.19
2. Drexel W. AUT 1.37.03
3. Gfölner I. AUT 1.38.18

**St. Moritz**
1. Proell A. AUT 1.58.09
2. Gfölner I. AUT 2.00.46
3. Drexel W. AUT 2.01.35

### GIANT SLALOM

**Saalbach**
1. Proell A. AUT 1.17.17
2. Kaserer M. AUT 1.18.62
3. Wenzel H. LIE 1.19.65

**Saint Gervais**
1. Proell A. AUT 2.27.30
2. Kaserer M. AUT 2.28.86
3. Rouvier J. FRA 2.29.72

**Les Contamines**
1. Kaserer M. AUT 1.23.10
2. Treichl T. BRD 1.23.42
3. Cochran M. USA 1.23.88

**Abetone**
1. Kaserer M. AUT 1.44.64
2. Treichl T. BRD 1.45.11
3. Poulsen S. USA 1.45.81

**Québec**
1. Proell A. AUT 1.31.62
2. Zurbriggen B. SUI 1.31.64
3. Nadig M.-T. SUI 1.32.03

**Mt-Alyeska**
1. Zurbriggen B. SUI 1.23.21
2. Kaserer M. AUT 1.23.52
3. Kreiner K. CAN 1.24.21

**Naeba**
1. Cochran M. USA 1.36.83
2. Giordani C. ITA 1.37.23
3. Proell A. AUT 1.37.38

**Heavenly Valley**
1. Emonet P. FRA 1.41.86
2. Kaserer M. AUT 1.43.79
3. Rolland L. FRA 1.44.33

### SLALOM

**Val d'Isère**
1. Behr P. BRD 1.24.35
2. Chalvin D. FRA 1.25.71
3. Emonet P. FRA 1.26.15

**Maribor**
1. Emonet P. FRA 1.57.09
2. Behr P. BRD 1.57.80
3. Mittermaier R. BRD 1.58.42

**Grindelwald**
1. Kaserer M. AUT 1.19.06
2. Mittermaier R. BRD 1.19.51
3. Crawford J. CAN 1.19.79

**Chamonix**
1. Cochran M. USA 1.30.14
2. Mittermaier R. BRD 1.30.73
3. Kaserer M. AUT 1.32.37

**Schruns**
1. Mittermaier R. BRD 1.31.33
2. Emonet P. FRA 1.32.79
3. Puig C. SPA 1.32.93

**Québec**
1. Emonet P. FRA 1.29.59
2. Debernard D. FRA 1.30.47
3. Lafforgue B. FRA 1.31.51

**Naeba**
1. Debernard D. FRA 1.29.97
2. Wenzel H. LIE 1.32.09
3. Cochran B. USA 1.32.88

**Heavenly Valley**
1. Emonet P. FRA 1.28.82
2. Serrat F. FRA 1.30.14
3. Zechmeister C. BRD 1.30.41

## MEN 1973/74

### DOWNHILL

**Val d'Isère**
1. Plank H. ITA 2.11.39
2. Grissmann W. AUT 2.12.33
3. Klammer F. AUT 2.12.42

**Zell am See**
1. Cordin K. AUT 1.47.43
2. Collombin R. SUI 1.47.77
3. Walcher J. AUT 1.48.26
Grabler M. AUS 1.48.26
Feyersinger P. AUT 1.48.26

**Schladming**
1. Klammer F. AUT 1.41.77
2. Collombin R. SUI 1.42.12
3. Russi B. SUI 1.42.13

**Garmisch-Partenk. AK**
1. Collombin R. SUI 1.45.17
2. Klammer F. AUT 1.45.41
3. Plank H. ITA 1.45.72

**Avoriaz**
1. Collombin R. SUI 1.48.31
2. Klammer F. AUT 1.48.85
3. Roux P. SUI 1.49.18

**Wengen**
1. Collombin R. SUI 1.56.22
2. Klammer F. AUT 1.56.38
3. Plank H. ITA 1.56.75

**Kitzbühel**
1. Collombin R. SUI 2.03.29
2. Anzi S. ITA 2.03.47
Besson G. ITA 2.03.47

### GIANT SLALOM

**Val d'Isère**
1. Hinterseer H. AUT 3.05.09
2. Schmalz H. ITA 3.05.23
3. Gros P. ITA 3.05.53

**Saalbach**
1. Berchtold H. AUT 3.24.98
2. Hauser T. AUT 3.26.21
3. Hinterseer H. AUT 3.26.45

**Berchtesgaden**
1. Gros P. ITA 2.07.00
2. Thoeni G. ITA 2.09.23
3. Stricker E. ITA 2.09.83

**Morzine**
1. Gros P. ITA 2.56.67
2. Hinterseer H. AUT 2.57.64
3. Thoeni G. ITA 2.58.67

**Adelboden**
1. Thöni G. ITA 2.22.06
2. Gros P. ITA 2.23.67
3. Hinterseer H. AUT 2.24.10

**Voss**
1. Thoeni G. ITA 3.16.74
2. Hinterseer H. AUT 3.17.02
3. Stenmark I. SWE 3.17.84

**Vysoke Tatry**
1. Gros P. ITA 2.37.58
2. Stenmark I. SWE 2.39.23
3. Hinterseer H. AUT 2.39.36

### SLALOM

**Vipiteno**
1. Gros. P. ITA 1.38.04
2. Kniewasser J. AUT 1.40.72
3. Neureuther C. BRD 1.40.95

**Garmisch-Partenk. AK**
1. Neureuther C. BRD 1.25.07
2. Thoeni G. ITA 1.25.11
3. Schlager H.-J. BRD 1.25.20

**Wengen**
1. Neureuther C. BRD 1.32.23
2. Radici F. ITA 1.32.28
3. Zwilling D. AUT 1.33.00

**Kitzbühel**
1. Hinterseer H. AUT 1.46.80
2. Kniewasser J. AUT 1.47.77
3. Thoeni G. ITA 1.48.14

**Voss**
1. Gros P. ITA 1.48.44
2. Stenmark I. SWE 1.49.33
3. Kniewasser J. AUT 1.49.52

**Zakopane**
1. Fernand.-O. F. SPA 1.58.50
2. Thoeni G. ITA 1.59.24
3. Hinterseer H. AUT 1.59.92

**Vysoke Tatry**
1. Thoeni G. ITA 1.31.62
2. Stenmark I. SWE 1.32.06
3. Fernand.-O.-F. SPA 1.32.12

## WOMEN 1973/74

### DOWNHILL

**Val d'Isère**
1. Moser-Proell A. AUT 1.29.42

2. Gföllner I. AUT 1.31.59
3. Drexel W. AUT 1.31.95

**Zell am See**
1. Moser-Proell A. AUT 1.28.68
2. Drexel W. AUT 1.30.04
3. Nadig M.-T. SUI 1.30.29

**Pfronten**
1. Moser-Proell A. AUT 1.12.93
2. Drexel W. AUT 1.14.25
3. Clifford B. CAN 1.14.38

**Grindelwald**
1. Nelson C. USA 1.52.54
2. Moser-Proell A. AUT 1.52.31
3. Nadig M.-T. SUI 1.52.62

**Badgastein**
1. Moser-Proell A. AUT 2.08.01
2. Nadig M.-T. SUI 2.10.41
3. Drexel W. AUT 2.10.50

### GIANT SLALOM

**Pfontein**
1. Kreiner K. CAN 1.20.43
2. Morerod L.-M. SUI 1.21.40
3. Serrat F. FRA 1.21.43

**Zell am See**
1. Wenzel H. LIE 1.24.06
2. Nadig M.-T. SUI 1.24.72
3. Treichl T. BRD 1.24.83

**Les Gets**
1. Giordani C. ITA 1.19.37
2. Cochran B. USA 1.19.45
3. Wenzel H. LIE 1.19.53

**Grindelwald**
1. Kaserer M. AUT 1.12.78
2. Wenzel H. LIE 1.13.37
3. Zechmeister C. BRD 1.13.71

**Badgastein**
1. Serrat F. FRA 1.20.03
2. Morerod L.-M. SUI 1.20.38
3. Mittermaier R. BRD 1.20.66

**Vysoke Tatry**
1. Kaserer M. AUT 1.18.57
2. Moser-Proell A. AUT 1.18.96
3. Morerod L.-M. SUI 1.19.23

### SLALOM

**Val d'Isère**
1. Zechmeister C. BRD 1.20.72
2. Wenzel H. LIE 1.21.57
3. Cochran M. USA 1.22.13

**Les Gets**
1. Zechmeister C. BRD 1.20.01
2. Cochran L. USA 1.20.22
3. Moser-Proell A. AUT 1.20.60

**Les Diablerets**
1. Zechmeister C. BRD 1.22.54
2. Serrat F. FRA 1.22.71
3. Mittermaier R. BRD 1.23.06

**Badgastein**
1. Zechmeister C. BRD 1.12.46
2. Serrat F. FRA 1.13.41
3. Kaserer M. AUT 1.13.63

**Abetone**
1. Mittermaier R. BRD 1.27.36
2. Moser-Proell A. AUT 1.27.92
3. Serrat F. FRA 1.28.22

**Vysoke Tatry**
1. Mittermaier R. BRD 1.28.07
2. Debernard D. FRA 1.28.14
3. Wenzel H. LIE 1.28.49

## MEN 1974/75

### DOWNHILL

**Val d'Isère**
1. Klammer F. AUT 2.03.19
2. Grissmann W. AUT 2.04.01
3. Veith M. BRD 2.04.09

**St. Moritz**
1. Klammer F. AUT 1.54.72
2. Plank H. ITA 1.56.08
3. Grissmann W. AUT 1.56.60

**Garmisch-Partenkirchen**
1. Klammer F. AUT 1.43.31
2. Grissman W. AUT 1.44.70
3. Walcher S. AUT 1.44.96

**Wengen**
1. Klammer F. AUT 2.35.19
2. Plank H. ITA 2.38.73
3. Haker E. NOR 2.38.85

**Kitzbühel**
1. Klammer F. AUT 2.03.22
2. Thoeni G. ITA 2.03.23
3. Grissmann W. AUT 2.03.30

**Innsbruck**
1. Klammer F. AUT 1.55.78
2. Russi B. SUI 1.56.27
3. Plank H. ITA 1.56.61

**Megêve**
1. Vesti W. SUI 2.03.11
2. Berthod R. SUI 2.03.18
3. Roux P. SUI 2.03.79

**Jackson Hole**
1. Klammer F. AUT 1.55.64
2. Veith M. BRD 1.57.82
3. Berthod R. SUI 1.57.84

**Val Gardena**
1. Klammer F. AUT 2.01.22
2. Haker E. NOR 2.01.84
3. Russi B. SUI 2.02.27

### GIANT SLALOM

**Val d'Isère**
1. Gros P. ITA 3.10.03
2. Stenmark I. SWE 3.10.95
3. Haker E. NOR 3.11.27

**Madonna di Campiglio**
1. Gros P. ITA 3.05.38
2. Jones G. USA 3.06.08
3. Pietrogiovana T. ITA 3.06.68

**Adelboden**
1. Gros P. ITA 2.42.60
2. Thoeni G. ITA 2.42.88
3. Mattle W. SUI 2.45.31

**Fulpmes**
1. Haker E. NOR 2.55.66
2. Stenmark I. SWE 2.56.47
3. Hinterseer H. AUT 2.57.31

**Naeba**
1. Stenmark I. SWE 3.29.58
2. Haker E. NOR 3.29.64
3. Hinterseer H. AUT 3.29.74

**Garibaldi**
1. Stenmark I. SWE 3.18.00
2. Hemmi H. SUI 3.19.83
3. Thoeni G. ITA 3.19.86

**Sun Valley**
1. Stenmark I. SWE 2.39.08
2. Gros P. ITA 2.42.06
3. Thoeni G. ITA 2.42.31

### SLALOM

**Madonna di Campiglio**
1. Stenmark I. SWE 1.51.02
2. De Chiesa P. ITA 1.51.21
3. Radici F. ITA 1.51.34

**Garmisch-Partenkirchen**
1. Gros P. ITA 1.22.40
2. Thöni G. ITA 1.22.45
3. Radici F. ITA 1.22.88

**Wengen**
1. Stenmark I. SWE 1.39.87
2. Gros P. ITA 1.39.91
3. De Chiesa P. ITA 1.42.12

**Kitzbühel**
1. Gros P. ITA 1.51.35
2. Stenmark I. SWE 1.52.21
3. De Chiesa P. ITA 1.52.40

**Chamonix**
1. Thoeni G. ITA 1.42.11
2. Stenmark I. SWE 1.43.30
3. Hinterseer H. AUT 1.43.31

**Naeba**
1. Hinterseer H. AUT 1.26.46
2. Stenmark I. SWE 1.26.52
3. Neureuther C. BRD 1.26.87

**Sun Valley**
1. Thoeni G. ITA 1.49.88
2. Gros P. ITA 1.50.06
3. Stenmark I. SWE 1.50.49

### PARALLEL SLALOM

**Val Gardena (P)**
1. Thoeni G. ITA
2. Stenmark I. SWE
3. Tresch W. SUI

## WOMEN 1974/75

### DOWNHILL

**Val d'Isère**
1. Drexel W. AUT 1.25.90
2. Zurbriggen B. SUI 1.26.16
3. Debernard D. FRA 1.26.74

**Cortina d'Ampezzo**
1. Moser-Proell A. AUT 1.29.45
2. Nelson C. USA 1.29.92
3. Drexel W. AUT 1.30.79

**Saalbach**
1. Nelson C. USA 1.36.26
2. Nadig M.-T. SUI 1.36.49
3. Mittermaier R. BRD 1.37.00

**Grindelwald**
1. Moser-Proell A. AUT 1.53.80
2. Mittermaier R. BRD 1.54.36
3. Nadig M.-T. SUI 1.54.81

**Schruns**
1. Zurbriggen B. SUI 1.27.53
2. Schmid-G.I. AUT 1.28.83
3. Nadig M.-T. SUI 1.29.22

**Innsbruck**
1. Nadig M.-T. SUI 1.46.95
2. Moser-Proell A. AUT 1.47.31
3. Rouvier J. FRA 1.48.32

**Chamonix**
1. Zurbriggen B. SUI 1.33.09
2. Moser-Proell A. AUT 1.33.43
3. Nadig M.-T. SUI 1.33.70

**Jackson Hole**
1. Nadig M.-T. SUI 1.43.27
2. Zurbriggen B. SUI 1.44.49
3. Moser-Proell A. AUT 1.45.63

### GIANT SLALOM

**Val d'Isère**
1. Moser-Proell A. AUT 1.22.22
2. Kaserer M. AUT 1.22.74
3. Serrat F. FRA 1.22.82

**Grindelwald I**
1. Moser-Proell A. AUT 1.21.60
2. Wenzel H. LIE 1.23.00
3. Mittermaier R. BRD 1.23.39

**Grindelwald II**
1. Moser-Proell A. AUT 1.20.34
2. Serrat F. FRA 1.20.94
3. Wenzel H. LIE 1.21.54

**Jahorina**
1. Moser-Proell A. AUT 1.14.79
2. Morerod L.-M. SUI 1.15.07
3. Mittermaier R. BRD 1.15.15

**Naeba**
1. Moser-Proell A. AUT 1.27.57
2. Kaserer M. AUT 1.28.29
3. Tisot C. ITA 1.28.45

**Garibaldi**
1. Nelson C. USA 1.32.34
2. Serrat F. FRA 1.32.72
3. Kreiner K. CAN 1.32.85

**Sun Valley**
1. Morerod L.-M. SUI 1.14.91
2. Kaserer M. AUT 1.14.94
3. Serrat F. FRA 1.15.41

### SLALOM

**Cortina d'Ampezzo**
1. Mittermaier R. BRD 1.31.73
2. Serrat F. FRA 1.33.73
3. Zechmeister C. BRD 1.34.27

**Garmisch-Partenkirchen**
1. Morerod L.-M. SUI 1.37.32
2. Zechmeister C. BRD 1.38.26
3. Fjeldstad T. NOR 1.41.68

**Schruns**
1. Zechmeister C. BRD 1.21.49
2. Moser-Proell A. AUT 1.22.28
3. Wenzel H. LIE 1.22.35

**St. Gervais**
1. Morerod L.-M. SUI 1.23.41
2. Wenzel H. LIE 1.23.57
3. Mittermaier R. BRD 1.23.99

**Naeba**
1. Wenzel H. LIE 1.27.91
2. Morerod L.-M. SUI 1.28.94
3. Zechmeister C. BRD 1.31.33

**Sun Valley**
1. Wenzel H. LIE 1.24.23
2. Moser-Proell A. AUT 1.25.17
3. Zechmeister C. BRD 1.25.36

**Val Gardena**
1. Morerod L.-M. SUI 1.10.39
2. Moser-Proell A. AUT 1.11.29
3. Kaserer M. AUT 1.11.61

### PARALLEL SLALOM

**Val Gardena**
1. Kaserer M. AUT
2. Giordani C. ITA
3. Serrat F. FRA

## MEN 1975/76

### DOWNHILL

**Val d'Isère**
1. Read K. CAN 2.04.97
2. Plank H. ITA 2.05.58
3. Russi B. SUI 2.05.62

**Madonna di Campiglio**
1. Klammer F. AUT 1.39.95
2. Roux Ph. SUI 1.40.89
3. Haker E. NOR 1.40.92

**Schladming**
1. Irwin D. CAN 2.00.84
2. Eberhard K. AUT 2.02.45
3. Plank H. ITA 2.02.51

**Wengen I**
1. Plank H. ITA 2.08.48
2. Klammer F. AUT 2.08.68
3. Russi B. SUI 2.08.72

**Wengen II**
1. Klammer F. AUT 2.40.36
2. Roux Ph. SUI 2.42.58
3. Hunter J. CAN 2.42.68

**Avoriaz**
1. Klammer F. AUT 1.54.24
2. Russi B. SUI 1.54.33
3. Steiner A. AUT 1.54.88

**Kitzbühel**
1. Klammer F. AUT 2.03.79
2. Haker E. NOR 2.05.85
3. Walcher S. AUT 2.06.47

**Aspen**
1. Klammer F. AUT 1.54.12
2. Berthod R. SUI 1.54.24
3. Winkler E. AUT 1.55.14

### GIANT SLALOM

**Val d'Isère**
1. Thoeni G. ITA 3.23.36
2. Stenmark I. SWE 3.23.66
3. Gros P. ITA 3.24.77

**Madonna di Campiglio**
1. Pargätzi E. SUI 3.09.52
2. Good E. SUI 3.10.58
3. Gros. P. ITA 3.10.62

**Adelboden**
1. Thoeni G. ITA 2.58.94
2. Stenmark I. SWE 3.00.43
3. Pagätzi E. SUI 3.01.86

**Avoriaz**
1. Bieler F. ITA 2.59.32
2. Gros P. ITA 2.59.78
3. Stenmark I. SWE 3.00.31

**Zwiesel**
1. Stenmark I. SWE 2.28.96
2. Thoeni G. ITA 2.29.13
3. Hinterseer H. AUT 2.29.95

**Copper Mountain**
1. Jones G. USA 3.20.51
2. Mahre P. USA 3.20.83
3. Pargätzi E. SUI 3.21.47

**Mont-Sainte-Anne**
1. Hemmi H. SUI 2.55.38
2. Gros P. ITA 2.58.25
3. Good E. SUI 2.59.01

### SLALOM

**Vipiteno**
1. Stenmark I. SWE 1.51.65
2. Hinterseer H. AUT 1.52.25
3. Gros P. ITA 1.52.99

**Schladming**
1. Hinterseer H. AUT 1.45.32
2. Stenmark I. SWE 1.45.44
3. Gros P. ITA 1.45.49

**Garmisch-Partenkirchen**
1. Radici F. ITA 1.25.81
2. Gros P. ITA 1.25.90
3. Stenmark I. SWE 1.26.23

**Wengen**
1. Stenmark I. SWE 1.40.96
2. Gros P. ITA 1.40.99
3. Neureuther C. BRD 1.41.00

**Kitzbühel**
1. Stenmark I. SWE 1.47.74
2. Thoeni G. ITA 1.48.10
3. Gros P. ITA 1.48.60

**Copper Mountain**
1. Stenmark I. SWE 1.37.75
2. Mahre S. USA 1.37.85
3. Thoeni G. ITA 1.38.51

**Aspen**
1. Stenmark I. SWE 1.49.76
2. Mahre P. USA 1.51.34
3. Thoeni G. ITA 1.51.64

## WOMEN 1975/76

### DOWNHILL

**Val d'Isère**
1. Zurbriggen B. SUI 1.26.07
2. Epple I. BRD 1.26.67
3. Nadig M.-T. SUI 1.26.86

**Aprica**
1. Totschnig B. AUT 1.47.49
2. Deufl E. AUT 1.47.85
3. Nelson C. USA 1.47.91

**Cortina d'Ampezzo**
1. Mittermaier E. BRD 1.42.82
2. Totschnig B. AUT 1.42.95
3. Zurbriggen B. SUI 1.43.51

**Meiringen-Hasliberg I**
1. Totschnig B. AUT 1.37.62
2. Spiess N. AUT 1.38.74
3. Lukasser I. AUT 1.39.37

**Meiringen-Hasliberg II**
1. Zurbriggen B. SUI 1.37.23
2. Lukasser I. AUT 1.37.31
3. Spiess N. AUT 1.37.34

**Badgastein**
1. De Agostini D. SUI 2.29.19
2. Oberholzer M. SUI 2.29.77
3. Deufl E. AUT 2.29.88

**Aspen**
1. Totschnig B. AUT 1.22.24
2. Debernard D. FRA 1.22.63
3. Mittermaier R. BRD 1.22.75

### GIANT SLALOM

**Val d'Isère**
1. Morerod L.-M. SUI 1.16.15
2. Mittermaier R. BRD 1.17.37
3. Kaserer M. AUT 1.17.50

**Meiringen-Hasliberg**
1. Kaserer M. AUT 1.20.71
2. Debernard D. FRA 1.20.91
3. Nadig M.-T. SUI 1.21.00

**Les Gets**
1. Morerod L.-M. SUI 1.08.40
2. Mittermaier R. BRD 1.10.56
3. Kaserer M. AUT 1.10.74

**Berchtesgaden**
1. Debernard D. FRA 1.02.17
2. Morerod L.-M. SUI 1.02.24
3. Kaserer M. AUT 1.02.64

**Kranjska Gora**
1. Morerod L.-M. SUI 1.24.83
2. Mittermaier R. BRD 1.26.05
3. Zurbriggen B. SUI 1.27.77

**Copper Mountain**
1. Mittermaier R. BRD 1.28.45
2. Nelson C. USA 1.29.77
3. Zurbriggen B. SUI 1.30.10

**Aspen**
1. Morerod L.-M. SUI 1.28.10
2. Debernard D. FRA 1.29.19
3. Kaserer M. AUT 1.29.32

**Mont-Saint-Anne**
1. Kaserer M. AUT 1.52.43
2. Serrat F. FRA 1.52.84
3. Kreiner K. CAN 1.52.85

### SLALOM

**Aprica**
1. Morerod L.-M. SUI 1.32.65
2. Mittermaier R. BRD 1.35.51
3. Giordani C. ITA 1.35.81

**Cortina d'Ampezzo**
1. Serrat F. FRA 1.51.23
2. Behr P. BRD 1.51.54
3. Mittermaier R. BRD 1.52.65

**Les Diablerets**
1. Morerod L.-M. SUI 1.21.24
2. Mittermaier R. BRD 1.21.97
3. Emonet P. FRA 1.22.04

**Les Gets**
1. Debernard D. FRA 1.42.60
2. Berwein M. BRD 1.42.74
3. Emonet P. FRA 1.42.75

**Berchtesgaden**
1. Zechmeister C. BRD 1.50.47
2. Debernard D. FRA 1.50.59
3. Wenzel H. LIE 1.50.62

**Badgastein**
1. Mittermaier R. BRD 1.18.09
2. Giordani C. ITA 1.18.57
3. Nelson C. USA 1.18.99

**Kranjska Gora**
1. Morerod L.-M. SUI 1.41.25
2. Mittermaier R. BRD 1.42.27
3. Sackl R. AUT 1.42.37

**Copper Mountain**
1. Mittermaier R. BRD 1.47.78
2. Kaserer M. AUT 1.47.94
3. Morerod L.-M. SUI 1.48.06

## MEN 1976/77

### DOWNHILL

**Val Gardena I**
1. Klammer F. AUT 2.03.80
2. Plank H. ITA 2.04.91
3. Haker E. NOR 2.05.27

**Val Gardena II**
1. Klammer F. AUT 2.05.71
2. Walcher J. AUT 2.06.66
3. Russi B. SUI 2.07.30

**Garmisch-Partenkirchen**
1. Klammer F. AUT 2.02.63
2. Winkler E. AUT 2.03.38
3. Wirnsberger P. AUT 2.05.13

**Kitzbühel**
1. Klammer F. AUT 2.09.71
2. Berthod R. SUI 2.10.64
3. Russi B. SUI 2.10.81

**Wengen**
1. Klammer F. AUT 2.35.66
2. Ferstl S. BRD 2.36.65
3. Russi B. SUI 2.36.78

**Morzine-Avoriaz I**
1. Russi B. SUI 1.45.57
2. Walcher J. AUT 1.46.16
3. Winkler E. AUT 1.46.18

**Morzine-Avoriaz II**
1. Walcher J. AUT 1.43.61
2. Plank H. ITA 1.43.70
3. Russi B. SUI 1.43.82

**Laax**
1. Klammer F. AUT 1.59.10
2. Ferstl S. BRD 1.59.51
3. Russi B. SUI 1.59.54

**Heavenly Valley I**
1. Walcher J. AUT 1.36.44
2. Grissmann W. AUT 1.37.14
3. Russi B. SUI 1.37.20

**Heavenly Valley II**
1. Gensbichler B. AUT 1.46.91
2. Winkler E. AUT 1.47.13
3. Fischer P. BRD 1.47.52

### GIANT SLALOM

**Val d'Isère I**
1. Mahre P. USA 3.32.21
2. Stenmark I. SWE 3.33.27
3. Heidegger K. AUT 3.33.73

**Val d'Isère II**
1. Hemmi H. SUI 2.50.79
2. Gros P. ITA 2.51.92
3. Mahre P. USA 2.52.19

**Ebnat-Kappel**
1. Hemmi H. SUI 3.11.22
2. Hemmi C. SUI 3.13.39
3. Thoeni G. ITA 3.14.67

**Garm.-Partenkirchen**
1. Heidegger K. AUT 3.22.29
2. Hemmi H. AUT 3.22.30
3. Frommelt W. LIE 3.23.19

**Adelboden**
1. Hemmi H. SUI 3.07.94
2. Stenmark I. SWE 3.08.73
3. Heidegger K. AUT 3.10.09

**Furano**
1. Hinterseer H. AUT 3.11.58
2. Brunner M. AUT 3.12.10
3. Good E. SUI 3.12.27

**Sun Valley**
1. Stenmark I. SWE 2.32.36
2. Hemmi Ch. SUI 2.33.18
3. Hemmi H. SUI 2.34.05

**Voss**
1. Heidegger K. AUT 2.59.47
2. Gros P. ITA 3.00.03
3. Mahre P. USA 3.00.35

**Åre**
1. Stenmark I. SWE 2.46.00
2. Heidegger K. AUT 2.48.20
3. Sochor M. CSF 2.48.32

**Sierra Nevada**
1. Stenmark I. SWE 2.55.51
2. Hemmi H. SUI 2.55.70
3. Hemmi C. SUI 2.58.28

### SLALOM

**Madonna di Campiglio**
1. Radici F. ITA 1.48.11
2. Gros P. ITA 1.48.15
3. Thoeni G. ITA 1.48.53

**Laax**
1. Stenmark I. SWE 1.40.25
2. Frommelt P. LIE 1.41.65
3. Tresch W. SUI 1.41.73

**Berchtesgaden**
1. Stenmark I. SWE 1.43.26
2. Heidegger K. AUT 1.43.66
3. Morgenstern A. AUT 1.44.11

**Kitzbühel**
1. Stenmark I. SWE 1.39.63
2. Gros P. ITA 1.40.06
3. Bieler F. ITA 1.40.70

**Wengen**
1. Stenmark I. SWE 1.35.36
2. Frommelt P. LIE 1.36.31
3. Heidegger K. AUT 1.37.06

**St. Anton a. Arlberg-AK**
1. Stenmark I. SWE 1.50.38
2. Heidegger K. AUT 1.50.47
3. Frommelt P. LIE 1.50.52

**Furano**
1. Heidegger K. AUT 1.57.65
2. Stenmark I. SWE 1.57.88
3. Nöcker B. ITA 1.57.99

**Sun Valley**
1. Mahre P. USA 1.47.15
2. Stenmark I. SWE 1.47.25
3. Mahre S. USA 1.47.64

**Voss**
1. Stenmark I. SWE 1.32.11
2. Gros P. ITA 1.32.77
3. Neureuther C. BRD 1.32.97

**Åre**
1. Stenmark I. SWE 1.38.93
2. Bieler F. ITA 1.40.52
3. Thoeni G. ITA 1.41.27

## WOMEN 1976/77

### DOWNHILL

**Cortina d'Ampezzo**
1. Moser-Proell A. AUT 1.34.43
2. Matous E. IRA 1.36.06
3. Habersatter B. AUT 1.36.33

**Zell am See I**
1. Habersatter B. AUT 1.30.65
2. Moser-Proell A. AUT 1.30.90
3. Spiess N. AUT 1.31.24

**Zell am See II**
1. Habersatter B. AUT 1.30.51
2. Spiess N. AUT 1.31.95
   Nadig M.-T. SUI 1.31.95

**Pfronten**
1. Moser-Proell A. AUT 1.20.09
2. Nadig M.-Th. SUI 1.20.86
3. Epple I. BRD 1.21.45

**Garmisch-Partenkirchen**
1. Moser-Proell A. AUT 1.51.00
2. Zurbriggen B. SUI 1.51.11
3. Nadig M.-Th. SUI 1.51.27

**Schruns-Montafon**
1. Zurbriggen B. SUI 1.23.49
2. Mittermaier E. BRD 1.23.85
3. Nadig M.-Th. SUI 1.23.95

**Crans-Montana**
1. Habersatter B. AUT 1.28.73
2. Mittermaier E. BRD 1.28.90
3. Moser-Proell A. AUT 1.29.05

**Heavenly Valley I**
1. Habersatter B. AUT 1.41.00
2. Mittermaier E. BRD 1.41.55
3. De Agostini D. SUI 1.41.69

### GIANT SLALOM

**Val d'Isère**
1. Morerod L.-M. SUI 1.16.91
2. Fischer A. USA 1.17.10
3. Moser-Proell A. AUT 1.17.29

**Courmayeur**
1. Habersatter B. AUT 1.40.26
2. Sölkner L. AUT 1.41.07
3. Wenzel H. LIE 1.41.49

**Arosa**
1. Morerod L.-M. SUI 1.19.66
2. Kreiner K. CAN 1.20.15
3. Kaserer M. AUT 1.20.26

**Megêve**
1. Kaserer M. AUT 1.34.87
2. Morerod L.-M. SUI 1.34.89
3. Moser-Proell A. AUT 1.35.06

**Maribor**
1. Morerod L.-M. SUI 1.12.04
2. Kaserer M. AUT 1.12.13
3. Serrat F. FRA 1.12.91

**Furano**
1. Kaserer M. AUT 1.37.32
2. Morerod L.-M. SUI 1.38.54
3. Moser-Proell A. AUT 1.40.02

**Sun Valley**
1. Morerod L.-M. SUI 1.22.54
2. Kreiner K. CAN 1.22.95
3. Fischer A. USA 1.23.18

**Sierra Nevada**
1. Morerod L.-M. SUI 1.33.38
2. Eberle I. AUT 1.34.55
3. Konzett U. LIE 1.34.66

### SLALOM

**Cortina d'Ampezzo**
1. Morerod L.-M. SUI 1.26.62
2. Wenzel H. LIE 1.27.97
3. Giordani C. ITA 1.28.14

**Oberstaufen**
1. Morerod L.-M. SUI 1.35.17
2. Wenzel H. LIE 1.35.61
3. Emonet P. FRA 1.35.88

**Schruns-Montafon**
1. Morerod L.-M. SUI 1.38.30
2. Serrat F. FRA 1.39.08
3. Behr P. BRD 1.39.18

**Crans-Montana**
1. Pelen P. FRA 1.26.66
2. Morerod L.-M. SUI 1.26.69
3. Serrat F. FRA 1.27.25

**St. Gervais**
1. Pelen P. FRA 1.23.60
2. Emonet P. FRA 1.24.41
3. Kaserer M. AUT 1.24.70

**Maribor**
1. Giordani C. ITA 1.40.44
2. Kaserer M. AUT 1.40.77
3. Pelen P. FRA 1.40.82

**Furano**
1. Sackl R. AUT 1.51.99
2. Moser-Proell A. AUT 1.52.13
3. Giordani C. ITA 1.52.76

**Sun Valley**
1. Pelen P. FRA 1.42.58
2. Giordani C. ITA 1.43.19
3. Kaserer M. AUT 1.43.36

## MEN 1977/78

### DOWNHILL

**Val d'Isère**
1. Klammer F. AUT 2.07.61
2. Plank H. ITA 2.07.89
3. Walcher J. AUT 2.07.95

**Val Gardena**
1. Plank H. ITA 2.01.47
2. Wirnsberger P. AUT 2.02.60
3. Klammer F. AUT 2.03.32

**Cortina**
1. Plank H. ITA 1.50.99
2. Russi B. SUI 1.51.13
3. Wirnsberger P. AUT 1.51.24

**Kitzbühel I**
1. Walcher J. AUT 2.06.90
2. Vesti W. SUI 2.06.97
3. Antonioli R. ITA 2.07.05

**Kitzbühel II**
1. Walcher J. AUT 2.07.81
   Ferstl S. BRD 2.07.81
3. Veith M. BRD 2.07.85

**Chamonix**
1. Read K. CAN 2.08.11
2. Murray D. CAN 2.08.27
3. Veith M. BRD 2.08.46

**Laax I**
1. Spieß U. AUT 1.57.96
2. Klammer F. AUT 1.58.18
3. Haker E. NOR 1.58.55

**Laax II**
1. Klammer F. AUT 1.55.76
2. Haker E. NOR 1.55.79
3. Spieß U. AUT 1.56.16

### GIANT SLALOM

**Val d'Isère**
1. Stenmark I. SWE 3.14.15
2. Hemmi H. SUI 3.16.23
3. Fournier J. L. SUI 3.16.84

**Madonna di Campiglio**
1. Stenmark I SWE 2.49.91
2. Hemmi H. SUI 2.50.06
3. Wenzel A. LIE 2.50.09

**Zwiesel**
1. Stenmark I. SWE 2.34.00
2. Mahre P. USA 2.34.42
3. Wenzel A. LIE 2.35.36

**Adelboden**
1. Wenzel A. LIE 2.34.36
2. Stenmark I. SWE 2.34.89
3. Gros P. ITA 2.35.07

**Stratton-Mountain**
1. Mahre P. USA 2.41.04
2. Hemmi H. SUI 2.41.04
3. Stenmark I. SWE 2.41.65

**Waterville Valley**
1. Wenzel A. LIE 2.52.22
2. Mahre P. USA 2.53.02
3. Stenmark I. SWE 2.53.38

**Arosa**
1. Stenmark I. SWE 2.30.71
2. Wenzel A. LIE 2.31.06
3. Luescher P. SUI 2.31.18

### SLALOM

**Madonna di Campiglio**
1. Stenmark I. SWE 110.81
2. Heidegger K. AUT 112.13
3. Krizaj B. JUG 112.51

**Oberstaufen**
1. Stenmark I. SWE 109.81
2. Heidegger K. AUT 110.60
3. Gros P. ITA 110.89

**Zwiesel**
1. Stenmark I. SWE 112.39
2. Bernardi M. ITA 113.50
3. Mahre P. USA 113.56

**Wengen**
1. Heidegger K. AUT 90.79
2. Popangelov P. BUL 91.09
3. Bernardi M. ITA 91.47

**Kitzbühel**
1. Heidegger K. AUT 103.95
2. Popangelov P. BUL 103.99
3. Wenzel A. LIE 104.76

**Chamonix**
1. Mahre Ph. USA 118.26
2. Stenmark I. SWE 119.85
3. De Chiesa P. ITA 120.40

**Stratton-Mountain**
1. Mahre S. USA 1.50.47
2. Stenmark I. SWE 1.50.87
3. Luescher P. SUI 1.51.65

### PARALLEL SLALOM

**Aspen**
1. Mahre P. USA
2. Stenmark I. SWE
3. Stock L. AUT

## WOMEN 1977/78

### DOWNHILL

**Val d'Isère**
1. Nadig M.-T. SUI 1.24.18
2. Moser-Proell A. AUT 1.24.30
3. Bader M. BRD 1.25.25

**Pfronten**
1. Moser-Proell A. AUT 1.19.47
2. Nelson C. USA 1.19.57
3. De Agostini D. ITA 1.19.71

**Pfronten**
1. Moser-Proell A. AUT 1.17.14
2. Nelson C. USA 1.18.27
3. Nadig M.-T. SUI 1.18.62

**Les Diablerets**
1. Moser-Proell A. AUT 1.29.38
2. Mittermaier E. BRD 1.30.36
3. Epple I. BRD 1.31.00

**Badgastein**
1. Mittermaier E. BRD 1.31.92
2. Moser-Proell A. AUT 1.32.43
3. Nadig M.-T. SUI 1.32.73

**Bad Kleinkirchheim**
1. Moser-Proell A. AUT 1.46.71
2. Nelson C. USA 1.47.25
3. Mittermaier E. BRD 1.47.51

**Bad Kleinkirchheim**
1. Moser-Proell A. AUT 1.48.68
2. Nelson C. USA 1.48.81
3. Nadig M.-T. SUI 1.48.96

### GIANT SLALOM

**Val d'Isère**
1. Morerod L.-M. SUI 2.32.36
2. Epple M. BRD 2.34.03
3. Kaserer M. AUT 2.34.49

**Madonna di Campiglio**
1. Wenzel H. LIE 3.02.13
2. Kaserer M. AUT 3.02.68
3. Morerod L.-M. SUI 3.02.89

**Les Diablerets**
1. Morerod L.-M. SUI 2.59.31
2. Wenzel H. LIE 3.01.73
3. Epple M. BRD 3.02.62

**Les Diablerets**

1. Wenzel H. LIE 2.52.77
2. Kaserer M. AUT 2.53.78
3. Serrat F. FRA 2.54.24

**St Gervais**

1. Morerod L.-M. SUI 2.36.85
2. Moser-Proell A. AUT 2.38.44
3. Serrat F. FRA 2.38.91

**Stratton Mountain**

1. Wenzel H. LIE 2.22.38
2. Epple M. BRD 2.23.54
3. Morerod L.-M. SUI 2.24.20

**Waterville Valley**

1. Morerod L.-M. SUI 2.25.20
2. Dorsey B. USA 2.26.75
3. Serrat F. FRA 2.27.73

**Arosa**

1. Moser-Proell A. AUT 2.26.54
2. Epple I. BRD 2.27.91
3. Morerod L.-M. SUI 2.28.14

### SLALOM

**Cervinia**

1. Pelen P. FRA 79.00
2. Serrat F. FRA 79.01
3. Wenzel H. LIE 79.76

**Badgastein**

1. Morerod L.-M. SUI 75.92
2. Wenzel H. LIE 76.06
3. Pelen P. FRA 76.38

**Marburg**

1. Wenzel H. LIE 85.37
2. Epple M. BRD 85.86
3. Sölkner L. AUT 85.88

**Berchtesgaden**

1. Wenzel H. LIE 1.15.77
2. Morerod L.-M. SUI 1.16.35
3. Pelen P. FRA 1.16.49

**Berchtesgaden**

1. Wenzel H. LIE 1.05.75
2. Serrat F. FRA 1.05.84
3. Morerod L.-M. SUI 1.06.81

**Megêve**

1. Pelen P. FRA 84.35
2. Sölkner L. AUT 84.90
3. Serrat F. FRA 85.17

**Stratton Mountain**

1. Pelen P. FRA 1.37.07
2. Serrat F. FRA 1.37.12
3. Wenzel H. LIE 1.37.99

### PARALLEL SLALOM

**Arosa**

1. Moser-Proell A. AUT
2. Zechmeister C. BRD
3. Fleckenstein V. USA

## MEN 1978/79

### DOWNHILL

**Schladming**

1. Read K. CAN 1.32.11
2. Murray D. CAN 1.32.17
3. Makeev V. SOV 1.32.24

**Gröden I**

1. Walcher J. AUT 2.11.86
2. Müller P. SUI 2.12.16
3. Vesti W. SUI 2.12.91

**Gröden II**

1. Haker E. NOR 2.06.37
2. Müller P. SUI 2.07.63
3. Read K. CAN 2.08.45

**Morzine-Avoriaz**

1. Podborski S. CAN 1.43.97
2. Plank H. ITA 1.44.41
3. Spieß U. AUT 1.44.60

**Montana**

1. Bürgler T. SUI 1.58.19
2. Müller P. SUI 1.58.43
3. Read K. CAN 1.59.10

**Kitzbühel**

1. Ferstl S. BRD 2.04.48
2. Wirnsberger P. AUT 2.04.68
3. Spieß U. AUT 2.05.45

**Garmisch**

1. Wirnsberger P. AUT 1.57.44
2. Spieß U. AUT 1.57.82
3. Plank H. ITA 1.57.85

**Villars**

1. Müller P. SUI 1.45.97
2. Stock L. AUT 1.46.19
3. Grissmann W. AUT 1.46.20

**Lake Placid**

1. Wirnsberger P. AUT 1.42.88
2. Müller P. SUI 1.42.91
3. Murray D. CAN 1.42.99

### GIANT SLALOM

**Schladming**

1. Stenmark I. SWE 3.02.24
2. Luescher P. SUI 3.04.10
3. David L. ITA 3.04.37

**Kranjska Gora**

1. Stenmark I. SWE 2.28.51
2. Luescher P. SUI 2.29.91
3. Krizaj B. JUG 2.30.53

**Courchevel**

1. Stenmark I. SWE 2.54.33
2. Luescher P. SUI 2.58.06
3. Krizaj B. JUG 2.58.13

**Adelboden**

1. Stenmark I. SWE 2.24.16
2. Wenzel A. LIE 2.25.70
3. Lüthy J. SUI 2.26.07

**Jasna**

1. Stenmark I. SWE 2.53.47
2. Krizaj B. JUG 2.57.53
3. Hemmi H. SUI 2.57.68

**Åre**

1. Stenmark I. SWE 2.25.09
2. Mahre P. USA 2.27.17
3. Lüthy J. SUI 2.27.18

**Lake Placid**

1. Stenmark I. SWE 2.38.93
2. Enn H. AUT 2.41.01
3. Luescher P. SUI 2.41.10

**Heavenly Valley**

1. Stenmark I. SWE 2.11.72
2. Krizaj B. JUG 2.12.43
3. Enn H. AUT 2.13.23

**Steinach**

1. Stenmark I. SWE 3.00.01
2. Luescher P. SUI 3.00.98
3. Wenzel A. LIE 3.01.38

**Furano**

1. Stenmark I. SWE 2.58.59
2. Hemmi H. SUI 3.00.15
3. Fournier J.-L. SUI 3.00.41

### SLALOM

**Madonna di Campiglio**

1. Donnet M. SUI 91.59
2. Luescher P. SUI 91.87
3. Neureuther C. BRD 92.05

**Kranjska Gora**

1. Stenmark I. SWE 106.67
2. Frommelt P. LIE 106.77
3. David L. ITA 107.96

**Crans Montana I**

1. Neureuther C. BRD 105.27
2. Popangelov P. BUL 105.49
3. Trojer K. ITA 105.90

**Crans Montana II**

1. Frommelt P. LIE 105.33
2. Wenzel A. LIE 105.50
3. Stenmark I. SWE 106.19

**Garmisch**

1. Luescher P. SUI 86.11
2. Mahre P. USA 86.14
3. Popangelov P. BUL 86.26

**Jasna**

1. Mahre P. USA 103.03
2. David L. ITA 103.81
3. Stenmark I. SWE 104.65

**Oslo**

1. David L. ITA 89.15
2. Stenmark I. SWE 89.22
3. Mahre Ph. USA 89.31

**Åre**

1. Stenmark I. SWE 1.35.77
2. Mahre Ph. USA 1.36.67
3. Thoeni G. ITA 1.36.78

**Kitzbühel**

1. Neureuther C. BRD 101.16
2. Stenmark I. SWE 101.42
3. Mahre P. USA 101.53

**Furano**

1. Stenmark I. SWE 108.14
2. Neureuther C. BRD 108.91
3. Frommelt P. LIE 109.29

## WOMEN 1978/79

### DOWNHILL

**Piancavallo**

1. Moser-Proell A. AUT 1.46.06
2. De Agostini D. SUI 1.47.79
3. Dirren E. SUI 1.48.00

**Val d'Isère**

1. Moser-Proell A. AUT 1.20.58
2. Mittermaier E. BRD 1.20.56
3. Zurbriggen B. SUI 1.20.60

**Les Diablerets**

1. Moser-Proell A. AUT 1.28.83
2. Mittermaier E. BRD 1.30.64
3. Nadig M.-T. SUI 1.31.19

**Lake Placid**

1. Moser-Proell A. AUT 1.43.07
2. Nadig M.-T. SUI 1.43.17
3. Zurbriggen B. SUI 1.43.49

**Meiringen**

1. Moser-Proell A. AUT 1.36.14
2. Epple I. BRD 1.37.44
3. Zurbriggen B. SUI 1.37.66

**Schruns**

1. Moser-Proell A. AUT 1.21.99
2. Nelson C. USA 1.24.34
3. Epple I. BRD 1.24.39

**Pfronten**

1. Nelson C. USA 1.18.62
2. Attia C. FRA 1.18.64
3. Epple I. BRD 1.18.65

### GIANT SLALOM

**Piancavallo**

1. Wenzel H. LIE 2.43.80
2. Nadig M.-T. SUI 2.44.14
3. Epple I. BRD 2.44.52

**Les Gets**

1. Kinshofer C. BRD 2.12.77
2. Wenzel H. LIE 2.14.72
3. Sackl R. AUT 2.15.05

**Berchtesgaden**

1. Kinshofer C. BRD 2.10.76
2. Epple I. BRD 2.12.23
3. Moser-Proell A. AUT 2.12.55

**Furano**

1. Nadig M.-T. SUI 2.46.03
2. Moser-Proell A. AUT 2.51.23
3. Epple I. BRD 2.51.42

**Val d'Isère**

1. Kinshofer C. BRD 2.19.85
2. Wenzel H. LIE 2.20.32
3. Nadig M.-T. SUI 2.20.41

**Aspen**

1. Kinshofer C. BRD 2.30.81
2. Epple I. BRD 2.31.25
3. Nadig M.-T. SUI 2.32.77

**Heavenly Valley**

1. Kinshofer C. BRD 2.19.62
2. Wenzel H. LIE 2.20.19
3. Epple I. BRD 2.20.82

### SLALOM

**Piancavallo**

1. Fisher A. USA 109.81
2. Pelen P. FRA 109.82
3. McKinney T. USA 109.94

**Les Gets**

1. Sackl R. AUT 86.58
2. Pelen P. FRA 87.05
3. Moser-Proell A. AUT 87.08

**Meiringen**

1. Sackl R. AUT 85.24
2. Giordani C. ITA 85.37
3. Kurz M. AUT 85.71

**Schruns**

1. Sölkner L. AUT 99.84
2. Giordani C. ITA 101.62
3. Moser-Proell A. AUT 101.78

**Mellau**

1. Quario R.-M. ITA 87.99
2. Moser-Proell A. AUT 88.45
3. Pelen P. FRA 89.00

**Pfronten**

1. Wenzel H. LIE 97.49
2. Serrat F. FRA 97.58
3. Sackl R. AUT 98.89

**Maribor**

1. Wenzel H. LIE 92.71
2. Kinshofer C. BRD 93.52
3. Quario R.-M. ITA 93.82

**Furano**

1. Pelen P. FRA 90.05
2. Wenzel H. LIE 90.06
3. Moser-Proell A. AUT 91.24

## MEN 1979/80

### DOWNHILL

**Val d'Isère**

1. Wirnsberger P. AUT 2.01.83
2. Plank H. ITA 2.02.13
3. Haaker E. NOR 2.02.37

**Gröden**

1. Müller P. SUI 2.03.94
2. Haaker E. NOR 2.40.72
3. Grissmann W. AUT 2.04.84

**Pra Loup**

1. Müller P. SUI 1.53.56
2. Plank H. ITA 1.54.37
3. Haaker E. NOR 1.54.44

**Kitzbühel**

1. Read K. CAN 2.04.93
2. Weirather H. AUT 2.05.51
3. Plank H. ITA 2.05.61

**Wengen I**

1. Read K. CAN 2.31.31
2. Walcher J. AUT 2.31.34
3. Wirnsberger P. AUT 2.31.58

**Wengen II**

1. Müller P. SUI 2.30.56
2. Read K. CAN 2.30.58
3. Podborski S. CAN 2.30.66

**Lake Louise**

1. Plank H. ITA 1.50.47
2. Weirather H. AUT 1.51.24
3. Grissmann W. AUT 1.51.47

### GIANT SLALOM

**Val d'Isère**

1. Stenmark I. SWE 2.37.61
2. Krizaj B. JUG 2.38.12
3. Enn H. AUT 2.38.24

**Madonna di Campiglio**

1. Stenmark I. SWE 2.49.71
2. Lüthy J. SUI 2.50.03
3. Krizaj B. JUG 2.50.86

**Adelboden**

1. Stenmark I. SWE 2.50.21
2. Lüthy J. SUI 2.50.47
3. Gaspoz J. SUI 2.52.21

**Waterville Valley**

1. Enn H. AUT 2.45.10
2. Wenzel A. LIE 2.46.23
3. Halsnes J. NOR 2.46.32

**Mt. St. Anne**

1. Stenmark I. SWE 3.14.03
2. Mahre Ph. USA 3.14.09
3. Zeman B. CSR 3.15.28

**Oberstaufen**

1. Wenzel A. LIE 2.14.93
2. Lüthy J. SUI 2.15.12
3. Stenmark I. SWE 2.15.50

**Cortina**

1. Stenmark I. SWE 3.05.64
2. Enn H. AUT 3.08.25
3. Gaspoz J. SUI 3.08.82

**Saalbach**

1. Stenmark I. SWE 2.37.23
2. Gaspoz J. SUI 2.38.78
3. Enn H. AUT 2.39.26

### SLALOM

**Madonna di Campiglio**

1. Stenmark I. SWE 1.37.20
2. Krizaj B. JUG 1.37.59
3. Frommelt P. LIE 1.38.74

**Lenggries**

1. Popangelov P. BUL 96.17
2. Zhirov A. SOV 96.66
3. Stenmark I. SWE 96.92

**Kitzbühel**

1. Wenzel A. LIE 1.41.10
2. Neureuther C. BRD 1.41.78
3. Lüthy J. AUT 1.41.91

**Wengen**

1. Krizaj Bojan JUG 1.27.30
2. Stenmark I. SWE 1.27.47
3. Frommelt P. LIE 1.27.84

**Chamonix**

1. Stenmark I. SWE 2.01.18
2. Krizaj B. JUG 2.01.34
3. Orlainsky C. AUT 2.01.60

**Waterville Valley**

1. Stenmark I. SWE 1.42.04
2. Neureuther C. BRD 1.43.02
3. Heidegger K. AUT 1.43.08

**Cortina**

1. Stenmark I. SWE 1.30.92
2. Zhirov A. SOV 1.31.32
3. Orlainsky C. AUT 1.31.37

**Saalbach**

1. Stenmark I. SWE 1.33.58
2. Mahre S. USA 1.33.67
3. Popangelov P. BUL 1.33.84

## WOMEN 1979/80

### DOWNHILL

**Val d'Isère**

1. Nadig M.-T. SUI 1.20.76
2. Nelson C. USA 1.21.08
3. Graham L. CAN 1.21.98

**Piancavallo**

1. Nadig M.-T. SUI 1.41.29
2. Moser-Proell A. AUT 1.41.48
3. Soltysova J. CSR 1.41.66

**Zell am See**

1. Nadig M.-T. SUI 1.30.56
2. Soltysova J. CSR 1.31.06
3. Moser-Proell A. AUT 1.31.11

**Pfronten**

1. Moser-Proell A. AUT 1.19.84
2. Nadig M.-T. SUI 1.20.20
3. Wenzel H. LIE 1.21.58

**Pfronten**

1. Nadig M.-T. SUI 1.21.22
2. Pröll C. AUT 1.21.41
3. De Agostini D. SUI 1.21.60

**Arosa**

1. Nadig M.T. SUI 1.39.79
2. Moser-Proell A. AUT 1.39.90
3. Wenzel H. LIE 1.41.21

**Badgastein**

1. Nadig M.T. SUI 1.58.09
2. Moser-Proell A. AUT 1.58.39
3. Wenzel H. LIE 1.59.38

### GIANT SLALOM

**Val d'Isère**

1. Nadig M.-T. SUI 2.45.09
2. Pelen P. FRA 2.45.24
3. Hess E. SUI 2.45.85

**Limone Piemonte**

1. Wenzel H. LIE 2.23.19
2. Hess E. SUI 2.24.42
3. Serrat F. FRA 2.25.14

**Berchtesgaden**

1. Wenzel H. LIE 2.11.72
2. Pelen P. FRA 2.12.64
3. Giordani C. ITA 2.13.22

**Arosa**

1. Wenzel H. LIE 2.18.15
2. Nadig M.-T. SUI 2.18.44

Pelen P. FRA 2.19.85

**St. Gervais/Megêve**

1. Wenzel H. LIE 2.20.37

2. Pelen P. FRA 2.35.39
3. Nadig M.-T. SUI 2.35.44

**Waterville Valley**
1. Wenzel H. LIE 2.16.38
2. Epple M. BRD 2.17.13
3. Epple I. BRD 2.17.57

**Mt. St. Anne**
1. Nadig M.-T. SUI 2.48.75
2. Epple I. BRD 2.50.89
3. Wenzel H. LIE 2.50.98

**Saalbach**
1. Epple I. BRD 2.17.87
2. Pelen P. FRA 2.18.04
3. Serrat F. FRA 2.18.32

### SLALOM

**Piancavallo**
1. Moser-Proell A. AUT 1.57.04
2. Pelen P. FRA 1.57.31
3. Giordani C. ITA 1.57.45

**Berchtesgaden**
1. Pelen P. FRA 1.38.51
2. Giordani C. ITA 1.39.61
3. Zini D. ITA 1.39.66

**Badgastein**
1. Wenzel H. LIE 1.32.44
2. Pelen P. FRA 1.32.79
3. Hess E. SUI 1.33.10

**Marburg**
1. Wenzel H. LIE 1.18.11
2. Pelen P. FRA 1.18.73
3. Moser-Proell A. AUT 1.18.98

**Waterville Valley**
1. Pelen P. FRA 1.48.44
2. Patrakeeva M. SOV 1.49.25
3. Wenzel H. LIE 1.49.26

**Vysoke Tatry**
1. Pelen P. FRA 1.27.07
2. Serrat F. FRA 1.27.14
3. McKinney T. USA 1.27.51

**Vysoke Tatry**
1. Zini D. ITA 1.27.29
2. Wenzel H. LIE 1.27.42
3. Hess E. SUI 1.27.60

**Saalbach**
1. Giordani C. ITA 1.30.24
2. Kinshofer C. BRD 1.30.41
3. Wenzel H. LIE 1.30.56

**St. Gervais/Megêve**
1. Pelen P. FRA 1.21.46
2. Moser-Proell A. AUT 1.22.79
3. Zini D. ITA 1.23.54

## MEN 1980/81

### DOWNHILL

**Val d'Isère**
1. Spieß U. AUT 2.00.15
2. Read K. CAN 2.00.52
3. Podborski S. CAN 2.00.71

**Gröden I**
1. Müller P. SUI 2.01.24
2. Weirather H. AUT 2.01.59
3. Podborski S. CAN 2.02.00

**Gröden II**
1. Weirather H. AUT 1.52.96
2. Spieß U. AUT 1.53.09
3. Müller P. SUI 1.53.36

**St. Moritz**
1. Podborski S. CAN 1.54.31
2. Wirnsberger P. AUT 1.54.41
3. Müller P. SUI 1.54.88

**Garmisch**
1. Podborski S. CAN 1.55.48
2. Müller P. SUI 1.56.05
3. Weirather H. AUT 1.56.31

**Kitzbühel**
1. Podborski S. CAN 2.03.76
2. Müller P. SUI 2.04.16
3. Wirnsberger P. AUT 2.04.74

**Wengen**
1. Bürgler T. SUI 2.27.91
2. Weirather H. AUT 2.28.27
3. Podborski S. CAN 2.28.46

**St. Anton**
1. Weirather H. AUT 1.59.67
2. Wirnsberger P. AUT 1.59.73
3. Podborski S. CAN 2.00.15

**Aspen**
1. Tsyganov V. SOV 1.52.95
2. Weirather H. AUT 1.53.11
3. Pfaffenbichler G. AUT 1.53.18

**Aspen**
1. Weirather H. AUT 1.52.21
2. Podborski S. CAN 1.52.49
3. Heinzer F. SUI 1.52.59

### GIANT SLALOM

**Madonna di Campiglio**
1. Stenmark I. SWE 2.42.14
2. Zhirov A. SOV 2.42.66
3. Jäger Gerhard AUT 2.43.14

**Ebnat-Kappel**
1. Orlainsky C. AUT 2.41.41
2. Enn H. AUT 2.41.50
3. Fournier J.-L. SUI 2.41.58

**Morzine**
1. Stenmark I. SWE 3.06.26
2. Gaspoz J. SUI 3.06.77
3. Krizaj B. JUG 3.06.83

**Adelboden**
1. Stenmark I. SWE 2.45.00
2. Orlainsky C. AUT 2.46.70
Strel B. JUG 2.46.70

**Schladming**
1. Stenmark I. SWE 2.34.80
2. Enn H. AUT 2.35.71
3. Fournier J.-L. SUI 2.35.82

**Voss**
1. Stenmark I. SWE 3.08.60
2. Zhirov A. SOV 3.10.09
3. Nöckler B. ITA 3.11.42

**Åre**
1. Stenmark I. SWE 2.40.96
2. Zhirov A. SOV 2.42.43
3. Mahre P. USA 2.42.84

**Aspen**
1. Mahre P. USA 3.12.76
2. Stenmark I. SWE 3.12.90
3. Mahre S. USA 3.15.22

**Furano**
1. Zhirov A. SOV 3.00.41
2. Jäger G. AUT 3.01.54
3. Stenmark I. SWE 3.01.63

**Borovetz**
1. Zhirov A. SOV 2.29.39
2. Stenmark I. SWE 2.30.55
3. Gaspoz J. SUI 2.30.67

**Laax**
1. Zhirov A. SOV 2.39.80
2. Mahre P. USA 2.40.05
3. Stenmark I. SWE 2.40.24

### SLALOM

**Madonna di Campiglio**
1. Stenmark I. SWE 1.41.05
2. Frommelt P. LIE 1.41.62
3. Krizaj B. JUG 1.41.76

**Garmisch**
1. Mahre S. USA 80.07
2. Popangelov P. BUL 80.57
3. Frommelt P. LIE 80.63

**Oberstaufen**
1. Frommelt P. LIE 1.44.41
2. Stenmark I. SWE 1.44.43
3. Mahre S. USA 1.44.78

**Kitzbühel**
1. Stenmark I. SWE 1.40.47
2. Andreev V. SOV 1.41.12
3. Orlainsky C. AUT 1.41.34

**Wengen**
1. Krizaj B. JUG 1.34.27
2. Girardelli M. LUX 1.34.69
3. Stenmark I. SWE 1.34.84

**St. Anton**
1. Stenmark I. SWE 1.40.94
2. Mahre Ph. USA 1.41.06
3. Halsnes J. NOR 1.41.62

**Oslo**
1. Stenmark I. SWE 1.32.51
2. Fjaelberg B. SWE 1.33.09
3. Andreev V. SOV 1.33.16

**Åre**
1. Mahre P. USA 1.34.36
2. Stenmark I. SWE 1.34.39
3. Gruber F. AUT 1.34.51

**Furano**
1. Mahre P. USA 1.36.97
2. Krizaj B. JUG 1.37.21
3. Stenmark I. SWE 1.37.46

**Borovetz**
1. Zhirov A. SOV 1.52.34
2. Mahre S. USA 1.52.75
3. Mahre P. USA 1.53.17

## WOMEN 1980/81

### DOWNHILL

**Val d'Isère**
1. Nadig M.-T. SUI 1.33.10
2. Kreiner C. CAN 1.34.07
3. Epple I. BRD 1.34.77

**Piancavallo**
1. Nadig M.-T. SUI 1.41.38
2. Fjeldstad T. NOR 1.41.64
3. De Agostini D. SUI 1.41.93

**Altenmarkt**
1. Soltysova J. CSR 1.25.11
2. De Agostini D. SUI 1.25.19
3. Fjeldstad T. NOR 1.25.36

**Pfronten**
1. Pröll C. AUT 1.19.36
2. De Agostini D. SUI 1.19.54
3. Flanders H. USA 1.19.75

**Schruns**
1. De Agostini D. SUI 1.17.92
2. Nelson C. USA 1.18.46
3. Epple I. BRD 1.18.78

**Montana**
1. Nadig M.-T. SUI 1.44.50
2. De Agostini D. SUI 1.44.60
3. Kinshofer C. BRD 1.45.05

**Megêve I**
1. De Agostini D. SUI 1.21.20
2. Nadig M.-T. SUI 1.21.70
3. Fjeldstad T. NOR 1.21.86

**Megêve II**
1. Nadig M.-T. SUI 1.21.05
2. De Agostini D. SUI 1.21.13
3. Pröll C. AUT 1.21.69

**Haus**
1. Sorensen G. CAN 1.39.27
2. Epple I. BRD 1.39.35
3. Pröll C. AUT 1.39.47

**Aspen**
1. Kirchler E. AUT 1.25.07
2. Moesenlechner R. BRD 1.25.12
3. Nelson C. USA 1.25.16

### GIANT SLALOM

**Val d'Isère**
1. Epple I. BRD 2.16.92
2. Pelen P. FRA 2.17.49
3. Kinshofer C. BRD 2.17.72

**Limone Piemonte**
1. Nadig M.-T. SUI 2.50.45
2. Zini D. ITA 2.50.57
3. Serrat F. FRA 2.50.76

**Haute Nendaz**
1. McKinney T. USA 2.35.09
2. Wenzel H. LIE 2.35.53
3. Epple I. BRD 2.35.60

**Les Gets**
1. McKinney T. USA 2.05.96
2. Kinshofer C. BRD 2.07.65
3. Wenzel H. LIE 2.08.08

**Zwiesel**
1. Epple M BRD 2.18.69
2. Kinshofer C BRD 2.18.83
3. McKinney T. USA 2.19.04

**Maribor**
1. Nadig M.-T. SUI 2.31.40
2. Epple M. BRD 2.32.01
3. Epple I. BRD 2.32.16

**Aspen**
1. McKinney T. USA 2.23.59
2. Hess E. SUI 2.24.09
3. Bieler W. ITA 2.25.16

**Furano**
1. Nadig. M.-T. SUI 2.34.05
2. Wenzel H. LIE 2.34.44
3. Cooper C. USA 2.34.86

**Wangs**
1. Hess E. SUI 2.20.46
2. Cooper C. USA 2.21.54
3. Wenzel H. LIE 2.21.79

### SLALOM

**Piancavallo**
1. Serrat F. FRA 1.51.85
2. Hess E. SUI 1.52.96
3. Quario M.-R. ITA 1.53.26

**Altenmarkt**
1. Pelen P. FRA 1.28.13
2. Kinshofer C. BRD 1.28.35
3. Zini D. ITA 1.28.43

**Bormio**
1. Pelen P. FRA 1.37.23
2. Patrakeeva N. SOV 1.37.58
3. Hess E. SUI 1.37.64

**Schruns**
1. Hess E. SUI 1.30.28
2. Giordani C. ITA 1.32.01
3. McKinney T. USA 1.32.04

**Montana**
1. Hess E. SUI 1.33.46
2. Cooper C. USA 1.33.90
3. Wenzel H. LIE 1.34.46

**Les Diablerets**
1. Hess E. SUI 1.17.98
2. Cooper C. USA 1.18.84
3. Zini D. ITA 1.18.87

**Zwiesel**
1. Hess E. SUI 1.34.12
2. Zini D. ITA 1.34.64
3. Cooper C. USA 1.34.74

**Furano**
1. Hess E. SUI 1.19.18
2. Cooper C. USA 1.19.36
3. Epple M. BRD 1.19.59

**Wangs**
1. Hess E. SUI 1.29.96
2. Zini D. ITA 1.31.09
3. Walliser M. SUI 1.31.44

## MEN 1981/82

### DOWNHILL

**Val d'Isère**
1. Klammer F. AUT 2.05.22
2. Müller P. SUI 2.05.48
3. Bürgler T. SUI 2.05.63

**Gröden**
1. Resch E. AUT 2.07.41
2. Bartelski K. GBR 2.07.52
3. Stock L. AUT 2.07.81

**Crans Montana**
1. Podborski S. CAN 2.09.22
2. Müller P. SUI 2.09.37
3. Read K. CAN 2.09.83

**Kitzbühel I**
1. Weirather H. AUT 1.57.20
2. Podborski S. CAN 1.57.89
3. Read K. CAN 1.57.97

**Kitzbühel II**
1. Podborski S. CAN 1.57.24
2. Klammer F. AUT 1.57.78
3. Read K. CAN 1.57.90

**Wengen**
1. Weirather Harti AUT 2.04.43
2. Resch E. AUT 2.04.93
3. Wirnsberger P. AUT 2.04.96

**Garmisch**
1. Podborski S. CAN 1.50.52
2. Cathomen K. SUI 1.50.81
3. Weirather H. AUT 1.50.94

**Whistler Mountain**
1. Müller P. SUI 2.14.38
2. Podborski S. CAN 2.15.53
3. Irwin D. CAN 2.15.73

**Aspen I**
1. Müller P. SUI 1.47.17
2. Weirather H. AUT 1.47.28
3. Cathomen C. SUI 1.47.55

**Aspen II**
1. Müller P. SUI 1.46.50
2. Brooker T. CAN 1.47.18
3. Höflehner H. AUT 1.47.31

### GIANT SLALOM

**Aprica**
1. Gaspoz J. SUI 2.38.49
2. Mahre P. USA 2.40.47
3. Stenmark I. SWE 2.40.52

**Cortina**
1. Strel B. JUG 2.41.06
2. Mahre P. USA 2.41.33
3. Gaspoz J. SUI 2.41.43

**Morzine/FRA**
1. Stenmark I. SWE 2.34.04
2. Mahre P. USA 2.34.57
3. Girardelli M. LUX 2.35.00

**Adelboden**
1. Stenmark I. SWE 2.34.25
2. Mahre P. USA 2.36.41
3. Julen M. SUI 2.36.82

**Kirchberg**
1. Stenmark I. SWE 2.52.06
2. Mahre P. USA 2.52.98
3. Girardelli M. LUX 2.54.05

**Jasna**
1. Mahre S. USA 2.15.07
2. Enn H. AUT 2.15.10
3. Mahre P. USA 2.15.21

**Bad Kleinkirchheim**
1. Mahre S. USA 2.34.16
2. Mahre P. USA 2.34.23
3. Zurbriggen P. SUI 2.34.71

**San Sicario**
1. Zurbriggen P. SUI 2.42.37
2. Girardelli M LUX 2.43.03
3. Mahre P. USA 2.43.15

**Kranjska Gora**
1. Mahre P. USA 2.23.65
2. Enn H. AUT 2.23.91
3. Girardelli M. LUX 2.24.40

### SLALOM

**Madonna di Campiglio**
1. Mahre P. USA 1.38.89
2. Stenmark I. SWE 1.39.04
3. De Chiesa P. ITA 1.39.68

**Cortina**
1. Mahre S. USA 1.44.64
2. Mahre P. USA 1.44.72
3. Stenmark I. SWE 1.45.70

**Bad Wiessee**
1. Stenmark I. SWE 1.38.96
2. Gruber F. AUT 1.39.33
2. Mahre P. USA 1.39.76

**Kitzbühel**
1. Stenmark I. SWE 1.42.64
2. Mahre P. USA 1.45.80
3. Mahre S. USA 1.46.76
De Chiesa P. ITA 1.46.76

**Wengen**
1. Mahre P. USA 1.33.48
2. Stenmark I. SWE 1.33.77
3. Frommelt P. LIE 1.33.90

**Garmisch**
1. Mahre S. USA 1.35.79
2. Mahre P. USA 1.36.86
3. De Chiesa P. ITA 1.37.16

**Jasna**
1. Mahre P. USA 1.27.92
2. Stenmark I. SWE 1.29.51
3. Mahre S. USA 1.29.93
Steiner A. AUT 1.29.93

**Kranjska Gora**
1. Krizaj B. JUG 1.38.89
2. Stenmark I. SWE 1.38.93
3. Gruber F. AUT 1.39.10

**Montgenevre**
1. Mahre P. USA 1.39.41
2. Stenmark I. SWE 1.40.07
3. Gaspoz J. SUI 1.40.09

## WOMEN 1981/82

### DOWNHILL

**Saalbach I**
1. Gros-Gaudenier FRA 1.41.00
2. De Agostini D. SUI 1.42.00
3. Wolf S. AUT 1.42.31

**Saalbach II**
1. De Agostini D. SUI 1.13.71
2. Gros-Gaudenier FRA 1.13.96
3. Epple I. BRD 1.14.00

**Grindelwald I**
1. Sörensen G. CAN 2.00.54
2. Gros-Gaudenier FRA 2.00.86
3. Chaud E. FRA 2.01.29

**Grindelwald II**
1. Sorensen G. CAN 2.00.14
2. Epple I. BRD 2.00.59
3. Nelson C. USA 2.00.72

**Badgastein I**
1. Flanders H. USA 1.57.65
2. Sölkner L. AUT 1.57.94
3. Eder S. AUT 1.57.95

**Badgastein II**
1. Eder S. AUT 1.58.10
2. Chaud E. FRA 1.58.27
3. Flanders H. USA 1.58.33

**Arosa I**
1. Flanders H. USA 1.36.62
2. Nelson C. USA 1.36.80
3. Walliser M. SUI 1.36.94

**Arosa II**
1. De Agostini D. SUI 1.36.67
2. Walliser M. SUI 1.36.93
3. Sörensen G. CAN 1.37.10

### GIANT SLALOM

**Val d'Isère**
1. Epple I. BRD 2.30.24
2. Hess E. SUI 2.30.91
3. McKinney T. USA 2.31.29

**Pila**
1. Epple I. BRD 2.34.62
2. Wenzel H. LIE 2.34.89
3. McKinney T. USA 2.35.27

**St. Gervais**
1. Chaud E. FRA 2.58.14
2. Epple I. BRD 2.58.44
3. Hess E. SUI 2.58.59

**Pfronten/BRD**
1. Epple I. BRD 2.24.70
2. Hess E. SUI 2.25.81
3. Epple M. BRD 2.25.92

**Oberstaufen**
1. Epple M. BRD 2.27.79
2. Cooper C. USA 2.27.97
3. Hess E. SUI 2.28.35

**Waterville Valley**
1. Epple I. BRD 2.11.85
2. Epple M. BRD 2.12.11
3. McKinney T. USA 2.12.92

**Aspen**
1. Epple M. BRD 2.13.51
2. Hess E. SUI 2.13.67
3. Epple I. BRD 2.14.16

**Alpe d'Huez**
1. Hess E. SUI 2.12.05
2. McKinney T. USA 2.12.09
3. Cooper C. USA 2.13.07

**San Sicario**
1. Epple M. BRD 2.23.97
2. Hess E. SUI 2.24.33
3. Cooper C. USA 2.24.70

### SLALOM

**Piancavallo I**
1. Wenzel H. LIE 1.45.17
2. Hess E. SUI 1.45.55
3. Konzett U. LIE 1.46.03

**Piancavallo II**
1. Hess E. SUI 1.45.64
2. Wenzel H. LIE 1.46.44
3. Quario M.-R. ITA 1.46.63

**Chamonix**
1. Hess E. SUI 1.40.40
2. Krobichler A. AUT 1.41.22
3. Konzett U. LIE 1.41.51

**Maribor**
1. Hess E. SUI 1.37.58
2. Quario M.-R. ITA 1.38.43
3. Charvatova O. CSR 1.38.53

**Badgastein**
1. Hess E. SUI 1.30.66
2. Konzett U. LIE 1.31.16
3. Serrat F. FRA 1.32.15

**Lenggries**
1. Konzett U. LIE 1.39.55
2. Kronbichler A. AUT 1.39.56
3. Hess E. SUI 1.40.25

**Berchtesgaden**
1. Cooper C. USA 1.36.53
2. Pelen P. FRA 1.36.79
3. Konzett U. LIE 1.37.11

**Waterville Valley**
1. Konzett U. LIE 1.29.55
2. Quario M.-R. ITA 1.29.85
3. McKinney T. USA 1.29.86

**Alpe d'Huez**
1. Hess E. SUI 1.41.65
2. Zini D. ITA 1.42.57
3. McKinney T. USA 1.42.90

**Montgenevre**
1. Cooper C. USA 1.32.25
2. Epple M. BRD 1.33.55
3. Tlalka D. POL 1.33.65

## MEN 1982/83

### DOWNHILL

**Lagalb/Pontresina**
1. Weirather H. AUT 1.42.13
2. Klammer F. AUT 1.43.15
3. Müller P. SUI 1.43.21

**Gröden I**
1. Cathomen Conr. SUI 2.09.54
2. Resch E. AUT 2.09.87
3. Klammer F. AUT 2.10.09

**Gröden II**
1. Klammer F. AUT 2.08.91
2. Müller P. SUI 2.09.39
3. Räber U. SUI 2.09.61

**Val d'Isère I**
1. Resch E. AUT 1.59.26
2. Luescher P. SUI 1.59.44
3. Cathomen Conr. SUI 1.59.56

**Val d'Isère II**
1. Cathomen Conr. SUI 1.59.20
2. Read K. CAN 1.59.32
3. Sbardellotto D. ITA 1.59.66

**Kitzbühel I**
1. Kernen B. SUI 2.06.68
2. Podborski S. CAN 2.06.79
3. Räber U. SUI 2.07.10

**Kitzbühel II**
1. Brooker T. CAN 2.01.96
2. Räber U. SUI 2.02.19
3. Read K. CAN 2.20.47

**Sarajevo**
1. Pfaffenbichler G. AUT 1.48.81
2. Podborski S. CAN 1.49.02
3. Klammer F. AUT 1.49.07

**St. Anton**
1. Luescher P. SUI 2.04.22
2. Meli S. SUI 2.04.82
3. Weirather H. AUT 2.05.00

**Aspen**
1. Brooker T. CAN 1.47.87
2. Mair M. ITA 1.48.24
3. Höflehner H. AUT 1.48.58

**Lake Louise**
1. Höflehner H. AUT 1.40.52
2. Klammer F. AUT 1.40.75
3. Cathomen C. SUI 1.40.77

### GIANT SLALOM

**Adelboden**
1. Zurbriggen P. SUI 2.24.94
2. Julen M. SUI 2.25.19
3. Lüthy J. SUI 2.25.92

**Kranjska Gora**
1. Enn H. AUT 2.24.19
2. Julen M. SUI 2.24.45
3. Stenmark I. SWE 2.24.89

**Todtnau**
1. Stenmark I. SWE 2.45.66
2. Julen M. SUI 2.46.68
3. Zurbriggen P. SUI 2.46.71

**Gällivare**
1. Stenmark I. SWE 2.29.11
2. Julen M. SUI 2.30.83
Mahre P. USA 2.30.83

**Aspen**
1. Mahre P. USA 2.31.49
2. Girardelli M. LUX 2.31.73
3. Stenmark I. SWE 2.32.09

**Vail**
1. Mahre P. USA 3.03.00
2. Stenmark I. SWE 3.03.14
3. Julen M. SUI 3.03.52

**Furano**
1. Mahre P. USA 2.35.20
2. Julen M. SUI 2.35.21
3. Stenmark I. SWE 2.35.27

### SUPER-G

**Val d'Isère**
1. Müller P. SUI 1.35.16
2. Luescher P. SUI 1.35.22
3. Zurbriggen P. SUI 1.35.77

**Madonna**
1. Mair M. ITA 1.43.71
2. Enn H. AUT 1.43.86
3. Zurbriggen P. SUI 1.43.95

**Garmisch**
1. Luescher P. SUI 1.36.45
2. Zurbriggen P. SUI 1.36.65
3. Enn H. AUT 1.37.60

### SLALOM

**Courmayeur**
1. Stenmark I. SWE 102.12
2. Strand S. SWE 102.43
3. Mahre P. USA 102.86

**Madonna**
1. Strand S. SWE 98.99
2. Stenmark I. SWE 99.23
3. Mahre P. USA 99.26

**Parpan**
1. Mahre S. USA 98.96
2. Lüthy J. SUI 100.73
3. Wenzel A. LIE 100.92

**Kitzbühel**
1. Stenmark I. SWE 105.43
2. Orlainsky C. AUT 106.37
3. Mahre P. USA 106.56

**Kranjska Gora**
1. Gruber F. AUT 88.62
2. Strand S. SWE 88.96
3. Canac M. FRA 89.43

**St. Anton**
1. Mahre S. USA 111.44
2. Wenzel A. LIE 111.49
3. Mahre P. USA 111.61

**Markstein I**
1. Stenmark I. SWE 104.54
2. De Chiesa P. ITA 105.04
3. Mahre P. USA 105.23

**Markstein II**
1. Krizaj B. JUG 98.98
2. Fjällberg B. SWE 99.42
3. Orlainsky C. AUT 99.56

**Tärnaby**
1. Wenzel A. LIE 10.48
2. Strand S. SWE 100.98
3. Krizaj B. JUG 101.20

**Gällivare**
1. Girardelli M. LUX 92.49
2. Strand S. SWE 93.88
3. Stenmark I. SWE 94.08

**Furano**
1. Strand S. SWE 92.31
2. Wenzel A. LIE 92.82
3. Krizaj B. JUG 93.32

### PARALLEL SLALOM

**Furano**
1. Stenmark I. SWE
2. Mahre P. USA
3. Wenzel A. LIE

## WOMEN 1982/83

### DOWNHILL

**Val d'Isère**
1. De Agostini D. SUI 1.22.58
2. Sölkner L. AUT 1.22.96
3. Walliser M. SUI 1.23.61

**Sansicario**
1. Attia C. FRA 1.24.57
2. Emonet C. FRA 1.24.86
3. Wiesler H. BRD 1.25.16

**Schruns**
1. De Agostini D. SUI 1.24.57
2. Chaud E. FRA 1.24.69
3. Attia C. FRA 1.24.89

**Megêve I**
1. Walliser M. SUI 1.24.52
2. Maricich M. USA 1.24.71
3. Waldmeier M.-L. FRA 1.24.78

**Megêve II**
1. Kirchler E. AUT 1.23.31
2. De Agostini D. SUI 1.23.40
3. Attia C. FRA 1.23.69

**Les Diablerets**
1. De Agostini D. SUI 1.24.65
2. Kirchler E. AUT 1.25.13
3. Vitzthum V. AUT 1.25.44

**Sarajevo/Jahorina**
1. Walliser M. SUI 1.19.88
2. Kirchler E. AUT 1.20.67
3. Ehrat A. SUI 1.21.10

**Mt. St. Anne**
1. Graham L. CAN 1.32.53
2. Walliser M. SUI 1.32.93
3. Figini M. SUI 1.33.52

### GIANT SLALOM

**Val d'Isère**
1. Hess E. SUI 2.22.12
2. McKinney T. USA 2.22.87
3. Wenzel H. LIE 2.23.66

**St. Gervais**
1. McKinney T. USA 2.29.60
2. Cooper C. USA 2.30.62
3. Merle C. FRA 2.30.96

**Mt. St. Anne**
1. Rey A.-F. FRA 2.22.48
2. Epple M. BRD 2.22.57
3. Hess E. SUI 2.23.71

**Waterville Valley I**
1. McKinney T. USA 2.18.44
2. Epple M. BRD 2.19.15
3. Serrat F. FRA 2.19.54

**Waterville Valley II**
1. McKinney T. USA 2.18.72
2. Epple M. USA 2.19.25
3. Nelson C. USA 2.19.74

**Vail**
1. McKinney T. USA 2.23.43
2. Nelson C. USA 2.24.05
3. Hess E. SUI 2.25.32

**Furano**
1. Wenzel H. LIE 2.31.33
2. Serrat F. FRA 2.33.18
3. Walliser M. SUI 2.33.40

### SUPER-G

**Verbier I**
1. Epple I. BRD 1.16.70
2. Wenzel H. LIE 1.16.94
3. McKinney T. USA 1.16.96

**Verbier II**
1. Nelson C. USA 1.08.56
2. Haas Z. SUI 1.09.16
3. Epple I. BRD 1.09.41

### SLALOM

**Limone-Piemonte**
1. McKinney T. USA 96.61
2. Hess E. SUI 96.77
3. Wenzel H. LIE 97.17

**Piancavallo**
1. Hess E. SUI 107.04
2. Pelen P. FRA 107.08
3. Cooper C. USA 107.91

**Davos**
1. McKinney T. USA 85.26
2. Hess E. SUI 85.44
3. Pelen P. FRA 85.73

**Schruns**
1. Kronbichler A. AUT 98.35
2. Quario R.-M. ITA 98.54
Tlalka M. POL 98.54

**Les Diablerets**
1. Quario M.-T. ITA 81.72
2. Wenzel H. LIE 82.29
3. Tlalka D. POL 82.50

**Maribor**
1. Hess E. SUI 102.68
2. Wenzel H. LIE 102.96
3. Kronbichler A. AUT 103.10

**Vysoke Tatry**
1. Quario M.-R. ITA 93.40
2. Hess E. SUI 93.71
3. Tlalka M. POL 94.29

**Waterville Valley**
1. Steiner R. AUT 93.84
2. McKinney T. USA 94.21
3. Wenzel H. LIE 94.23

**Furano**
1. McKinney T. USA 71.80
2. Hess E. SUI 72.00
3. Tlalka M. POL 72.12

### PARALLEL SLALOM

**Furano**
1. Rey A.-F. FRA
2. Wenzel H. LIE
3. Kronbichler A. AUT

## MEN 1983/84

### DOWNHILL

**Schladming**
1. Resch E. AUT 1.58.50
2. Weirather H. AUT 1.58.89
3. Podborski S. CAN 1.58.90

**Val d'Isère**
1. Heinzer F. SUI 2.01.56
2. Brooker T. CAN 2.01.57
3. Weirather H. AUT 2.01.62

**Gröden**
1. Räber U. SUI 1.56.80
2. Brooker T. CAN 1.57.41
3. Podborski S. CAN 1.57.79

**Laax**
1. Räber U. SUI 1.56.75
2. Klammer F. AUT 1.56.86
3. Mair M. ITA 1.57.30

**Wengen**
1. Johnson B. USA 2.10.89
2. Steiner A. AUT 2.11.00
3. Resch E. AUT 2.11.06

**Kitzbühel**
1. Klammer F. AUT 2.02.82
2. Resch E. AUT 2.03.39
3. Steiner A. AUT 2.03.43

**Garmisch**
1. Podborski S. CAN 1.56.95
2. Resch E. AUT 1.57.20
3. Klammer F. AUT 1.57.44

**Cortina**
1. Höflehner H. AUT 1.51.81
2. Räber U. SUI 1.43.05
3. Cathomen C. SUI 1.53.06

**Aspen**
1. Johnson B. USA 1.49.60
2. Höflehner H. AUT 1.49.85
Steiner A. AUT 1.49.85

**Whistler Mountain**
1. Johnson B. USA 2.02.85
2. Höflehner H. AUT 2.03.17
3. Zurbriggen P. SUI 2.03.18

### GIANT SLALOM

**Les Diablerets**
1. Julen M. SUI 3.17.68

| | | |
|---|---|---|
| 2. Zurbriggen P. | SUI | 3.18.27 |
| 3. Franko J. | JUG | 3.19.33 |

| **Adelboden** | | |
|---|---|---|
| 1. Stenmark I. | SWE | 2.27.36 |
| 2. Strolz H. | AUT | 2.28.04 |
| 3. Zurbriggen P. | SUI | 2.28.16 |

| **Kirchberg** | | |
|---|---|---|
| 1. Stenmark I. | SWE | 3.13.96 |
| 2. Girardelli M. | LUX | 3.15.21 |
| 3. Sundquist J. | SWE | 3.16.36 |

| **Borovetz** | | |
|---|---|---|
| 1. Stenmark I. | SWE | 2.29.60 |
| 2. Girardelli M. | LUX | 2.30.13 |
| 3. Erlacher R. | ITA | 2.20.38 |

| **Aspen** | | |
|---|---|---|
| 1. Zurbriggen P. | SUI | 2.32.40 |
| 2. Girardelli M. | LUX | 2.33.28 |
| 3. Mahre Ph. | USA | 2.33.33 |

| **Vail** | | |
|---|---|---|
| 1. Stenmark I. | SWE | 2.50.58 |
| 2. Zurbriggen P. | SUI | 2.51.43 |
| 3. Enn H. | AUT | 2.51.69 |

| **Åre** | | |
|---|---|---|
| 1. Enn H. | AUT | 1.25.27 |
| 2. Strolz H. | AUT | 2.25.43 |
| 3. Stenmark I. | SWE | 2.25.50 |

| **Oslo** | | |
|---|---|---|
| 1. Enn H. | AUT | 2.17.65 |
| 2. Giorgi A. | ITA | 2.17.89 |
| 3. Bürgler T. | SUI | 2.17.98 |

### SUPER-G

| **Val d'Isère** | | |
|---|---|---|
| 1. Enn. H. | AUT | 1.36.26 |
| 2. Zurbriggen P. | SUI | 1.36.73 |
| 3. Franko J. | JUG | 1.37.02 |

| **Gröden** | | |
|---|---|---|
| 1. Zurbriggen P. | SUI | 1.35.33 |
| 2. Hangl M. | SUI | 1.35.76 |
| 3. Stock L. | AUT | 1.36.63 |

| **Garmisch** | | |
|---|---|---|
| 1. Wenzel A. | LIE | 1.36.53 |
| 2. Zurbriggen P. | SUI | 1.36.62 |
| 3. Enn H. | AUT | 1.37.55 |

| **Oppdal** | | |
|---|---|---|
| 1. Zurbriggen P. | SUI | 1.24.30 |
| 2. Girardelli M. | LUX | 1.25.50 |
| 3. Franko J. | JUG | 1.25.80 |

### SLALOM

| **Kranjska Gora** | | |
|---|---|---|
| 1. Wenzel A. | LIE | 1.39.55 |
| 2. Popangelov P. | BUL | 1.40.30 |
| 3. Frommelt P. | LIE | 1.40.49 |

| **Courmayeur** | | |
|---|---|---|
| 1. Stenmark I. | SWE | 1.48.97 |
| 2. Krizaj B. | JUG | 1.49.13 |
| 3. Mahre S. | USA | 1.50.19 |

| **Madonna di Campiglio** | | |
|---|---|---|
| 1. Stenmark I. | SWE | 1.36.89 |
| 2. Zoller R. | AUT | 1.37.09 |
| 3. Popangelov P. | BUL | 1.37.58 |

| **Parpan I** | | |
|---|---|---|
| 1. Girardelli M. | LUX | 1.47.19 |
| 2. De Chiesa P. | ITA | 1.47.83 |
| 3. Wenzel A. | LIE | 1.47.87 |

| **Parpan II** | | |
|---|---|---|
| 1. Stenmark I. | SWE | 1.47.36 |
| 2. Girardelli M. | LUC | 1.47.63 |
| 3. Gruber F. | AUT | 1.48.58 |

| **Kitzbühel** | | |
|---|---|---|
| 1. Girardelli M. | LUX | 1.38.24 |
| 2. Gruber F. | AUT | 1.38.91 |
| 3. Krizaj B. | JUG | 1.38.93 |

| **Borovetz** | | |
|---|---|---|
| 1. Girardelli M. | LUX | 1.49.21 |
| 2. Stenmark I. | SWE | 1.49.40 |
| 3. Gruber F. | AUT | 1.49.76 |

| **Vail** | | |
|---|---|---|
| 1. Zoller R. | AUT | 1.41.11 |
| 2. Popangelov P. | BUL | 1.41.56 |
| 3. Halvarsson L. | SWE | 1.41.73 |
| Mahre Ph. | USA | 1.41.73 |

| **Åre** | | |
|---|---|---|
| 1. Girardelli M. | LUX | 1.28.84 |
| 2. Gruber F. | AUT | 1.28.91 |
| 3. Halvarsson L. | SWE | 1.29.47 |

| **Oslo** | | |
|---|---|---|
| 1. Girardelli M. | LUX | 1.23.43 |
| 2. Stenmark I. | SWE | 1.24.04 |
| 3. De Chiesa P. | ITA | 1.24.58 |

### PARALLEL SLALOM

| **Oslo** | |
|---|---|
| 1. Enn H. | AUT |
| 2. Steiner A. | AUT |
| 3. Stenmark I. | SWE |

## WOMEN 1983/84

### DOWNHILL

| **Val d'Isère** | | |
|---|---|---|
| 1. Epple I. | BRD | 1.21.72 |
| 2. Ehrat A. | SUI | 1.21.80 |
| 3. Attia C. | FRA | 1.22.34 |

| **Val d'Isère** | | |
|---|---|---|
| 1. Walliser M. | SUI | 1.20.99 |
| 2. Epple I. | BRD | 1.21.13 |
| 3. Sölkner L. | AUT | 1.21.27 |

| **Haus/Ennstal** | | |
|---|---|---|
| 1. Wenzel H. | LIE | 1.44.67 |
| 2. Epple I. | BRD | 1.45.00 |
| 3. Walliser M. | SUI | 1.45.03 |

| **Puy St. Vincent** | | |
|---|---|---|
| 1. Sörensen G. | CAN | 1.40.44 |
| 2. Vitzthum V. | AUT | 1.41.82 |
| 3. Walliser M. | SUI | 1.42.02 |

| **Badgastein** | | |
|---|---|---|
| 1. Wenzel H. | LIE | 1.58.88 |
| 2. Epple I. | BRD | 1.58.92 |
| 3. Walliser M. | SUI | 1.59.11 |

| **Verbier** | | |
|---|---|---|
| 1. Walliser M. | SUI | 1.39.84 |
| 2. Flanders H.B. | USA | 1.39.99 |
| 3. Charvatova O. | CSR | 1.40.76 |

| **Megêve/St. Gervais** | | |
|---|---|---|
| 1. Figini M. | SUI | 1.26.49 |
| 2. Kirchler E. | SUI | 1.27.06 |
| 3. Eder S. | AUT | 1.27.16 |

| **Mt. St. Anne** | | |
|---|---|---|
| 1. Flanders H. | USA | 1.29.50 |
| 2. Waldmeier M. | FRA | 1.30.20 |
| 3. Eder S. | AUT | 1.30.21 |

### GIANT SLALOM

| **Val d'Isère** | | |
|---|---|---|
| 1. Hess E. | SUI | 2.24.11 |
| 2. Pelen P. | FRA | 2.25.06 |
| 3. Wenzel H. | LIE | 2.25.79 |

| **Haus Ennstal** | | |
|---|---|---|
| 1. Wenzel H. | LIE | 2.09.46 |
| 2. Epple M. | BRD | 2.09.57 |
| 3. Cooper C. | USA | 2.09.65 |

| **Megeve/St. Gervais** | | |
|---|---|---|
| 1. Hess E. | SUI | 2.24.05 |
| 2. Cooper C. | USA | 2.24.94 |
| 3. Merle C. | FRA | 2.25.13 |

| **Lake Placid** | | |
|---|---|---|
| 1 Cooper C. | USA | 2.38.38 |
| 2. Kiehl M. | BRD | 2.39.15 |
| 3. Epple M. | BRD | 2.39.36 |

| **Waterville Valley** | | |
|---|---|---|
| 1. McKinney T. | USA | 2.09.66 |
| 2. Hess E. | SUI | 2.10.16 |
| 3. Cooper C. | USA | 2.10.30 |

| **Jasna** | | |
|---|---|---|
| 1. Hess E. | SUI | 2.17.08 |
| 2. Figini M. | SUI | 2.17.89 |
| 3. Cooper C. | USA | 2.17.96 |

| **Zwiesel** | | |
|---|---|---|
| 1. McKinney T. | USA | 2.13.28 |
| 2. Hess E. | SUI | 2.14.05 |
| 3. Fernandez B. | SPA | 2.14.28 |

### SUPER-G

| **Puy St. Vincent** | | |
|---|---|---|
| 1. Graham L. | CAN | 1.15.73 |
| 2. Figini M. | SUI | 1.15.98 |
| 3. Armstrong D. | USA | 1.16.21 |

| **Mt. St. Anne** | | |
|---|---|---|
| 1. Kiehl M. | BRD | 1.24.44 |
| 2. Kirchler E. | AUT | 1.25.36 |
| 3. Cooper C. | USA | 1.25.61 |

### SLALOM

| **Kranjska Gora** | | |
|---|---|---|
| 1. Hess E. | SUI | 1.33.39 |
| 2. McKinney T. | USA | 1.34.01 |
| 3. Tlalka M. | POL | 1.35.85 |

| **Sestriere** | | |
|---|---|---|
| 1. Quario M.-R. | ITA | 1.37.66 |
| 2. Steiner R. | AUT | 1.37.99 |
| 3. Hess M. | SUI | 1.38.28 |

| **Piancavallo** | | |
|---|---|---|
| 1. Steiner R. | AUT | 1.34.05 |
| 2. Tlalka M. | POL | 1.34.33 |
| 3. Quario M.-R. | ITA | 1.34.72 |

| **Maribor** | | |
|---|---|---|
| 1. Hess E. | SUI | 1.26.94 |
| 2. McKinney T. | USA | 1.27.00 |
| 3. Cooper C. | USA | 1.27.10 |

| **Badgastein** | | |
|---|---|---|
| 1. Pelen P. | FRA | 1.34.47 |
| 2. Steiner R. | AUT | 1.35.05 |
| 3. Tlalka D. | POL | 1.35.08 |

| **Verbier** | | |
|---|---|---|
| 1. Kronbichler A. | AUT | 1.30.97 |
| 2. Epple M. | BRD | 1.31.07 |
| 3. Hess E. | SUI | 1.31.67 |

| **Limone Piemonte** | | |
|---|---|---|
| 1. Zini D. | ITA | 1.42.39 |
| 2. Quario M.-R. | ITA | 1.42.51 |
| 3. Cooper C. | USA | 1.42.62 |

| **Waterville Valley** | | |
|---|---|---|
| 1. McKinney T. | USA | 1.37.78 |
| 2. Gadient B. | SUI | 1.38.91 |
| 3. Pelen P. | FRA | 1.38.96 |

| **Jasna** | | |
|---|---|---|
| 1. Steiner R. | AUT | 1.35.53 |
| 2. Pelen P. | FRA | 1.35.82 |
| 3. Magoni P. | ITA | 1.36.34 |

| **Zwiesel** | | |
|---|---|---|
| 1. Wenzel H. | LIE | 91.77 |
| 2. McKinney T. | USA | 91.96 |
| 3. Pelen P. | FRA | 92.58 |

| **Oslo** | | |
|---|---|---|
| 1. McKinney T. | USA | 1.29.21 |
| 2. Tlalka D. | POL | 1.30.15 |
| 3. Pelen P. | FRA | 1.30.31 |

### PARALLEL SLALOM

| **Oslo** | |
|---|---|
| 1. Charvatova O. | CSR |
| 2. Hess E. | SUI |
| 3. McKinney T. | USA |

## MEN 1984/85

### DOWNHILL

| **Val Gardena** | | |
|---|---|---|
| 1. Höflehner H. | AUT | 2.06.82 |
| 2. Cathomen C. | SUI | 2.07.66 |
| 3. Wirnsberger P. | AUT | 2.08.25 |

| **Kitzbühel** | | |
|---|---|---|
| 1. Zurbriggen P. | SUI | 2.08.65 |
| 2. Heinzer F. | SUI | 2.08.98 |
| 3. Wirnsberger P. | AUT | 2.09.33 |

| **Kitzbühel** | | |
|---|---|---|
| 1. Zurbriggen P. | SUI | 2.06.95 |
| 2. Höflehner H. | AUT | 2.07.21 |
| 3. Brooker T. | CAN | 2.08.10 |

| **Wengen** | | |
|---|---|---|
| 1. Höflehner H. | AUT | 2.36.04 |
| 2. Heinzer F. | SUI | 2.36.15 |
| 3. Wirnsberger P. | AUT | 2.36.59 |

| **Wengen** | | |
|---|---|---|
| 1. Wirnsberger P. | AUT | 2.35.97 |
| 2. Luescher P. | SUI | 2.36.19 |
| 3. Müller P. | SUI | 2.36.53 |

| **Garmisch-Partenkirchen** | | |
|---|---|---|
| 1. Höflehner H. | AUT | 1.54.56 |
| 2. Müller P. | SUI | 1.54.78 |
| 3. Steiner A. | AUT | 1.55.23 |

| **Bad Kleinkirchheim** | | |
|---|---|---|
| 1. Alpiger K. | SUI | 1.56.04 |
| 2. Müller P. | SUI | 1.56.43 |
| 3. Niederseer G. | AUT | 1.57.01 |

| **Furano** | | |
|---|---|---|
| 1. Brooker T. | CAN | 1.55.62 |
| 2. Wildgruber S. | BRD | 1.56.18 |
| 3. Kernen B. | SUI | 1.56.35 |

| **Aspen** | | |
|---|---|---|
| 1. Müller P. | SUI | 1.45.74 |
| 2. Alpiger K. | SUI | 1.45.91 |
| 3. Wildgruber S. | BRD | 1.46.58 |

| **Panorama** | | |
|---|---|---|
| 1. Müller P. | SUI | 2.03.12 |
| 2. Mahrer D. | SUI | 2.03.83 |
| 3. Höflehner H. | AUT | 2.03.86 |

### GIANT SLALOM

| **Puy-St. Vincent** | | |
|---|---|---|
| 1. Erlacher R. | ITA | 2.30.13 |
| 2. Hangl M. | SUI | 2.30.34 |
| 3. Pramotton R. | ITA | 2.30.40 |

| **Sestrière** | | |
|---|---|---|
| 1. Girardelli M. | LUX | 2.25.56 |
| 2. Wasmaier M. | BRD | 2.26.51 |
| 3. Julen M. | SUI | 2.26.73 |

| **Schladming** | | |
|---|---|---|
| 1. Bürgler T. | SUI | 2.36.65 |
| 2. Girardelli M. | LUX | 2.36.76 |
| 3. Hangl M. | SUI | 2.38.33 |

| **Adelboden** | | |
|---|---|---|
| 1. Enn H. | AUT | 3.07.14 |
| 2. Strolz H. | AUT | 3.07.21 |
| 3. Pramotton R. | ITA | 3.07.61 |

| **Kranjska Gora** | | |
|---|---|---|
| 1. Bürgler T. | SUI | 2.10.21 |
| 2. Zurbriggen P. | SUI | 2.10.22 |
| 3. Girardelli M. | LUX | 2.10.42 |

| **Aspen** | | |
|---|---|---|
| 1. Girardelli M. | LUX | 2.27.40 |
| 2. Stenmark I. | SWE | 2.27.72 |
| 3. Julen M. | SUI | 2.27.86 |

### SLALOM

| **Sestrière I** | | |
|---|---|---|
| 1. Girardelli M. | LUX | 1.46.80 |
| 2. Nilsson J. | SWE | 1.49.12 |
| 3. De Chiesa P. | ITA | 1.49.33 |

| **Sestrière II** | | |
|---|---|---|
| 1. Zurbriggen P. | SUI | 1.36.02 |
| 2. De Chiesa P. | ITA | 1.36.85 |
| 3. Edalini I. | ITA | 1.36.94 |

| **Madonna di Campiglio** | | |
|---|---|---|
| 1. Krizaj B. | JUG | 1.36.42 |
| 2. Wenzel A. | LIE | 1.37.05 |
| 3. Popangelov P. | BUL | 1.37.24 |

| **Bad Wiessee** | | |
|---|---|---|
| 1. Girardelli M. | LUX | 1.51.29 |
| 2. Beck F. | BRD | 1.53.74 |
| 3. Stenmark I. | SWE | 1.53.77 |

| **La Mongie** | | |
|---|---|---|
| 1. Wenzel A. | LIE | 1.33.58 |
| 2. Nilsson J. | SWE | 1.33.81 |
| 3. Frommelt P. | LIE | 1.34.04 |

| **Kitzbühel** | | |
|---|---|---|
| 1. Girardelli M. | LUX | 1.40.68 |
| 2. Tötsch O. | ITA | 1.40.86 |
| 3. Krizaj B. | JUG | 1.41.05 |

| **Wengen** | | |
|---|---|---|
| 1. Girardelli M. | LUX | 1.36.23 |
| 2. Stenmark I. | SWE | 1.37.61 |
| 3. Frommelt P. | LIE | 1.38.85 |

| **Kranjska Gora** | | |
|---|---|---|
| 1. Girardelli M. | LUX | 1.43.11 |
| 2. Stenmark I. | SWE | 1.43.16 |
| 3. Nilsson J. | SWE | 1.43.88 |
| Frommelt P. | LIE | 1.43.88 |

| **Park City** | | |
|---|---|---|
| 1. Girardelli M. | LUX | 1.47.24 |
| 2. Petrovic R. | JUG | 1.49.38 |
| 3. Frommelt P. | LIE | 1.50.50 |

| **Heavenly Valley** | | |
|---|---|---|
| 1. Girardelli M. | LUX | 1.48.66 |
| 2. Frommelt P. | LIE | 1.50.40 |
| 3. Zoller R. | AUT | 1.50.74 |

### SUPER-G

| **Puy-St Vincent** | | |
|---|---|---|
| 1. Zurbriggen P. | SUI | 1.43.89 |
| 2. Girardelli M. | LUX | 1.44.80 |
| 3. Bürgler T. | SUI | 1.45.12 |

| **Madonna di Campiglio** | | |
|---|---|---|
| 1. Girardelli M. | LUX | 1.41.87 |
| 2. Zurbriggen P. | SUI | 1.42.78 |
| 3. Hangl M. | SUI | 1.43.20 |

| **Garmisch-Partenkirchen** | | |
|---|---|---|
| 1. Girardelli M. | LUX | 1.34.09 |
| 2. Wenzel A. | LIE | 1.34.26 |
| 3. Stuffer H. | BRD | 1.34.59 |

| **Furano** | | |
|---|---|---|
| 1. Mahrer D. | SUI | 1.31.36 |
| Lee S. | AUS | 1.31.36 |
| 3. Stemmle B. | CAN | 1.31.64 |

| **Panorama** | | |
|---|---|---|
| 1. Zurbriggen P. | SUI | 1.47.10 |
| 2. Erlacher R. | ITA | 1.48.37 |
| 3. Bürgler T. | SUI | 1.48.62 |

## WOMEN 1984/85

### DOWNHILL

| **Puy-St. Vincent** | | |
|---|---|---|
| 1. Haas Z. | SUI | 1.26.30 |
| 2. Kiehl M. | BRD | 1.26.35 |
| 3. Epple I. | BRD | 1.26.55 |

| **Valfurva** | | |
|---|---|---|
| 1. Kirchler E. | AUT | 1.24.60 |
| 2. Vitzthum V. | AUT | 1.24.79 |
| 3. Gutensohn K. | AUT | 1.24.88 |

| **Bad Kleinkirchheim** | | |
|---|---|---|
| 1. Figini M. | SUI | 1.43.23 |
| 2. Oertli B. | SUI | 1.43.83 |
| 3. Ehrat A. | SUI | 1.44.32 |

| **Bad Kleinkirchheim** | | |
|---|---|---|
| 1. Figini M. | SUI | 1.41.72 |
| 2. Oertli B. | SUI | 1.42.35 |
| 3. Walliser M. | SUI | 1.42.58 |

| **Megêve** | | |
|---|---|---|
| 1. Figini M. | SUI | 1.32.23 |
| 2. Quittet C. | FRA | 1.32.42 |
| 3. Emonet C. | FRA | 1.32.94 |

| **Vail** | | |
|---|---|---|
| 1. Gutensohn K. | AUT | 1.47.95 |
| 2. Oertli B. | SUI | 1.48.43 |
| 3. Walliser M. | SUI | 1.48.57 |

| **Sunshine** | | |
|---|---|---|
| 1. Walliser M. | SUI | 1.21.05 |
| 2. Figini M. | SUI | 1.21.36 |
| 3. Graham L. | CAN | 1.21.65 |

| **Sunshine** | | |
|---|---|---|
| 1. Graham L. | CAN | 1.19.50 |
| 2. Figini M. | SUI | 1.19.89 |
| 3. Walliser M. | SUI | 1.20.28 |

### GIANT SLALOM

| **Madonna di Campiglio** | | |
|---|---|---|
| 1. Kiehl M. | BRD | 2.49.65 |
| 2. Walliser M. | SUI | 2.50.57 |
| 3. Haas Z. | SUI | 2.50.67 |

| **S. Caterina/Valfurva** | | |
|---|---|---|
| 1. Schneider V. | SUI | 2.36.56 |
| 2. McKinney T. | USA | 2.37.66 |
| 3. Epple M. | BRD | 2.38.15 |

| **Maribor** | | |
|---|---|---|
| 1. Figini M. | SUI | 2.33.43 |
| 2. Schneider V. | SUI | 2.34.04 |
| 3. Fernandez B. | SPA | 2.35.48 |

| **Pfronten** | | |
|---|---|---|
| 1. Figini M. | SUI | 1.23.13 |
| 2. Kiehl M. | BRD | 1.23.48 |
| 3. Walliser M. | SUI | 1.24.02 |

| **St. Gervais** | | |
|---|---|---|
| 1. Figini M. | SUI | 2.47.61 |
| 2. Kirchler E. | AUT | 2.47.85 |
| 3. Rey A.-F. | FRA | 2.47.93 |

| **Arosa** | | |
|---|---|---|
| 1. Kiehl M. | BRD | 1.25.07 |
| 2. Twardokens E. | USA | 1.25.41 |
| 3. Figini M. | SUI | 1.26.06 |

| **Vail** | | |
|---|---|---|
| 1. Fernandez B. | SPA | 2.26.88 |
| 2. Walliser M. | SUI | 2.27.49 |
| 3. Schneider V. | SUI | 2.28.12 |
| Haas Z. | SUI | 2.28.12 |

| **Lake Placid** | | |
|---|---|---|
| 1. Roffe D. | USA | 2.37.73 |
| 2. Svet M. | JUG | 2.37.87 |
| 3. Kiehl M. | BRD | 2.37.95 |

**Waterville Valley**
1. Schneider V. SUI 2.08.11
2. Roffe D. USA 2.08.31
3. Hächer T. BRD 2.08.66

### SLALOM

**Courmayeur**
1. Pelen P. FRA 1.34.18
2. Epple M. BRD 1.34.55
3. Magoni P. ITA 1.34.79

**Davos**
1. Guignard C. FRA 1.34.04
2. Hess E. SUI 1.34.26
3. Barbier H. FRA 1.34.88

**Madonna di Campiglio**
1. Tlalka D. POL 1.47.90
2. Gadient B. SUI 1.48.36
3. Guignard C. FRA 1.48.57

**Maribor**
1. McKinney T. USA 1.24.06
2. Charvatova O. CSR 1.24.24
3. Gadient B. SUI 1.24.57

**Bad Kleinkirchheim**
1. Guignard C. FRA 1.26.17
2. Quario M.-R. ITA 1.26.49
3. Hess E. SUI 1.27.48

**Pfronten**
1. Magoni P. ITA 1.47.18
2. Oertli B. SUI 1.48.50
3. Zini D. ITA 1.49.18

**Arosa**
1. Epple M. BRD 1.48.11
2. McKinney T. USA 1.48.12
3. Hess E. SUI 1.49.15

**Waterville Valley**
1. McKinney T. USA 1.33.10
2. Quario M.-R. ITA 1.33.45
3. Kronbichler A. AUT 1.34.21

**Park City**
1. Hess E. SUI 1.17.30
2. Pelen P. FRA 1.17.42
3. Quario M.-R. ITA 1.17.49

**Heavenly Valley**
1. Hess E. SUI 1.29.87
2. Pelen P. FRA 1.30.10
3. Tlalka M. POL 1.30.36

### SUPER-G

**Davos**
1. Hächer T. BRD 1.50.33
2. Walliser M. SUI 1.52.14
3. Kiehl M. BRD 1.52.15

**Sunshine**
1. Kiehl M. BRD 1.23.29
2. Figini M. SUI 1.23.78
3. Oertli B. SUI 1.24.70

## MEN 1985/86

### DOWNHILL

**Las Leñas I**
1. Alpiger K. SUI 1.47.74
2. Lewis D. USA 1.47.78
3. Höflehner H. AUT 1.47.97

**Las Leñas II**
1. Alpiger K. SUI 2.01.27
2. Müller P. SUI 2.01.38
3. Wasmeier M. BRD 2.01.73

**Val d'Isère**
1. Mair M. ITA 2.01.32
2. Girardelli M. LUX 2.01.66
3. Wirnsberger P. AUT 2.01.99

**Val Gardena**
1. Wirnsberger P. AUT 2.04.29
2. Müller P. SUI 2.04.82
3. Wildgruber S. BRD 2.05.28

**Schladming**
1. Wirnsberger P. AUT 1.56.87
2. Müller P. SUI 1.57.84
3. Resch E. AUT 1.57.92

**Kitzbühel I**
1. Wirnsberger P. AUT 2.01.77
2. Resch E. AUT 2.03.00
3. Zurbriggen P. SUI 2.03.12

**Kitzbühel II**
1. Wirnsberger P. AUT 2.02.04
2. Resch E. AUT 2.02.19
3. Mair M. ITA 2.02.52

**Morzine**
1. Steiner A. AUT 1.38.85
2. Oehrli G. SUI 1.38.92
3. Wirnsberger P. AUT 1.38.93

**Morzine**
1. Müller P. SUI 1.53.81
2. Stock L. AUT 1.54.86
3. Skaardal A. NOR 1.54.94

**Åre I**
1. Muller P. SUI 1.56.22
2. Mair Michael ITA 1.57.12
3. Girardelli M. LUX 1.57.58

**Åre II**
1. Heinzer F. SUI 1.55.74
2. Girardelli M. LUX 1.56.25
3. Assinger A. AUT 1.56.38

**Aspen**
1. Muller P. SUI 1.42.96
2. Wirnsberger P. AUT 1.43.25
3. Stock L. AUT 1.43.98

**Whistler Mountain**
1. Steiner A. AUT 2.09.78
2. Mair M. ITA 2.09.89
3. Stock L. AUT 2.10.14

### GIANT SLALOM

**Alta Badia**
1. Stenmark I. SWE 2.38.95
2. Strolz H. AUT 2.39.37
3. Erlacher R. ITA 2.39.90

**Kranjska Gora I**
1. Gaspoz J. SUI 2.16.88
2. Erlacher R. ITA 2.17.05
3. Strolz H. AUT 2.17.42

**Kranjska Gora II**
1. Gaspoz J. SUI 2.03.89
2. Strolz H. AUT 2.04.20
3. Wasmeier M. BRD 2.04.48

**Adelboden**
1. Pramotton R. ITA 2.36.08
2. Tonazzi M. ITA 2.36.38
3. Strolz H. AUT 2.36.51

**Hemsedal**
1. Stenmark I. SWE 2.26.04
2. Stuffer H. BRD 2.26.32
3. Strolz H. AUT 2.26.67

**Lake Placid I**
1. Stenmark I. SWE 2.40.90
2. Strolz H. AUT 2.40.94
3. Erlacher R. ITA 2.41.32

**Lake Placid II**
1. Gaspoz J. SUI 2.34.27
2. Erlacher R. ITA 2.34.84
3. Strolz H. AUT 2.35.01

### SLALOM

**Sestrière**
1. Petrovic R. JUG 1.40.79
2. Krizaj B. JUG 1.41.53
3. Edalini I. ITA 1.41.69

**Madonna di Campiglio**
1. Nilsson J. SWE 1.37.04
2. Krizaj B. JUG 1.37.67
3. Frommelt P. LIE 1.38.48

**Kranjska Gora**
1. Petrovic R. JUG 1.44.83
2. Nilsson J. SWE 1.45.63
3. Stangassinger T. AUT 1.46.92

**Berchtesgaden**
1. Wallner J. SWE 1.43.96
2. Krizaj B. JUG 1.44.05
3. Mougel D. FRA 1.44.76

**Kitzbühel**
1. Frommelt P. LIE 1.42.13
2. Stenmark I. SWE 1.43.14
3. Köhlbichler D. AUT 1.43.62
Wenzel A. LIE 1.43.62

**Parpan**
1. Bouvet D. FRA 1.33.03
2. Stenmark I. SWE 1.33.54
3. Bürgler T. SUI 1.33.71

**St. Anton I**
1. Stenmark I. SWE 1.47.59
2. Petrovic R. JUG 1.47.87
3. Nilsson J. SWE 1.47.93

**Wengen**
1. Petrovic R. JUG 1.31.14
2. Bouvet D. FRA 1.32.34
3. Krizaj B. JUG 1.32.76

**Åre**
1. Zurbriggen P. SUI 1.32.53
2. Frommelt P. LIC 1.33.52
3. Nilsson J. SWE 1.33.66

**Lillehammer**
1. Petrovic R. YUG 1.23.99
2. Stenmark I. SWE 1.24.12
3. Girardelli M. LUX 1.24.71

**Geilo**
1. Mader G. AUT 1.40.66
2. Frommelt P. LIC 1.41.47
3. Petrovic R. YUG 1.41.55

**Heavenly Valley**
1. Petrovic R. YUG 1.44.52
2. Zurbriggen P. SUI 1.45.45
3. Stenmark I. SWE 1.46.33

Bromont
1. Krizaj B. YUG 1.59.66
2. Frommelt P. LIC 1.59.88
3. Zurbriggen P. SUI 2.00.12

### SUPER G

**Crans-Montana I**
1. Müller P. SUI 1.39.32
2. Zurbriggen P. SUI 1.39.72
3. Wasmeier M. BRD 1.39.95

**Crans Montana II**
1. Girardelli M. LUX 1.47.34
2. Wasmeier M. BRD 1.47.46
3. Müller P. SUI 1.47.64

**Morzine**
1. Wasmeier M. BRD 1.22.32
2. Girardelli M. LUX 1.23.36
3. Strolz H. AUT 1.23.61

**Hemsedal**
1. Zurbriggen P. SUI 1.37.44
2. Wasmeier M. BRD 1.37.62
3. Stock L. AUT 1.38.72

### PARALLEL SLALOM

**Wien**
1. Edalini I. ITA
2. Wasmeier M. BRD
3. Steiner A. AUT

## WOMEN 1985/86

### DOWNHILL

**Val d'Isère I**
1. Gerg M. BRD 1.25.59
2. Graham L. CAN 1.25.70
3. Walliser M. SUI 1.25.75

**Val d'Isère II**
1. Graham L. CAN 1.25.01
2. Walliser M. SUI 1.25.13
3. Gerg M. BRD 1.25.68

**Badgastein I**
1. Gutensohn K. AUT 2.03.05
2. Savijarvi L. CAN 2.03.38
3. Graham L. CAN 2.03.95

**Badgastein II**
1. Walliser M. SUI 2.04.04
2. Winkler S. AUT 2.05.39
3. Gutensohn K. AUT 2.06.41

**Puy-St. Vincent**
1. Gutensohn K. AUT 1.31.17
2. Oertli B. SUI 1.31.23
3. Graham L. CAN 1.31.42

**Crans-Montana I**
1. Graham L. CAN 1.30.80
2. Oertli B. SUI 1.31.07
3. Gutensohn K. AUT 1.31.58

**Crans-Montana II**
1. Gutensohn K. AUT 1.27.64
2. Walliser M. SUI 1.28.36
3. Haas Z. SUI 1.28.55

**Furano**
1. Walliser M. SUI 1.19.92
2. Ortli B. SUI 1.20.11
3. Graham L. CAN 1.20.32

**Sunshine**
1. Walliser M. SUI 1.32.37
2. Gutensohn K. AUT 1.33.16
3. Percy K. CAN 1.33.44

**Vail**
1. Fletscher P. A. USA 1.54.28
2. Graham L. CAN 1.54.60
3. Walliser M. SUI 1.55.08

### GIANT SLALOM

**Maribor**
1. Schneider V. SUI 2.31.90
2. Figini M. SUI 2.33.01
3. Kiehl M. BRD 2.33.37

**Oberstaufen I**
1. Schneider V. SUI 2.14.53
2. Gerg M. BRD 2.15.45
3. Figini M. SUI 2.15.84

**Oberstaufen II**
1. Hächer T. BRD 2.23.45
2. Schneider V. SUI 2.24.40
3. Charvatova O. CSR 2.24.76

**Valzoldana**
1. Walliser M. SUI 2.34.00
2. Svet M. JUG 2.34.97
3. Charvatova O. CSR 2.35.89

**Vysoke Tatry**
1. Svet M. JUG 1.48.71
2. Fernandez B. SPA 1.49.19
3. Hächer T. BRD 1.49.47

**Sunshine**
1. Haecher T. BRD
2. Walliser M. SUI
3. Zacj K. YUG

**Waterville Valley**
Schneider V. SUI 2.13.42
2. Wachter A. AUT 2.15.15
3. Charvatova O. TCH 2.16.29

**Bromont**
1. Svet M. YUG 2.17.16
2. Charvotova O. TCH 2.18.76
3. Schneider V. SUI 2.19.27

### SLALOM

**Sestrière**
1. Steiner R. AUT 1.30.02
2. Hess E. SUI 1.30.22
3. Oertli B. SUI 1.30.32

**Savognin**
1. Hess E. SUI 1.42.89
2. Gadient B. SUI 1.43.36
3. Bonfini N. ITA 1.43.37

**Maribor**
1. Steiner R. AUT 1.19.12
2. Hess E. SUI 1.19.89
3. Ladstätter I. AUT 1.20.33

**Badgastein**
1. Kronbichler A. AUT 1.36.53
2. Hess E. SUI 1.37.69
3. Schneider V. SUI 1.38.45

**St. Gervais I**
1. Steiner R. AUT 1.31.04
2. Pelen P. FRA 1.31.60
3. Svet M. JUG 1.31.64

**St. Gervais II**
1. Steiner R. AUT 1.31.04
2. Pelen P. FRA 1.31.60
3. Svet M. JUG 1.31.64

**Piancavallo**
1. Charvatova O. CSR 1.28.08
2. Pelen P. FRA 1.28.11
3. Oertli B. SUI 1.28.19

**Vysoke Tatry**
1. Schmidh C. SUI 1.24.57
2. Bonfini N. ITA 1.24.73
3. Hess E. SUI 1.25.13

**Park City**
1. Hess E. SUI 1.39.95
2. Charvatova O. TCH 1.40.85
3. Pelen P. FRA 1.41.08

**Waterville Valley**
1. Steiner R. AUT 1.34.17
2. Tlalka-Mogore M. FRA 1.34.31
3. Hess E. SUI 1.34.66

### SUPER-G

**Sestriere**
1. Kiehl M. BRD 1.28.44
2. Gerg M. BRD 1.28.66
3. Svet M. JUG 1.29.14

**Puy-St. Vincent**
1. Hächer T. BRD 1.15.46
2. Walliser M. SUI 1.16.09
3. Schneider V. SUI 1.16.37

**Megêve I**
1. Marzola M. ITA 1.20.73
2. Kirchler E. AUT 1.20.83
3. Hächer T. BRD 1.21.01

**Megêve II**
1. Marzola M. ITA 1.20.73
2. Kirchler E. AUT 1.20.83
3. Hächer T. BRD 1.21.01

**Furano**
1. Savijarvi L. CAN 1.20.43
2. Winkler S. AUT 1.21.04
3. Fletcher P. USA 1.21.09

**Vail**
1. Kiehl M. BRD 1.23.40
2. Wachter A. AUT 1.23.64
3. Savijarvi L. CAN 1.23.90


## ACKNOWLEDGEMENTS

We would like to thank the following for their valuable contributions in the preparation of this book.

For translating the original French manuscript
D. Wryte Price, Gavin Bell

**Editorial**
Nigel Cawthorne

**Designers**
Kevin Ryan
Lesley Cook
Rachel Foster
Ralph Pitchford

**Map and Diagram Artwork**
Martin Woodford

**Photographers**
Serge Lang
Kjell Langset
ART FOTO
Giorgio Keller
Gerard Berthoud
J P Maeder
SCI
Reportagebild

**Typesetting**
I C Dawkins (Typesetters) Ltd.
S X Composing Ltd.

**Colour Separation**
Columbia Offset Ltd.
Excel Ltd.